THE GAA
AND THE WAR OF
INDEPENDENCE

Tim Pat Coogan is Ireland's best-known historical writer. His 1990 biography of Michael Collins rekindled interest in Collins and his era. He is also the author of *The IRA*; *De Valera: Long Fellow, Long Shadow*; *Wherever Green is Worn*; *The Famine Plot*; *1916: The Mornings After* and *The Twelve Apostles*.

Rival captains in a hurling match at the
1932 Tailteann Games.

THE GAA
AND THE WAR OF
INDEPENDENCE

TIM PAT COOGAN

HEAD
of ZEUS

An Apollo Book

This is an Apollo book, first published in 2018 by Head of Zeus Ltd

Copyright © Tim Pat Coogan 2018

The moral right of Tim Pat Coogan to be identified as the author
of this work has been asserted in accordance with the Copyright,
Designs and Patents Act of 1988.

1 3 5 7 9 10 8 6 4 2

A CIP catalogue record for this book is available from
the British Library.

Image credits GAA Museum: Frontispiece, 4, 9, 10, 12; Getty
Images: 13, 15, 18; National Library of Ireland: 8, 14; courtesy
of RTÉ archives: 7; courtesy of J. J. Barrett: 16, 19;
Wikimedia: 1, 2, 3, 5, 6, 11, 17.

ISBN (HB) 9781786697035
ISBN (E) 9781786697028

Upon the fields of friendly strife
Are sown the seeds that upon
Other fields on other days,
Will bear the fruits of victory.

Words of General Douglas MacArthur, inscribed on
the wall of West Point Military Academy gymnasium

*To my daughters Thomond, Jackie and Olwen
and my grandchildren Jessica, Olwen and Peadar
for all the invaluable help and research
they gave me in compiling this book*

Contents

Acknowledgements

Coming from outside the GAA, I am particularly indebted to people within the association who helped me; and of course to the many custodians of source material, who placed this at my disposal. I would like to express my gratitude to Peter McKenna (development officer of the GAA) and Mark Reynolds (the association's archivist) for the continuing help and guidelines provided to me during the course of this book's preparation.

In relation to the material on Northern Ireland, I have relied on my own involvement in the H Block controversy and on *On the Blanket*, my book exploring the 'dirty protest'. But I also found that Mark Reynolds's paper on the involvement of the GAA in the H Block saga was of particular benefit. Where matters Northern are concerned, I – like anyone else interested in the subject – also have reason to be grateful for the writings of Dónal McAnallan.

I must also thank my friends John O'Mahony and Joe Joe Barrett (both GAA men, and more importantly Kerrymen to their core) for their input. Joe Joe provided valuable suggestions and in addition was good enough to read the manuscript for me. His opinions would not always coincide with mine, but in true GAA fashion we found accommodation for opposing views!

While the GAA itself is an impressive institution, researching this book brought me into contact with another organization which plays a most useful role in contemporary Ireland. I speak, of course, of Ireland's library service. Through my local library in Dalkey I received information by way of books or pamphlets from every part of the country. What was sought in Dalkey arrived from every quarter, from Cork to Armagh. I wish to thank particularly Maria O'Sullivan, Mary Reynolds, Deanna Ortiz, Elaine Mooney, Martina O'Sullivan and Aline Santos da Silva.

In addition, librarians in other parts of the country were immensely helpful. I want to thank Petrina Mee from Galway, Helen Hehir from Kilkenny, Kieran Wyse from Cork, Celestine Murphy from Wexford, and Peter Beirne from Clare.

The provincial press was particularly helpful to me in publishing my requests for information: and here I would like to single out James Laffey, the editor of *Western People* in Ballina, Co. Mayo, for sending me his excellent book *The Road to 51: The Making of Mayo Football*. Jim Maher of Kilkenny, who is a justly respected local historian, also drew my attention to his useful work *The Flying Column: West Kilkenny 1916–1921*.

Others who provided me with help and information include Jack Ryan, Mary Guinan, Syl Cassidy, John Mahon, Paddy Coen, Liam Burke, Harry Roberts, Mary O'Hanlon, John

Kennedy, Charles Mooney, James Durney, Simon Mullen, Gary Carville, Colm Gannon and Peter Rabbitte.

A special thanks to Geraldine Reardon for research and typing.

I am particularly grateful for the frequent contribution of information from Diarmuid Grainger, Seamus McPhillips and Kieran Wyse.

Amongst my fellow practitioners of the black art of journalism, I found the writings of Martin Brehony, Sean Kilfeather and Patrick Moran particularly valuable.

I also consulted the records of the Tomás Ó'Fiaich Library in Armagh. Liam Mulcahy's advice on photographic sources was invaluable.

As I was helped by so many people, it is possible that I may have omitted a name or names from the foregoing. If I have inadvertently done so, I humbly apologize.

Cuala: My Local Club

PADDY DARCY PONDEROUSLY FILLED HIS PIPE AND THEN delivered an unexpected reminiscence in his characteristically pedantic style:

> We engaged the Freestaters at Ulverton Road and inflicted some casualties on them. Then we moved off towards Bray. We marched in good order until we came to Loughlinstown, where a fusillade was directed at us from the hospital. The column returned fire and there was a vigorous engagement before we silenced our opponents and marched off again without suffering any casualties. They told us afterwards that we had killed a nun. Not a lot of people knew that!

The seaside village of Dalkey, on the outskirts of south Dublin, is among the most well-heeled and prosperous of the city's neighbourhoods – and back in the day, Paddy Darcy was generally regarded as the Village Sage, energetic and active in all manner of local agitations and controversies. A retired civil servant, Darcy used to sit of a morning surrounded by a group of his disciples, in the atmospheric surroundings of the Men's Bathing Place on the rocks below the northern end of the Vico Road. His respectful hearers were in the habit of waiting for Darcy to set the agenda for their day's intellectual activity, his quotations and observations kicked off via his reading of that morning's *Irish Times* editorial and Letters to the Editor column.

As for me, in those days, I was less of a participant and more of an observer of the local Dalkey scene. I was a younger man: and besides, I wasn't a fully paid-up member of this illustrious group of retired civil servants, bankers, business people and commentators on the affairs of Dalkey, the nation and the world – of course, in that exact order. I did, however, have a stake in proceedings: I was perched on the Vico rocks because I was a swimmer, and because I appreciated fully the singular beauty of my surroundings.

This of course meant that I respected Paddy Darcy himself – and admired the work he had put in to safeguard this stretch of coast. In 1954, Darcy had been prominent in a campaign against overdevelopment along the scenic Vico Road – a campaign which, from that time until the present day, has been largely responsible for preserving one of the great views of Ireland from the predations of the greedy and the unscrupulous. The view, of course, is of Killiney Bay, curving spectacularly from Dalkey Island and the Bullock Harbour in the north all the way to the great dark nose of Bray Head in the south. The fact was that Darcy had done us all some service, and we knew it.

In my mind, Paddy Darcy was essentially a gentle person, averse to violence of any kind. Indeed, he had once upbraided me personally, for what he considered to be my cruelty in spearing flatfish while snorkelling off the strand at Killiney. But he seemed averse in general to confrontation of any sort – almost to a fault. I was aware, for example, that he had courted a local girl of both beauty and character for several years – but had not met her at the altar because (so the story went) he quailed at the thought of bringing home a bride to the sisters with whom he lived.

As for his experiences in the years when Ireland fought for independence, the fact was that none of us knew much about this period in Darcy's life. As was the case with very many of our veterans, he had allowed the portcullis of years to come down between his generation and mine. The result was that I had never associated Paddy Darcy with deeds involving physical courage – never, that is, until that day sitting on the rocks below the Vico Road.

Paddy's reminiscences concerning the nun had a powerful effect on those present, including myself. In fact, I am responsible – albeit inadvertently – for prompting his war reminiscence in the first place. I had done this by asking him his opinion regarding the IRA's so-called 'border campaign' which had broken out in Northern Ireland in the mid-1950s. This general subject, once raised, had extended gradually in scope, with the result that an altogether new Paddy Darcy was revealed to me.

Later, I delved deeper into Darcy's background, and unearthed further details of which I had previously been unaware. I discovered, for example, that Paddy and his friend

Charlie Somers had been founder members in 1918 of what was originally called the Cuala Hurling Club, based in Dalkey village itself. 2018, then, is a significant year for Cuala, as it celebrates not only its status as one of the foremost Gaelic Athletic Association (GAA) clubs in the country, but also its centenary. And with this in mind, Cuala players in 2018 celebrated their club's anniversary in considerable style by picking up their hurleys, taking to the pitch, and winning the All-Ireland Club Championship for the second year in a row.

I mention Cuala, because – as we will see – it can be taken as an important symbol both of the GAA's roots in the independence movement and its role in the development of Irish society in the years since the club's foundation. Paddy Darcy and Charlie Somers, for example, played significant roles in both. These two men took part in the 1916 Easter Rising, fighting in Jacob's Biscuit Factory in Dublin's south inner city. Their friend Eoghan O'Keeffe, writing to Cuala stalwart Harry Roberts, left a description of Somers which unconsciously encapsulated a great deal both about the kind of men they were, and the forces that shaped them.

> After the surrender he [Somers] just made his way home and as soon as possible turned up at his office like some other civil servants – notably Diarmuid O'Hegarty, afterwards Secretary to the Free State Cabinet! Nobody challenged them and they challenged nobody. But when called upon, Charlie agreed to act as a justice of the Dalkey Republican Court.[1]

The role of these courts – the so-called 'Dáil courts' established in June 1920 by order of the first Dáil Éireann – was to replace the trappings of British rule in both the civil and military spheres in Ireland. Somers, Darcy and others who shared their views – fellow Cuala founder members including John McGuinness, Eamon Kirk, Paddy Delaney and Noel Glynn – saw the role of their new club and of the GAA as another aspect, and an intrinsic aspect, of this process of de-Anglicisation. They saw the distinctively Irish sports of Gaelic football, hurling, camogie and handball as part of a continuum, part of this steady and unstoppable move in the Ireland of those years towards independence.

As for the word *Cuala* itself: this is an Irish term describing the rugged granite terrain that runs from Dalkey through to the nearby seaside town of Bray and on to the Sugar Loaf Mountain – landscapes so emblematic of coastal Co. Wicklow. And indeed, it was fitting that the terrain in which the club first found its feet was at least as rugged as anything to be found on the slopes of the Sugar Loaf. Initially the club played its games in Dalkey Quarry, behind Darcy's home. It was from these quarry works that the granite was extracted by the Victorians to build the great pincer walls of Kingstown – now Dún Laoghaire – harbour.

One of the reasons I have enjoyed writing this book is because I live close to the playing fields of contemporary Cuala. The history of this club exemplifies the subject of this book: the relationship between the political evolution of the modern island of Ireland and the GAA, the country's most influential sporting organization. For the GAA has, in its time, mirrored both Ireland's joys and its sorrows. To give just one glancing and painful example: Somers and Darcy, these sporting friends, these organizational partners, these brothers in arms – it would be their fate to take opposite sides in Ireland's bitter and fratricidal Civil War, which I will describe later in this book.

I hail from a rugby background – and for most of my earliest years, I was only vaguely aware that there was a clubhouse and a pitch in Dalkey on which GAA games were played, occasionally attracting sizeable crowds. As the years passed, however, I began to realize that this club was a symbol of modern Ireland, in both its good and bad aspects. I realized that one could chart both the growth of joyful and challenging times by observing the scene in the environs of the club's grounds.

For example, just outside the club gates there stands a bus stop that for long periods appeared to be part of a service mainly engaged in taking young people off, their bags packed, to the ferry port and the airport – to emigration. Passing the bus stop on their way into the Cuala grounds on weekend mornings, however, one could *also* see crowds of parents accompanying their children into the club to compete in various training sessions and junior leagues.

Over the years, it became noticeable that, as economic times got better, the bus passengers seemed to be mainly intent not on emigration so much as leisure – either going on holidays or coming from them. The composition of the parent-and-children traffic also changed: the cars grew bigger and more indicative of affluence. In latter years, it has become normal to find as many as six hundred or more kids arriving at the Cuala grounds, deposited from parental SUVs and Audis, Mercs and BMWs. Of course less affluent families continued to come – and more and more of them, too. The modern Cuala club has grown so large, in fact, that these days it can field over ninety teams a week: hurling and camogie and football, women and men – to say nothing of children as young as four years old.

In keeping with the fundamental ethos of the GAA, these manifold team activities are made possible, in Cuala as in other GAA clubs up and down the land, by the organizational efforts of the members. And these efforts have been recognized in a steady flow of awards to team clubs: for example, the AIB Leinster Club Hurling Championship (2016 and 2017); the AIB All-Ireland Club Hurling Championship (2017 and 2018); the Dublin Senior Hurling League & Championship (1989, 1991, 1994, 2015, 2016, and 2017); and the Leinster Junior Club League and Ladies' Football (2017).

The crucial aspect of this success, of course, is *voluntarism*: Cuala, like every GAA club in Ireland, depends wholly on the voluntary efforts of all its people – as selectors, as mentors, as organizers, as passionate planners for the future. I will expand on this particular – and crucial – point throughout this book.

The success and strength of the modern Cuala club is also the result of other factors that nurture and bolster the GAA in general: namely, the Irish-language movement; and the parish tradition. In Cuala's case, we can glance back to 1952, when a small group of Irish-language enthusiasts founded Scoil

Lorcáin, a primary school in nearby Monkstown. From this seed later sprouted a boys' secondary school (Coláiste Eoin, founded in 1969), and a girls' secondary school (Coláiste Iosagáin, founded in 1971). All three schools were to provide a new stream of camogie players, hurlers and Gaelic footballers to strengthen the Cuala tradition – and this continues to be the case today.

The parish tradition and its role in raising Irish social standards of education and of living, meanwhile, are also perfectly illustrated in the story of Cuala's growth. Around the time of Scoil Lorcáin's foundation, Dalkey's local National (or primary) School contained some committed Irish cultural nationalists, with none more fervent in the cause than the school's vice principal Proinsias O'Maoláin. The pupils of the school – for the most part the children of local tradesmen, labourers, shop assistants and so on – were reared in an environment in which the notion of a university education was entirely foreign to their frames of reference. After leaving primary school in their early teens they went either to a technical school or in a few cases to a Christian Brothers-run secondary school in nearby Dún Laoghaire.

In their years of primary school at Dalkey, however, these young people received a good grounding in the three Rs. More pertinently, they received the sort of instruction in the Irish language that shaped a great many of them for success in later life – even if at school many of them groaned at having to learn a language that they never heard spoken once they stepped outside the school gates.

Corporal punishment was the order of the day at Dalkey National School, as at other schools up and down the land – in this case visited upon those erstwhile pupils who did not do their homework. O'Maoláin was a small, energetic man: he made clear his preference for pupils who worked at the Irish language by seating them at the front of the classroom, while the English-language laggards were placed at the back. He was a tireless GAA exponent and is remembered to this day for his extraordinary ability to carry the full complement of hurling sticks for a team of fifteen plus substitutes on his bicycle, as he cycled the long hilly roads from Dalkey to the Dún Laoghaire Corporation playing fields in Sallynoggin several miles away. From the ranks of his former pupils, names are still recalled in Cuala club history: these include Pat Dalton, and the Wallace brothers. In addition, O'Maoláin strengthened Cuala further by proposing the amalgamation of two small local clubs – Dalkey Mitchells and St Begnet's – into the Cuala organization, thus safeguarding the future of Cuala itself.

These days, one can also meet with another Cuala club stalwart, and another embodiment of the tradition of the GAA Fenianism, in the person of Michael O'Brien. You would be likely to meet O'Brien climbing a ladder and festooned in bunting, in this neighbourhood or that neighbourhood in the borough of Dún Laoghaire, proclaiming to the populace that Cuala is once more engaged in serious combat. Take the scene in March 2018 when Cuala, under the tutelage of its remarkable coach Mattie Kenny – who can take much of the credit for the club's recent successes – emerged victorious in the game I mentioned a moment ago: the AIB All-Ireland Club of Hurling Championship Final Replay against the great Limerick club Na Piarsaigh.

It's safe to say that the periods leading up to the original match and then to the replay were frenetic for Michael O'Brien and his bunting. The district exploded with Cuala colours – while on the day itself, thousands marched to the local train station to board a special train to take them to the GAA stadium at O'Moore Park at Portlaoise in the Irish midlands.

As for the game itself – or rather the replay, which took place on 24 March 2018: this has since been lauded as one of the great displays of hurling in the modern game. Not a foul was struck; and the collisions and the aerial skills displayed were remarkable. The winning goal came from Mark Schutte, who flitted through a cloud of defenders like a swallow through starlings with the ball balanced on his hurley, before shortening his grip and burying the ball in the back of the net. His brother, team captain Paul Schutte, then won a place in hurling history for a sporting acceptance speech – delivered in Irish – in which he said that the better team had lost and congratulated his opponents at least as much as his own team mates. His sentiments were applauded by the thousands of Cuala supporters who had travelled from Dublin to Portlaoise that day.

My sense was that the explosion of support and enthusiasm for a GAA fixture in Dalkey and its environs that day was something that could not have been dreamt of in my boyhood days – when, let us not forget, the village of Dalkey and its environs was a considerable redoubt of British cultural influence.

The extraordinary point to be remembered about Cuala, in the face of such popular local support and success, is that it doesn't even have a proper senior playing pitch of its own. Instead, it is obliged to share its grounds with Dalkey United soccer club; and it trains and plays in three other different local venues – at Shankill, Bray and Sallynoggin. Four separate pitches dispersed widely across south Co. Dublin and north Co. Wicklow – and again, it cannot be stressed enough that the spirit of voluntarism shown by such men as Michael O'Brien, building on the spirit of voluntarism shown by Paddy Darcy, Charlie Somers and others, is the cement that binds this club together, in the face of such challenging logistics.

Here is another interesting point – one which underscores the fact that the GAA is a broad church. I first met O'Brien in the 1970s when he was upholding the long tradition of physical-force republicanism, which – as we will see in the course of this book – forms a crucial element in GAA history. I was on an information tour of Portlaoise Gaol, and O'Brien was the leader of the Provisional IRA prisoners held in this high-security prison. As I shook hands with him that day, he remarked that he had often seen me coming to his father's dairy in Glasthule, near Dalkey, to buy manure for my garden. To my shame I replied (with that coruscating wit for which I am of course justly infamous): 'Yes – and now you're in the shit, Michael.' Today, the times have moved on: Michael O'Brien intersperses his ladder-climbing activities on behalf of Cuala with his role as a distinguished member of the Sinn Féin party; and shares his GAA enthusiasms with yet another Cuala personality – the RTE sports commentator Des Cahill. Truly the GAA has grown to be an immensely broad society.

And it *is* a society: sport is central to its DNA, of course, but this is a multifaceted organization. The GAA fosters a benign consciousness of being Irish that makes the movement a serious contender for the title Most Valuable Institution in the Country. Its reach, moreover, is truly global. Today, the buses that pull up at the stop outside Cuala's gates are helping to disperse young Irish people all over the world: many can and will come back to Ireland – but those who do not come back have access to an enduring bond with Ireland through the good offices of the GAA.

This did not happen overnight. All over the world I have met people who make the GAA possible. They undertake seemingly simple, but in fact difficult and sometimes tiring and tedious tasks – such as rising early on a Sunday morning to drive around the homes of young men and women, be they in Boston or Birmingham or Brisbane, and dragging them out (hangover or no hangover) to play their games and sustain their consciousness of being Irish. They see to it that the pitches are maintained, that the showers work, that tickets are collected, that social activities are organized in advance, and that they proceed smoothly. In Chicago, New York and San Francisco, Melbourne and Sydney and Perth, Wellington and Auckland, such individuals put in the time training teams – and casting the net wider still by helping to get jobs for new Irish immigrants.

The reach of the GAA is astounding: it is, for example, a remarkable fact that hurling and Gaelic football are spreading so far afield that in 2017 a successful Asian Games was staged in Singapore. And it's the same, or a variant of the same, in every club in Ireland: be it Cuala in Dalkey, or Slaughtneil in Derry or Kerins O'Rahilly's in Kerry. This is not done for monetary return – although granted, expenses are now more common than of yore and there are fringe benefits previously unheard of.

It isn't all good news, of course. The poor performance of a Waterford hurling team against Kilkenny, in the month this Prologue was written, was attributed by one commentator to the effects of a two-week holiday in Cancún. And yet the case could have been a whole lot worse: for the team might have been granted a one-week holiday in a certain Co. Kilkenny village. Ballyragget would normally win, without much competition, the title of Sleepiest Village in Ireland. Lately, however, it briefly came to world attention as a result of a twenty-first birthday celebration staged for one of its players by the members of Ballyragget GAA Club – a celebration that disgraced the club and tainted the GAA itself. For in their wisdom, the organizers of this celebration decided to enliven the proceedings in a manner which would not have met with the approval of Archbishop Thomas Croke and the legions of Catholic clergy who defended and nurtured the original GAA – but which, by all accounts, was met with great approval by those present at the celebration.

They hired a stripper.

The occasion was (of course) filmed on a mobile phone, duly distributed – and the public lewdness on show that night went viral, and ended up involving the police. The occasion was deeply embarrassing to the GAA as an organization – but my sense is that both Ballyragget in particular and the GAA in general can be relied upon to surmount such problems in the future. The reasons I say this with confidence should shortly emerge from these pages. For now, allow me to conclude this Prologue by declaring that I want this book to recognize both the efforts of today's volunteers in building an organization to be proud of, and the efforts of their like-minded forebears in creating both the GAA itself and shaping modern Ireland in the turbulent years of the War of Independence. Individuals such as Paddy Darcy, who could in his later years sit in the sunshine on the warm rocks below the Vico Road and reflect on a life that fused sport and politics and culture, the private and the public and the social – to remarkable effect.

These are my aims – some of them – in writing this book. I hope I have succeeded.

Introduction

I T IS MY CONTENTION – ONE I HOPE TO AMPLIFY IN THE
course of this book – that the Gaelic Athletic Association
is the most socially valuable organization in Ireland. A unique
national institution, it has become a cornerstone of Irish
society – and in addition has spread internationally, so that its
games are played wherever green is worn: in North America
and Europe, New Zealand and Australia – and of course in
Great Britain. This growth has not been without heartache,
for the GAA acts as an accurate barometer of the health of
Ireland itself.

The initial growth of GAA clubs in the United States, for
example, was fuelled by mass emigration that accompanied
the trauma of the Great Famine in Ireland and its poverty-
stricken aftermath. And today, rural depopulation threatens
the viability of many GAA clubs in western Ireland.

In modern times too, the increasing urbanization of Irish
society has made Dublin the dominant Gaelic football county.
The intensity of its cousin sport of hurling, meanwhile, has
passed into everyday parlance: when the going gets tough in
business or in politics, in this or in that situation, participants
are apt to remark drily that 'this is senior hurling'.

The GAA has contributed richly to national development in both cultural and political terms. For over a century it has nurtured the ideal of voluntarism, and in so doing has contributed to a distinctive sense of national identity that would be hard to replicate anywhere in the world.

As for challenges posed to the GAA and its culture – these of course exist today too, and they flow, ironically, from the organization's very success. They are connected with sponsorship, the intrusion of the corporate sector into the life and finances of the GAA, television rights, and the financial rewards offered to coaches and county players: and the organization must juggle all of these issues while at the same time trying to maintain fidelity to its cherished voluntary tradition.

As for magical sporting occasions: the GAA has also provided its fair share of these – and sometimes they have assumed strange and unexpected forms. Take the scene at Croke Park in Dublin on Saturday 24 February 2007, when Ireland played host to England in the Six Nations rugby championship. On that day, the home team defeated the visitors soundly to record a 43–13 victory. Tries by Girvan Dempsey and David Wallace – both converted by Ronan O'Gara – contributed to this thrashing; and the Irish team, by common consent, played like a dream.

But this occasion was about more than the sport. Decades of hostility by the GAA towards rugby – and the other so-called 'garrison games' of soccer, hockey and cricket – were ending on this afternoon, to the accompaniment of rapturous applause from the 83,000 spectators who attended the game, and the millions who saw it on television screens all over the world. It was a signal moment in Irish sporting and cultural history.

For myself – and, I make bold to claim, most of the Irish rugby fans who watched the game that day – the era of measuring a person's patriotism by the shape of their football ended that afternoon in the electric atmosphere of Croke Park. The GAA has, after all, been traditionally associated with the Catholic Church in the minds of most people. And for good reason: literal parochialism has always been the organization's watchword, with players taking to the field and participating for the glory of their parish. Catholic clerics defended and protected the GAA in dangerous times; they used their education and administrative skills to bolster its day-to-day operations.

The local curate tended to act as secretary to the local club; the local bishop threw in the ball to kick off important matches. In late nineteenth- and early twentieth-century Ireland, Protestants gradually peeled away from the GAA; in Northern Ireland throughout its ill-starred existence, the GAA and the Protestant population have had little or nothing to say to one another. The GAA wore a hard varnish of Catholicism from its very beginnings – even though, as we shall see, this had not been the intention of its founders.

But times were changing – and on that late-winter day in 2007, people – or rather, the great majority of people – were entirely supportive of the decision by the GAA leadership to assist the Irish Rugby Football Union (IRFU) at this crucial moment. The IRFU was in the throes of rebuilding its own headquarters at Lansdowne Road, and the organization was in urgent need of a substitute ground for Six Nations and other games. By agreeing to lease Croke Park to the rugby authorities, important fixtures could be scheduled as normal, and important sources of revenue could be secured. The GAA also understood that its own national stadium would be filled to the brim on additional days in the year. This was a win-win for everyone involved.

This match has had a strange afterlife. After the final whistle sounded, rumours began to circulate that there may have been an even deeper significance to Girvan Dempsey's try. These rumours persisted and put down deeper roots: were they based on truth, or was an urban myth of some magnitude created on that day? My curiosity was whetted – and in due course, I decided to investigate. I contacted the GAA archivist, Mark Reynolds – and Reynolds introduced me to Peter McKenna, Croke Park's Development Officer.

McKenna had been closely involved in the reconstruction of Croke Park which concluded in 2004, and which resulted in the impressive stadium we see today. McKenna produced a set of architectural plans showing how the ground had changed in the decades since its construction on Jones Road in 1884 – and in particular how it had changed since a certain fateful day in 1920. Afterwards, he led me out to step on the sacred turf itself – the very grass on which every player of Gaelic football, camogie and hurling aspires to tread some day. And, with the aid of the plans we had just studied, we were able to establish that the rumours concerning Dempsey's try were not simply an urban myth.

Instead, they were based on fact.

For it chanced that the try had been scored on the very spot where, on the afternoon of 'Bloody Sunday' – 21 November 1920 – the Tipperary player Michael Hogan was shot dead by crown forces during a challenge football game between his county and Dublin. Early that day, Michael Collins's hit squad – the so-called 'Twelve Apostles' – had unexpectedly struck a body blow in a series of raids against a British military undercover death squad that had been making steady inroads into Collins's Irish intelligence network. In all, some nineteen British military personnel were either killed or wounded that day.

The response by British forces at Croke Park was immediate. A burst of firing, including by machine-guns, swept both players and spectators when troops invaded the stadium without warning, and exacted retribution for that morning's assassinations. A further thirteen civilians died alongside Hogan.

The British action that day was of course fundamentally wrong, in both legal and moral terms. But the British military commanders that day were fundamentally *correct* in their assessment that the GAA was one of the most powerful forces in the country ranged against them at this fraught moment in the Anglo-Irish relationship. In many ways, the GAA was – and indeed consciously laid claim to be – purely an Irish sporting organization, and an intrinsic part of the wave of cultural nationalism that spread across the country in the late nineteenth and early twentieth century. But to the British, who were at this moment in the throes of attempting to maintain by force a centuries-old system of colonization in Ireland, the GAA was recognizably an enemy, and a formidable advocate for the principle of de-Anglicization.

The importance of the deaths at Croke Park to the GAA and its supporters are symbolized in the naming of the Hogan Stand at the stadium itself. It is in the rooms within this stand that the ruling council of the GAA, the Ard Chomhairle, meets. It is within the Hogan Stand that the president, the taoiseach, and other dignitaries are invited to watch the more important games of the year. This is terrain charged with significance.

In addition, of course, the result of that first and ghastly Bloody Sunday was to underscore and maintain the GAA policy on retaining the ban on 'foreign' sports. This unique context, then, demonstrates the significance of the GAA decision in 2007 to permit the playing of rugby on the turf of Croke Park – a decision taken against a radically changing political context in Ireland, north and south. It also underscores, I think, the significance of the organization itself, and its place at the heart of Irish life and recent history. Put simply, it *mattered* that the GAA had decided to welcome rugby to Croke Park.

Let me now begin to trace the development of the GAA over the years, from a small grass-roots organization to a national movement close to the pulse of Irish culture and politics. And allow me to begin in – Korea.

CHAPTER ONE

New Beginnings

ROM THE VERY BEGINNINGS OF THE GAELIC ATHLETIC
Association as a national movement, late in the nineteenth
century, the British authorities in Dublin Castle were aware
of the organization's potential as a revolutionary seedbed and
future agent of unwelcome change. The result was that the GAA
was treated from the outset as a semi-subversive movement.

The context and motives behind the British view of the
GAA struck me forcibly in, of all places, South Korea. In the
course of a visit to the peninsula in 1983, I was entertained
by one of the South Korean president's most senior advisers.
This gentleman demonstrated a remarkable knowledge of
Irish history and culture: I was naturally curious about the
sources of this knowledge, and I asked him if he had gained his
information via an acquaintanceship with, say, Irish writers.
He replied in the negative – and went on to explain that his
knowledge had come about as a result of 'Korean history itself'.

He was referring to one incident in particular, which took
place prior to the Japanese annexation of the Korean peninsula
in 1910. Before the annexation, the Japanese sent abroad a team

of four professors to research the best model for colonizing a people and – even more importantly – keeping them in a state of subjection. The academics came to London: for the Japanese government had chosen to learn about imperialism through observation of the workings and administration of the British Empire. In particular, the Japanese were impressed by Britain's record in Ireland, including its extirpation of native culture, language, pastimes and dress.

In addition, the Japanese emissaries were interested in the means by which British colonialism had incubated in Ireland feelings of inferiority, and respect for the occupying power as being in some essential way possessed of superior culture and knowledge. They were engaged too by their reading of British successes in destroying existing systems of land ownership – with the whole backed up and reinforced by a strong security apparatus.

The Japanese professors had certainly chosen an excellent and highly practical model of subjugation – and a model that had over centuries been applied, refined, perfected. Various so-called 'plantations' and invasions, from the time of the Normans through those of the Tudors, Cromwell and many other English and British rulers, had resulted in the lands of Catholic Ireland being taken over by English and British dominant forms of culture. This was especially the case in the northeastern corner of the island, where the effects of such plantation can of course be detected even up to the present day.

The Catholics of Ireland suffered not only a loss of land, of course, but also of their own modes of cultural expression – and moreover, it is important to note that this loss was not inflicted by the actions of the English and British alone. From the time of the coming of the Normans in 1169, the influence of the papacy on the fortunes of Irish Catholics was perceptible, and the results were not always positive. At the time of the Norman invasion, the Irish Church was relatively free of excessive Roman influence: rather, it was decidedly independent-minded, and dominated economically and administratively by the indigenous Irish monasteries.

This state of affairs did not fit at all well with Rome's way of doing things. A succession of popes wished to control Irish practices – and more particularly, of course, Irish revenues – through the appointment of bishops selected by and answerable to Rome. Thus it came to pass that the pope, in the latter half of the twelfth century, watched as restless Norman landowners and militias in England and Wales looked abroad in search of lands to conquer – and looked in particular west, across the sea to Ireland. The Normans were coming – and in their mustering, Rome saw a chance to bring Ireland and its independent Church to heel.

The pope of the day happened to be English – Adrian IV, the only English Bishop of Rome to date: and Adrian bestowed on Henry II of England the permission, in the form of a so-called papal 'bull' or legal document, to invade and occupy Ireland – a momentous move duly begun in 1169. And so the Irish, whose monks had been responsible for the maintenance of Christianity in Europe during the Dark Ages, for their faithfulness found themselves subject to the effects of geopolitical skulduggery – beginning in the twelfth century and continuing without interruption in the centuries that were to follow.

Witness the fact that Pope Alexander VIII caused a Te Deum to be sung when the Protestant William of Orange defeated the Catholic King James of England at the Battle of the Boyne in 1690. It served the papacy's interests better to see James defeated, Catholic or not: for James was supported by Louis XIV of France – and the pope was at war with Louis at that time, as part of a European Great Game in which James was but a pawn.

Witness the fact too that the hierarchy of the Irish Catholic Church supported the Act of Union between Britain and Ireland which stunted Irish political growth from 1800 onwards. And witness the fact that this same hierarchy was supportive of Catholic Emancipation, passed by the Westminster parliament as the Roman Catholic Relief Act of 1829: this conferred freedoms on Irish (and British) Catholics of property, with the right to vote given to those whose landholdings were valued at forty shillings or more. There was nothing in Emancipation for Ireland's Catholic peasantry, which was doomed, for several generations, to political impotence – and the hierarchy was happy with this state of affairs. (And yet, Rome would continue to demand, and to receive, large financial subscriptions from Irish dioceses, even during the famine years of 1845–49 – and the hierarchy was supportive of this too.)

The fundamental point here, I think, is that in general Rome was happy to coexist with a system which gave it a degree of political control. This control took various forms as the years rolled on: by the middle of the nineteenth century, for example, the Catholic Church in Ireland was increasingly in a position of authority over the country's education system. It was also content with a state of affairs which enabled it to place its followers in respectable administrative roles within an English-speaking empire; and to send its priests to work within British-governed territories. In a country still influenced by a Protestant Ascendancy, these were important considerations.

And so the interests of the British authorities and the Catholic Church were fused – all too often to hellish effect.

Even if we set this particular context aside, however, we can see that nineteenth-century Ireland was a place of considerable drama, and a focus of gradually developing cultural and political ferment, in which various movements and organizations sought to stake claims in the country's future. Among these groups was the Catholic Church, of course: but also the Gaelic League, founded in 1893 with the intention of preserving and developing the Irish language; and the Irish Republican Brotherhood (IRB), established in 1858 in order to break, if it might, the link with Britain. Each of these parties, in its way, held a stake in the future: each was eager to mould the developing consciousness of what it was and what it meant to be Irish; each was concerned to, as James Joyce put it in 1904, 'forge in the smithy of my soul the uncreated conscience of my race'.

As the nineteenth century neared its end, the pieces of this greater national picture began to adhere, to create the political and economic conditions necessary for the process of nation-building itself. Economically, the land reforms initiated by the reformer and activist Michael Davitt began to bear fruit. Davitt had been instrumental in the formation of the Land Leagues, the first of which was established in Co. Mayo in 1879: this marked the beginning of what became known as the Land Wars, a period of agrarian unrest against a deeply unjust status quo in the matter of land ownership and tenants' rights.

Davitt and the Land Leagues pursued what became known as the 'Three Fs': fair rent, free sale, and fixity of tenure – achievement of which would transform the economic conditions for Irish farmers and agrarian workers. In the face of their sustained pressure, a succession of Land Acts was at length passed by a Westminster parliament which was struggling to cope with the changes now underway in Ireland. This legislation did indeed effect an economic transformation in rural Ireland by creating the conditions for a degree of economic security – and by, in effect, building a class of small and middling Catholic landowners where relatively few such had existed before.

Politically too, these were decades of steady and radical change. In 1882, the Irish Parliamentary Party was formed by Charles Stewart Parnell, a wealthy and well-connected Protestant landowner from Co. Wicklow. Parnell used a variety of tools – including the power of the mass rally, and the political arithmetic at Westminster – to influence the national conversation and to bring closer, if possible, his ultimate goal. This was Home Rule – a large degree of political autonomy for Ireland within the United Kingdom. Home Rule, indeed, was the defining political movement of the 1880s in Ireland and Britain. It was a bitterly divisive issue in the latter: elements in William Gladstone's Liberal Party favoured its introduction, while the Conservative Party set its collective face firmly against any move to, as it saw it, dilute the integrity of the United Kingdom.

As we will see, Realpolitik had its way – for that time: Parnell's political dreams of Home Rule would fade, the power of the Irish Parliamentary Party would diminish; and in the 1890s, the issue of Home Rule would retreat from the scene. But only temporarily: by the turn of the century, the so-called Irish Question would loom over politics once again, the Irish Parliamentary Party would rejuvenate under the leadership of John Redmond, and the issue of Home Rule would once more emerge, as if it had never gone away.

As for the shadowy IRB – better known as the Fenian movement – it too was playing its part on the Irish stage. It did so quietly and, as befitted a secret organization, in conditions as clandestine as could be managed. The movement had two wings: one organized in Ireland, the other in North America – and secrecy was woven into its very fabric. The IRB was arranged into a series of circles: at the heart of each circle was the so-called Centre, a single individual who was supposedly the only one to know the identity of all the members of that particular circle – and the only one to know the identity of the Centre of other circles, and so on.

Such, at any rate, was the theory. It is certainly the case that the IRB's cloak-and-dagger underground methods were successful in the sense that even today few people in Ireland realize the extent of the influence wielded by what was always in numerical terms a relatively small movement. In *practical* terms, however, complete secrecy could not be managed at all: the organization was of great interest to the Royal Irish Constabulary (RIC), the civil police force in colonial Ireland that was tasked with monitoring the activities of underground movements in the country, and infiltrating their ranks whenever the opportunity arose.

It was due in large part to such surveillance and infiltration of its ranks, for example, that the IRB uprising of 1867 failed – though with the benefit of hindsight it can also be seen that such bitter lessons were fully absorbed and applied by generations of future republicans including Michael Collins.

Incidentally, and in one of the happy chances of Irish history, the voluminous records and reports detailing the RIC's surveillance activities were handed over to the Irish government after independence, and are now safely lodged in the National Archives, thus making the IRB one of the more thoroughly studied underground movements in world history. (A sample of the RIC's reportage may be studied in the Appendix.)

Not that the IRB could reasonably grumble about State infiltration: after all, its own policy was to infiltrate every movement likely to advance its designs. And in this way its history begins to dovetail with that of the GAA. Sean O'Mahony is a noted collector of republican documents and the author of *Frongoch*, the standard work on a key interlude in republican history – and as he encapsulates it, pithily and with masterly understatement, the 'link between native games, hurling and Gaelic football, and the national movement is a strong one.' Put simply, the GAA was always a sporting organization – and it was always more than just a sporting organization.

And so, while Patrick Pearse may be considered by many to be a high priest of Irish nationalism, he was surely incorrect when he remarked that:

> The Gaelic League will be recognized in history as the most revolutionary influence that has ever come into Ireland. The Irish revolution really began when the seven pro-Gaelic Leaguers met in a back room in O'Connell Street. The germ of all future Irish History was in that backroom.

Or – not wholly incorrect. Pearse's analysis was, like the curate's egg, good in parts. The Gaelic League was indeed a highly significant cultural and political organization – but with the benefit of hindsight we can recognize that it was by no means the most influential such movement in Ireland.

That accolade belongs instead to the Gaelic Athletic Association.

This brief excursus into the political, economic and secret background of nineteenth-century Ireland is, as I hope I have shown, absolutely crucial to our story. It is important to glance at the wider geopolitical history, for example, because it helps in part to explain why the Irish nineteenth century assumed the character it did. The GAA was formed not only against the background of its own national drama, but against a European background too – and in response to, and in reaction against, a certain kind of historical experience. And in understanding this international drama and this historical experience, we come to understand our own national drama better too. It is certainly the case that this drama came fully into focus for me on that evening in South Korea, as in my mind I brought together a great many disparate threads to form a unified tapestry.

All this in turn explains the background against which a fateful meeting took place in a country town in central Ireland in November 1884. For if it is true that – as claimed by that famous Irishman, the Duke of Wellington – the Battle of Waterloo was won on the playing fields of Eton, then it could also be claimed that Ireland's War of Independence in the early part of the twentieth century was won on the playing fields of the GAA.

*

The Gaelic Athletic Association was founded by a group of seven Irishmen in the billiard room of the Hayes Hotel in Thurles, Co. Tipperary, on 1 November 1884. The aims of these men appeared relatively straightforward: they wished to establish an organization to cultivate and encourage the pursuit of Irish sport and Irish athletics. From these very earliest days, however, there was a political dimension to the GAA – even though it can readily be argued that sport and not politics *per se* was front and centre in the minds of most of its members. This political dimension came about partly because national-oriented culture in the Ireland of the late nineteenth century was unavoidably associated with politics; and partly as the result of the graft applied to the GAA in its very beginnings by the IRB.

A founder of the Fenians, John O'Mahony, had urged in public that an association be formed for the promotion of athletics and games, and that this organization be explicitly *nationalist* in outlook and *separatist* in its political aims. The result was that the temper and character of the GAA was set and established from the earliest times. Little wonder that by the early years of the twentieth century, the rank and file of the GAA were nationalist, supportive of independence for Ireland – and minded, incidentally, to support the Irish language too.

If we glance a little into the future, we can see that the dominant spirit within the organization found its apotheosis in the scenes surrounding the funeral of noted Fenian and republican Jeremiah O'Donovan Rossa, at Glasnevin Cemetery in August 1915. The funeral was a pretext for a considerable show of strength by the IRB – and the scene of the graveside oration by Pearse, when he delivered his famous remarks that 'they [the British authorities] have left us our Fenian dead. And while Ireland holds these graves, Ireland unfree shall never be at peace'. Pearse spoke his words surrounded by GAA members holding hurleys instead of rifles.

But at this moment of the GAA's formation, such seismic events lay far in the future.

The dream of a Gaelic games organization is generally agreed to have first taken flight in the course of a walk in Dublin's Phoenix Park in the summer of 1879. Present that day were two men: a Co. Clare-born teacher and IRB member named Michael Cusack, and his Co. Mayo-born friend and IRB colleague Patrick Nally. Cusack was in the habit of bringing teams to the park at weekends to play hurling, but on this occasion the two men were aware of a general sluggishness in the air: the playing fields and wide green spaces of the great park were largely empty of young people playing any sports – and traditional Irish sports least of all. Both men were further struck by the decay symbolized by this lack of vibrancy – and they decided there and then to stop talking, and do something about this situation.

Not that this state of affairs was of much actual surprise to either man; indeed, it could have been of little surprise to any casual observer of the contemporary Irish scene. Such were the levels of both urban and rural poverty at this time in nineteenth-century Ireland that sport was, reasonably enough, not foremost in the minds of many. In general terms, sport tended to be the prerogative of the Ascendancy, prosperous farmers and better-off shopkeepers and tradesmen. All manner of sports did, of course, have their devotees: cricket, in particular, was followed in communities up and down the land, in Ireland as in other British colonies: the sport had deep roots, and was followed with passionate interest. Soccer – traditionally the sport of the English working class – was also beginning to make inroads in Ireland. Gaelic games were not, however, widely followed.

Patrick Nally himself was a sportsman, of the most passionate stripe. Indeed, he was renowned as an athlete, accustomed to winning prizes in every competition he entered, and given to staging important, high-profile sports events on his father's extensive lands around Balla in central Co. Mayo – events at which the aristocracy were notably absent and the working classes notably present. Nally was also a key figure in the Mayo Land League, and he deserves to be regarded as having played an important role in the fall of feudalism in Ireland. Both Nally and his companion that day, then, were cultural nationalists and politicians to their fingertips, as well as being what we might call today 'sports-mad'. It was a heady combination – and an auspicious walk that acted as a considerable catalyst of change.

At this moment of genesis, then, we can see that the revolutionary IRB was already coupled with the GAA. After all, one of the governing briefs of the IRB was to take O'Mahony's strictures forward, to 'devise ways and means of bringing a national athletic body into existence, and to attract young people into its ranks'. Sport was to be firmly political, if the IRB had anything to do with it – and many young people would be attracted into the future GAA by that walk taken that day by Cusack and Nally.

In its aftermath, Cusack set to work on his plans. He expended a prodigious amount of energy in writing articles in support of his ideas – for over twenty newspapers – before the keynote sentiment described below appeared in identical pieces published simultaneously in two sympathetic newspapers on 11 October 1884. One was *United Ireland*, edited by the MP William O'Brien, a strong advocate for Home Rule in Ireland; and after Parnell himself, the most popular politician in the country. The other was the *Irishman*, edited by Richard Pigott: he also purported to support Home Rule and to be a nationalist of an even more advanced stripe than O'Brien – but he would later commit suicide, having been revealed as a forger involved in a notorious British plot to smear Parnell.

Cusack's historic article, 'A Word about Irish Athletics', contained the following sentiments:

> No movement having for its object the social and political advancement of a nation from the tyranny of imported and enforced customs and manners can be regarded as perfect if it has not made adequate provision for the preservation and cultivation of the national pastimes of the people; voluntary neglect of such pastimes is a sure sign of national decay and of approaching disillusion.

And so the starting pistol was fired.

Less than three weeks later, the auspicious meeting took place in that Thurles billiard room. It cannot, of course, have appeared especially auspicious at the time: there may have been as few as eight men in the room that night, and there were certainly no more than thirteen; and no women were present. These were small beginnings indeed.

The composition of this tiny group was, however, of some significance. It is generally accepted that there was a sprinkling of Fenians in the room that night, including John Wyse Power, who was one of seven on whose graves the GAA itself would later place plaques, regarding them as the organization's founding fathers. The others were Cusack, Maurice Davin, J.K. Bracken, John McKay, Joseph O'Ryan and Thomas McCarthy.

Bracken and McCarthy are two of the more interesting names on this list. Bracken was the father of Brendan Bracken, a player in Britain's Conservative Party, a close wartime ally of Winston Churchill and a minister in Churchill's wartime government, and a businessman who in 1945 was instrumental in the relaunch of the *Financial Times*. As for McCarthy: he very likely attended the Thurles meeting because of his friendship with Cusack, who had taught him at school. In other ways, his profile is at first glance curious in this context: for he played rugby for Ireland; and worked as a District Inspector in the RIC – though here, his career would suffer because of his association with the GAA. McCarthy survived the War of Independence, however, and lived to attend a fiftieth anniversary match in Croke Park in 1934 – although by this stage, the GAA was apparently unaware of his existence.

Today, McCarthy's memory is perpetuated by one of the most interesting GAA trophies: the Thomas McCarthy Cup which, as part of the peace process in Northern Ireland, is an annual competition held between the Republic's An Garda Síochána and the Police Service of Northern Ireland (PSNI) – a state of affairs which was of course enabled by the removal of a GAA ban on members of the British security forces joining the Association. (It is worth noting, however, that even though matches have been played at Croke Park, the names of participating PSNI players are still not released, a commentary in itself on the unfinished nature of the peace process.)

And what of Patrick Nally? – for readers will note the absence of Nally's name from the founders' list above. In 1881, he had been arrested in England and gaoled for allegedly conspiring to murder landlords' agents in and around Crossmolina, Co. Mayo. To say that foul play was suspected in his case is an understatement: there is very little evidence that Nally had conspired to do anything of the sort. He died in Dublin's Mountjoy Prison in 1891, shortly before he was due to be released. The *Irish Times* carried the following report on his inquest:

> Findings of the Jury on the evidence presented at the Inquest on P.W. Nally. The jury after an absence of 50 minutes returned the following verdict: That the said Patrick Nally died in the Infirmary in Mountjoy Gaol on the 9th November 1891 of Typhoid Fever, and we are of the opinion that the very harsh and cruel treatment to which the deceased was subjected to in [London's] Millbank Prison [...] so shattered his naturally strong constitution as to leave him susceptible to the disease to which he succumbed...

A significant part of the GAA's initial success was due, as we will see, to the presence amongst the founding seven at Hayes Hotel of Maurice Davin, who was an even greater athlete than Nally. If Nally can be thought of as representative of the Fenian vein in GAA history, Davin, a prosperous Tipperary farmer, epitomized the purely sporting concept of the GAA. His primary goal was to bring order into the chaotic state of Irish athletics; and like Cusack and Nally, to democratize Irish sport so that it became open to the labourer as well as the landlord and the upper classes. Davin was the most famous of a family of Tipperary brothers noted for their athletic prowess – and he himself was known in both Britain and Ireland for his exploits in hammer-throwing and other field events.

Davin's personal prestige and his organizational abilities were priceless assets for a fledgling sporting organization – albeit an organization which enjoyed the distinct benefit of being centre-stage in this era marked by a waxing and buoyant sense of confident cultural nationalism. As we have seen, an educated Catholic middle class was emerging, with money to spend and leisure time at its disposal: and while poverty continued to press close, this was nevertheless a good time for a new organization to take centre stage.

One senior IRB figure in this period of cultural ferment – and a man who would later play an important role in bringing the Irish Free State into existence in 1921, and sustaining it thereafter – has left a useful glimpse of the sustaining background against which the GAA was born. This was Patrick Sarsfield O'Hegarty, polymath, a noted historian, theatre critic, revolutionary and ultimately a senior civil servant who became Secretary of the Irish Department of Posts and Telegraphs. O'Hegarty has left a description of an afternoon in Cork early in 1902 during which a young man on the lowest rung of the service ladder suddenly heard the strains of an Irish concert in progress – and experienced an epiphany:

I was off duty and as I reached the Assembly Rooms and stopped to listen the impulse came to me to go in and see what it was like. So I went in and heard for the first time Irish songs properly sung and what happened to me then must have happened, in those years, to large numbers of people – there is no other way of explaining why so many different sorts of people, gentle and simple, rough and polished, of all classes, creeds and denominations, were drawn into the Gaelic League. Something in the songs – though I could understand only a few of the words – something in the music – something in the atmosphere – gripped me, and I seemed to be put into touch with something far back in the Race. Unknown depths in me were stirred, and across the centuries I seemed to be in touch with days when Irish speech and Irish manners and traditions were in every valley and on every hill and by every river. Is this mysticism? Oh no, it is actual fact. I understood, accepted and felt myself to be one with the Gael.

Similar experiences were being felt throughout Ireland. These were heady times – but challenges were bound to arise. In the next chapter, I want to illustrate how this extraordinary cultural and sporting energy was captured and channelled – and how the infant GAA confronted the inevitable challenges with which it was confronted in these first days of its existence.

CHAPTER TWO

Prairie Fire

Michael Cusack observed that the influence of the infant GAA soon spread across the land 'like a prairie fire'. It is safe to say that Cusack would certainly have known if this was indeed the case: he was himself a good hurler, noted for playing in matches alongside his students and for the remarkable interest he took in players – and so he could be depended upon to have his finger on the pulse.

Here is a recollection of Cusack from one of his protégés:

I can see him now so vividly as if time had rolled back almost two score years and I was taken again to that togging room at Jones Road [the home of Croke Park] where he moved amongst us, his great grey blue eyes glowing above his great grey beard. The shining blackthorn, firmly grasped in his right hand is raised and with a smile of real joy, he crashed it against the hurley of a waiting player and half shouts, half sings in his big husky voice, 'That's the ceol [music] that stirs the heart!' It was Michael Cusack's greatest delight, that mingling with the jersey gaels in the dressing room at Jones Road, clad in a big frieze coat he would move amongst us almost in a rapture of admiration, featuring his wonderful kind eyes on the athletic figures around him. I can clearly remember one Sunday after a big Dublin championship match, when, as we were receiving a rub down before dressing, he came up and delivered a vigorous smack with his bare hand and said with overwhelming enthusiasm: 'Man, is there anything grander than the smell of muscle!'[2]

But there was another side to Cusack. No smell of muscle permeates the coruscating portrait of the anti-Semitic, chauvinistic figure of the 'Citizen' of James Joyce's *Ulysses*, who is said to be based on Cusack. Whether this is true or not, there can certainly be no disputing the fact that Cusack's career exemplified the saying that the worst wounds are self-inflicted: for his confrontational style in controversy and his devotion (perhaps an over-devotion) to Irish sports cost him dearly.

Born in 1847 – in the teeth of the Great Famine – to Irish-speaking parents in the Burren area of Co. Clare, Cusack eventually went on to found a cramming institution in Dublin. Nineteenth-century teachers' salaries in the country's National Schools varied from a penny per pupil per week to twenty-five pence for the year. Conditions tended not to be pleasant: pupils in many cases were expected to bring with them a sod of turf for the fires in their generally small and chilly one-roomed schoolhouses. (These practices gave rise to the commonly heard expression that children were educated 'by the shilling and the sod of turf'.)

Cusack himself was spared the very worst of such conditions: he taught in secondary schools and as salary scales were slightly higher, he would have done a little better than many of his peers. Still, this salary would have paled by comparison with the income brought in by his Dublin crammer – a princely £1500 a year.

Cusack also – for a time, at any rate – found favour with Thomas Croke, who in 1874 had returned from his posting as Bishop of Auckland in New Zealand to take up the influential position of Archbishop of Cashel. Croke, like Cusack, is a pivotal figure in the story of these years; and Croke, like Cusack, was an immensely strong-willed individual – not to mention a skilled politician.

Upon his return from New Zealand, Croke had thrown himself – as much as a prelate could, and then some – into the Irish political scene. He allied himself to Parnell and the Irish Parliamentary Party, and to the reforming efforts of the Land League. Such overtly political activity occasionally landed Croke in trouble. His support for the Land League, for example, saw him summoned to Rome for a scolding – yet, remarkably, Croke remained undaunted. He let it be known that the papacy would be better off listening to the needs of the people – and that if it did, it would experience the same levels of popular support as he, Croke, enjoyed.

Upon his return to Ireland, indeed, Croke penned some irreverent verses to mark the occasion. One ran as follows:

'Presume not with politics iver to palter,
Give the platform and attend to the altar.'
So the Pontiff advised, and I wouldn't gainsay him,
But you'll see, darling boys, how I mane to obey him.
As for Bishopric's function, I own that I'm sick of it:
Dissension I love, and I am now in the thick of it.
Me and politics nothing on earth shall o'er siver,
So Hurrah for ould Ireland, now oulder than iver.

The context of Croke's summons to Rome is of considerable interest, in that it underlines the extent to which he came under enormous pressure from his own Church. Or rather, from elements in his own Church: from the 'Romans', as he called them – meaning those both in Ireland and in Rome who sought to maintain the so-called Ultramontane ascendancy epitomized by Cardinal Paul Cullen ('I forgot little old Paul Cullen,' cries Stephen Dedalus's father in Joyce's *A Portrait of the Artist as a Young Man*, 'Another apple of God's eye!'). Cullen and his faction preached strict adherence by the Irish Church to the rule of Rome, and disapproved of any kind of Irish independence of mind.

I have glanced at the long and tangled relationship between Rome and Ireland, and any longer discussion is outside the scope of this book – but it is worth remembering that it will have taken considerable strength on the part of Croke himself to withstand the sustained pressures to which he was subjected.

Obviously, then, Croke had a great deal on his plate: the daily administration of his Archbishopric, plus his support for

Parnell and the Land Leaguers were only some of the tasks that faced him. Busy and pressurized though he was, however, the assistance he offered to the GAA was unstinting, and is in large part the reason for the enduring strength and ethos of the GAA.

As for the relationship between these two men: Croke and Cusack were in many respects on the same wavelength. Both understood that, amid the general poverty of the country, sport provided a means of salvation for many people. Croke once wrote of the depressing sights he routinely saw: 'In driving through the country on my visitations, there was nothing that grieved me so much as to see fine strapping big fellows lying beside the ditches on their faces, or otherwise sneaking about with their hands in their pockets, and humps on them.'[3]

Croke, then, would readily have seen in Cusack's proposal for a new athletic association, a means whereby some of those 'humps' could be removed from the backs of the Irish peasantry – and so when Cusack approached him, he readily agreed to become (with Davitt and Parnell) a patron of the new organization. So readily, indeed, that his letter of acceptance became the Charter of the GAA and is reproduced in the Appendix to this book.

In the course of this letter, dated 18 December 1884, Croke wrote that:

The present aspect of things in this country, is derived from the ugly and irritating fact that we are daily importing from England not only her manufactured goods, which we cannot help doing, since she has practically strangled our own manufacturing appliances, but, together with her fashions, her accent, her vicious literature, her music, bar dances, and her manifold mannerisms, her games also and her pastimes to the utter discredit of our own grand national sports, and to the sore humiliation, as I believe, of every genuine son and daughter of the old land.

Croke was writing in a very specific context. The general culture of British governance of Irish sport was given a firm footing in 1880, with the establishment of the Amateur Athletics Association (AAA) – ostensibly the governing body of sports in England, but actually of all of the United Kingdom, including Ireland. The instant response of the AAA to the formation of the GAA was to publicly insist that it, and it alone, must function as the governing body for sport in Ireland as in Britain – a stance that made cooperation with the GAA impossible.

The GAA passed a retaliatory banning motion the following December stating that anyone competing at an athletic meeting held under the rules of another organization could not compete in GAA fixtures. This was arguably a perfectly reasonable response – but it was a significant moment, marking as it did the beginning of what became known as the 'ban'. This was, as we will see, a regime that would endure in one form or another for more than a century.

At this original moment, Croke, who did not want to see division in Irish sport, objected to the 'ban', and Cusack agreed to drop it. Later, however, as attitudes hardened in Ireland and the constitutional Home Rule movement was resisted by British and unionist forces, the 'ban' policy would re-emerge and became part of the GAA structure. Foreign games, including soccer, rugby, cricket and hockey, would be deemed beyond the pale; and even foreign dances would be prohibited. Attendances at such proscribed events would be subject to scrutiny by vigilantes – with GAA members expelled for attendance.

*

Later in the book, I will give sustained attention to what might be called the 'politics of naming' within the GAA – and in particular, the significance attached to the naming of a GAA stadium, or a stand within a stadium. For now, it is sufficient to emphasize the fact that the average GAA stadium or stand tends to be dedicated to the memory of members of the association – and to note that, with the exception of the GAA's Dublin headquarters (which of course bears Croke's own name), these titles together form an explicitly *republican* memorial, a powerful comment on the impact of the IRB and the physical-force tradition on the association.

It is not likely that Croke would appreciate the sight of such a list. Like Cusack and Davin, he wanted the new organization to be principally a sporting body, not a tool of the Irish Republican Brotherhood to be deployed in the promotion of revolution and violence. Throughout his life, indeed, Croke used his influence to withstand the takeover attempts of the secret society. His leadership ensured that priests in his archdiocese, and in others throughout the country, became active in the new organization;

and for many years the ranks of the Catholic clergy provided educated, dedicated administrators for the Association – while at the same time also acting as checks on the power and influence of the IRB.

Croke's influence can be detected in all manner of ways. Take the tradition of the Sunday Game, which is so central to GAA life. This derived from Croke's permission to hold matches on a Sunday – a radical move at the time, and one that contributed and indeed continues to contribute to the organization's strength. Croke's only stipulation was that the games be played at a time of day that allowed competitors and spectators to attend Mass first. An inspired decision, then – but there was one unwelcome consequence to this otherwise very sensible and practical Sunday rule. It meant that many Protestants, especially in the province of Ulster, declined to participate in GAA activities – for a Sunday game would mean breaking the Sabbath. This was a source of unhappiness for Cusack and for many others, for it worked against their ideal of the GAA as a truly national and non-sectarian body.

The GAA, then, was an organization that was able to call upon a good deal of energy and to rely on strong and powerful characters in its ranks – but such a state of affairs did not always work in its favour. This can be seen in the clash between Cusack and Croke – a clash which in hindsight seems inevitable, in spite of their common ideology. Croke took exception to Cusack's personal manner, his aggression and his use of violent and abusive language. And since it did not do to fall out with Archbishop Croke – or with any other

Irish Catholic prelate, come to that – Cusack was very much the loser.

He was ousted from his position as general secretary of the GAA in 1886, less than two years after his hard work had helped to create the organization. Four years later, his beloved wife Margaret died – another signal blow in the life of this commanding man. Cusack made sustained efforts to regain his position as general secretary – but he failed, and the remaining fabric of his life disintegrated. In 1887 he had founded a new newspaper, the *Celtic Times*: this was in itself a demanding experience, and it was shattering when the publication failed after a matter of months; it is said he pawned his watch in an attempt to keep the paper afloat.

His teaching career imploded too, and his crammer was eventually wound up. He died in 1906, a police report noting that he was 'broken down with drink'. But Michael Cusack deserves to be remembered for bringing bands, banners and heroes to a depressed land, and offering sustenance, where little had existed before, to many an inhabitant of Ireland.

*

I want to emphasize at this point that, despite the leadership of Croke, Davin and many others, the GAA did not step into a position of influence instantly and everywhere in the land. Certain Catholic prelates, for example, were more reluctant than the redoubtable Croke to step forward to offer support: and this in its turn meant that many anxious Catholic parents at first warned off their children from joining the ranks of a potentially suspect association. And waiting in the long grass were members of the Royal Irish Constabulary charged with monitoring and reporting back on the activities of this new and energetic organization with claims to national relevance.

Moreover, there could be personal danger involved with any open declaration of affiliation with the GAA. In Co. Kerry, for example, agrarian unrest and RIC counter-violence meant that, two years after the GAA began, the Killarney GAA club had to be founded late at night, by candlelight, in a gasworks, by a group whom the GAA historian Tom Looney aptly terms 'dangerous dreamers'. Police surveillance was such that those involved knew that they could pay for their actions by sanctions initiated by the police: severe sanctions such as losing a teaching or civil service post, or perhaps a contract to supply a government agency with goods or services.

The Catholic Church, meanwhile, was highly ambiguous in its attitude to the GAA as a political organization – in its attitude that is, to the Fenian stake in what was ostensibly a sporting body. The church in general and Thomas Croke in particular were obliged to undertake a delicate balancing act – both to protect the GAA itself and to defend and advance the interests of the church. It is certainly the case that Croke and his fellow priests helped to bring the Fenians in from the cold in so far as respectable opinion in Ireland was concerned. It was under the influence of IRB members within the GAA, for example, that the National Monuments Fund was established; this took place in 1887, and throughout the period of the next four years, this fund benefitted from tournaments held under GAA auspices which raised money to erect monuments over the graves of leading Fenians in Glasnevin Cemetery.

Croke himself had supported this fund. In a letter (with a cheque enclosed), he described his attitude to the Fenian rising of 1867. He wrote:

> The tragic incidents and deeds of daring so conspicuously associated with the abortive rising of 67, though in many ways to be deplored, were far from being barren in lasting and beneficent results; and the ashes of the men who chiefly figured in the memorable scenes of that eventful year should not, therefore, be allowed to remain unhonoured any longer on Irish soil.[4]

But it was inevitable that Croke, like the GAA itself, would suffer occasional falls from this tightrope that he himself had strung. In 1887, for example, Croke had found himself facing a Fenian-oriented situation once again: and this time, the politics and strategizing were clear for all to see. In that year, the IRB made a determined effort to take over the GAA at a convention held in Thurles. The Fenian faction backed Corkman P. M. Fitzgerald for the position of chairman – much to the disapproval of the church. In a heated atmosphere, one of Croke's priests, Jack Scanlan, attempted to deny the chair to Fitzgerald – but his move was rejected. Scanlan and his followers then left – or were driven out of – the meeting, and went on to convene one of their own. In their absence from the official convention, the IRB faction succeeded in electing another of their own – Clareman E. M. Bennett – as GAA president. The result was a bitter split which developed over the succeeding months, with many GAA clubs refusing to accept Bennett's appointment.

Croke intervened decisively in this angry dispute. Privately, he held a series of meetings involving all parties in Archbishop's House in Thurles. Publicly, he threatened to resign his position as a patron of the GAA, and he issued an influential statement to the newspapers in which he noted that the GAA (at this point, remember, still only three years old) had 'drifted away from its original designs, and those who had somehow secured the management of it were far more solicitous about individual supremacy and sectional tactics than about the success and development of our National Sports'.

Croke's threats and efforts bore fruit. Another convention was called for 1888, and was held once more in Thurles under Croke's own tutelage – and at this convention, the GAA was set on another course. Maurice Davin was elected president of the organization for a second time. The convention also adopted Croke's proposal to enable local clubs to take charge of their own affairs, with each subject to a county board. Thus, even if the IRB succeeded in taking over the annual convention – as they had done the previous November – the organization's *central* power would be diluted at *local* level. But Croke's proposal was not welcomed by all, with tensions emerging in the organization as a result.

Within the GAA, the split was worsened by the activities of both the IRB and the clergy following Davin's election as president. The IRB returned to the charge and in 1889, its members succeeded in taking control of the GAA Central Council. The clergy, whose support throughout the parishes was, we must remember, essential to the GAA, resisted: in spite of Croke's private ambiguities, the church was not prepared to allow itself to be used by the Fenians to bring potential recruits for an armed rebellion into the IRB's clutches. Bishops like John Coffey of Kerry and Edward O'Dwyer of Limerick warned their flock against fraternization with the GAA, and pulpits rang with denunciations of the organization.

Croke himself did not join in this public chorus of anger – and in this he had at least the tacit support of the powerful Archbishop of Dublin, William Walsh. But Croke *did* seek to nullify the IRB's creeping influence by encouraging his clergy to take an ever more active role in GAA affairs: and this tactic would, as I have mentioned, become his favourite way of introducing – quietly but effectively – checks and balances into the administration and ideological direction of the organization.

An incident in Kerry underscores the complexity of the relationship between church, the GAA and the Fenian in these years. Step forward Croke once more: for he was responsible for frustrating what could have been the authorities' greatest anti-GAA stroke: getting the Catholic Church in Kerry onside to publicly condemn the organization. This incident occurred in 1895, and arose out of the staging of a GAA game to raise funds for the local chapter of the Sisters of Charity. Bishop Coffey had initially granted permission for the game, but the RIC in the county appealed to him to change his mind – and Coffey very publicly withdrew his permission. He said that the GAA was connected with secret societies and that under no circumstances could he agree to any such fundraising effort taking place on his patch.

The GAA appealed to Croke to come to its rescue – and Croke rose to the occasion. But his reaction should not merely be assessed in terms of its value to the fledgling organization. It also, as we will see, laid down a template of using the Catholic doctrine of 'mental reservation': this enables one not to tell the truth while at the same time disguising this untruth so effectively (for example by withholding facts) that one cannot be accused of telling an actual lie.

At this very time, the GAA had arranged for the 1895 All-Ireland hurling final to be staged on Croke's own home patch of Thurles in his honour. Croke marked the occasion by issuing a statement saying that he was aware that the GAA 'had taken sides in the recent political dispute which was natural'. He then went on to remark that while he was aware of Coffey's denunciation of the GAA in Kerry, he himself was totally unaware of any links between the GAA and the IRB. He added that he entirely disbelieved that any such links existed, and that he was surprised that Coffey could have made such a statement. As far as he knew, Croke added, there was no foundation for such accusations.

This, about an organization connected intimately with the

IRB! This was a mental reservation writ large indeed!

Croke's ringing endorsement had the intended effect: it restored the GAA's standing in the minds of many of the doubtful. The Thurles game itself, however, did not: the match, between Dublin's Young Irelanders and Cork's Nils (shorthand for the Latin *nil desperandum*, do not despair) ended in a riot; and the GAA was fortunate that its reputation did not suffer worse damage. As for the links between the GAA and the IRB in Kerry: this was a deep and intimate relationship – and both the RIC and Croke were perfectly well aware of the fact. The county president Thomas Slattery, the secretary, Maurice Moynihan, and the treasurer, Michael Hanlon, were all senior figures in the IRB – and other members of the board were involved in the Brotherhood too.

*

In these closing decades of the nineteenth century, as we have seen, Home Rule was top of the agenda in Ireland and at Westminster – and Croke was an open and enthusiastic supporter of the measure, and of Parnell and his party. This was especially the case as the prospect of Home Rule inched ever closer to reality. There had been tension in the air in the course of the 1880s: alert readers will have noted Croke's gnomic reference, in his pronouncements on Kerry, Coffey and the IRB, to contemporary 'political developments'.

Or not so gnomic: though the archbishop could hardly have gone into detail, everyone in Ireland at this time would have understood what he meant. In 1887, Parnell was accused in the London *Times* of having been complicit in the murders in the Phoenix Park in May 1882 of two of the most important officials in the British administration in Ireland. The accusation caused a sensation: Parnell was able to prove that the accusations in *The Times* were utterly baseless – or rather, that they were based on letters forged on the direction of Richard Pigott, which would lead to Pigott's suicide – but this event was merely a forerunner of greater sensations to come.

In December 1889, a legal case initiated in London precipitated the downfall of Parnell. William O'Shea, one of his fellow Irish Party MPs, filed for divorce from his wife Katharine – and cited Parnell as co-respondent. The relationship between Katharine O'Shea and Parnell was of long standing, and had been an open secret in Irish and British political circles – but it was quite another matter to have the affair brought thus into the open.

In Ireland, the legal case had the effect of creating a split in the GAA. Its IRB members lined up to support Parnell, while the Catholic Church condemned his actions – in the process bringing many of its GAA followers with it. Prime Minister William Gladstone, meanwhile, was obliged to cut his previously close ties with Parnell: his own electoral base would not countenance an alliance with a man so, as many voters saw it, tainted by adultery.

Parnell refused to go quietly, railing against those who were snatching Home Rule from his grasp just when it appeared certain he was about to secure it. As for Croke, he too was appalled by the dashing of the hopes of Home Rule, but now he began to view Parnell, publicly at least (for of course he had been as aware as everyone else of his friend's relationship with Katharine O'Shea), as a 'maniac [...] rushing through the country every week setting Irish men at each other's throats, belauding himself and flinging filth and abuse at all who differ from him'.

Ultimately, the strain took its toll on Parnell, who died at Hove on 6 October 1891 at the age of forty-five. In the meantime, the emotions indicated by Croke's 'maniac' comment had been felt throughout the country. The GAA suffered badly from the position on Parnell adopted by the IRB, with club membership dwindling to something less than 200. In this climate, IRB influence on the GAA inevitably weakened – with the effect that figures rather more concerned with Gaelic games than Gaelic revolution came to the fore.

Two such, in particular, deserve mention for their efforts at healing the splits in the movement. One was a Meath farmer named Dick Blake; and the other was the Limerick native Frank Dineen. Under Blake, who became general secretary in 1895, a number of clubs which had left the GAA over the Parnellite split returned to the fold. In addition, he focused on reforming the games themselves. The GAA in this period also readdressed the issue of the 'ban'. The organization had, partly out of fear of British infiltration, discouraged members of the British security forces from membership: now, under Blake's direction, this ban was dropped.

This was a significant moment – though it should be noted that this was not emphatically the end of these bans. As time went on, as hostilities loomed, as attitudes hardened once again, the GAA would not only reinstitute the ban on British personnel, but would *extend* it to those who took the oath of allegiance to the British crown. This, of course, inevitably included public servants, and would lead, as we shall see, to further controversy and bitterness before the measure was in the fullness of time dropped.

Blake's spell at the helm ended in controversy in 1898 amid allegations of financial irregularity. Whether this was the real reason for the controversy is a moot point: it may have been due to the fact that he acted as referee in a highly combustible All-Ireland final between Cork and Limerick – which Cork lost. What is certain, however, is that during Blake's tenure, the GAA moved decisively away from overt politics – by, for example, outlawing political discussions at its annual convention. Henceforth, such discussions were not even to be held at lower levels of the association. The GAA was declared formally to be non-political and non-sectarian; and GAA clubs were forbidden from taking part in political movements or from using recognizably political labels in naming clubs.

In these endeavours to keep the GAA clear of politics, Blake received valuable support from a Parnellite MP. This was William Field, who was at this time treasurer, and he was joined by P. P. Sutton and Patrick Tobin, two other figures of honour in GAA history. Sutton and Tobin epitomize the term 'amateur' as it is used by the organization – describing as it does those individual members who devote time and energy without any expectation of financial or other return. For example, these two men managed to build bridges with some five hundred of the clubs which had disaffiliated at the time of the Parnellite split, and persuaded them to return to the fold.

Blake was succeeded by Dineen, a sportswriter who has left an indelible mark on the GAA. In 1908, when fourteen acres at Jones Road on the northside of Dublin came up for sale, Dineen bought the land for £3,250. Despite personal financial pressures (which caused him to sell a few acres of the site to nearby Belvedere College for use as playing fields), he managed to hold on to the greater part of this substantial patch of land for four years, until the GAA was able to raise the money to buy the rest of the ground from him – for the princely sum of £3,645, eight shillings and fivepence.

The rest, as they say, is history. That unprepossessing site on Jones Road became Croke Park – even if, in those early days, money was scarce and facilities even scarcer. The legendary sports writer Patrick D. Mehigan – better known as 'Carbery' – told a story which only he could write (and get away with) to illustrate the conditions in the early days of Croke Park. Carbery noted that:

> Croke Park was a rough dump without stands or sidelines. I recall one day – a day of dark November fog and drizzle with a dun red leather ball, battered and sodden: let the full back tell the story: 'The fog was terrible, with mist and rain. We were winning easily and only an occasional ball come to me out of the mist. Then I saw it soaring in;

I jumped up and caught with my left hand, a great catch; then I let fly ash. I hit and the next thing I was covered with feathers – I'd caught a Croke Park pigeon.'[5]

Carbery does not tell us the name of that fullback, but there is no doubt that feathers of another sort were about to fly in the next era of Croke Park's history – as we shall shortly see. Another GAA figure, a certain Luke O'Toole, was about to succeed Blake and Dineen in the familiar minuet of developing the games themselves while simultaneously dancing with the IRB and coping with the turmoil of Irish affairs.

First, however, let us examine the specific Gaelic games which all these figures helped to nurture.

CHAPTER THREE

Let the Games begin

I WANT IN THIS CHAPTER TO LOOK A LITTLE MORE CLOSELY AT the games developed into national pastimes by the Gaelic Athletic Association: hurling, camogie, handball and Gaelic football.

The last of these is of comparatively recent origin. One of the earliest mentions of the game we now call Gaelic football dates from 1812 when the Iberno-Celtic Society published a description of an energetic match between the young men of Meath and Louth. The game – it was sometimes called 'Caid' in those days, and was played with a ball made from the bladder of an ox – was conducted without much by way of rules, the object being simply for each team to drive the ball beyond a certain point in a field; to add to the drama, wrestling was frequently involved.

The game in those days, then, was certainly not for the faint-hearted. As can be imagined, these early encounters often became rather more productive of faction fights and riots than of sportsmanship, but the gradual evolution of the GAA put some flesh on the bones of this sport. The codification of sport as encouraged by the association led to the development of a set of rules to govern the playing of football. Players were limited to a fixed number of fifteen a side; and by 1911 the distinctive H-shaped goalposts of contemporary games made their first appearance.

Gaelic football was now set fair – and sure enough, it has since evolved to become the most popular form of football in Ireland, soccer notwithstanding. In addition, the strain of football known as Australian Rules – a version of the game heavily influenced by Irish emigrants – has become one of that country's most popular sports.

The game of Gaelic football involves physical contact, aerial fielding, and ground play. In addition, it requires a high degree of agility, because the rules on tackling – while they do not allow rugby's full-on embrace – do provide for fearsome charging and the knocking of the ball out of an opponent's grasp. And *fearsome* is the operative word: after all, a fist allegedly directed at a ball tucked under the chest can just as easily take out a player as the ball.

In the early days of the GAA, Gaelic football was rightly regarded as a game involving considerable precision. The Kerry footballer and legend Dick Fitzgerald, in a sports manual written in 1914, noted that the game ought best to be described as a *scientific* pursuit:

> It is necessary to lay this down at the very beginning, because some people have got an idea into their heads that the game is unscientific, and they have no scruple about saying so.

There was a time, indeed, when the game was anything but a scientific exposition. This was the case some twenty years ago, when the rough and tumble and the go-for-the-man system obtained. Then it was rather a trial of strength and endurance than an exhibition of skill. But all that is gone long since. Even as far back as the nineties, when as many as twenty-one men aside played, there were not wanting signs of development on the scientific side. Later on, when the game was confined to seventeen players a side, it became more and more a trial of skill, as in the Kerry v. Kildare matches, and, finally, when the number was reduced to fifteen aside, Science became the order of the day.

Can anyone say that Gaelic football is unscientific since the memorable encounters between Kerry and Louth in May and June, 1913? Some forty thousand people witnessed each of these strenuous tussles for supremacy, and it has been said on all sides that never in the history of outdoor games in Ireland have people gone home so well pleased with what they saw.

Fitzgerald himself was a true professional. Many of his recommendations for improvement of the game – including a regime of fully professional coaching, and an awareness of diet – are as relevant today as they were a century ago. It is fitting, and is doubtless a source of considerable pride to all Kerry players, that this great man is remembered in the naming of Fitzgerald Stadium in Killarney.

Given the careful distinctions drawn by Michael Cusack and others between 'Gaelic' games and the 'Anglo' pursuit of rugby football, it is amusing to think that Cusack may have been drawn to Gaelic football by his knowledge of – rugby! A historian of Blackrock College, Fr Michael Farragher (who had the dubious pleasure of being my English teacher), first suggested this idea to me. It was customary for students at late nineteenth-century Blackrock to play a form of running rugby known as 'tip rugby', in which the ball was passed when a player was touched. Tackling as such was outlawed for the good practical reason that the game was played in the College's unforgiving asphalt yard.

Farragher suggested to me – and it's a beguiling thought – that Cusack responded to the idea of embedding touch as a central rule of Gaelic football. He was, after all, a rugby player himself in his early days, and he understood the utility of the two-armed tackle as practised on the rugby field. Why not evolve a rule for Gaelic football that would draw inspiration from rugby while at the same time being unique and distinctive in its own right? And so the shoulder charge of Gaelic football was born – a charge that in its abrasiveness is the equal of any rugby move.

As it has evolved, Gaelic football – though enormously skilful and, particularly in the higher levels, calling for a high level of fitness – nevertheless leaves itself open to the possibility of persistent fouling. A player may not *tackle* another: but can attempt to *dislodge* the ball – and because a full-blooded tackle is not allowed, the dislodgement process can cause tempers to flare!

In addition, the ball may not be picked up directly from the ground: and it takes a skilful player to nudge it into the hands with a toe and still swerve past an opponent at full speed. As for hand-passing in Gaelic football: while in the past, high passes were common, a type of hand-passing has these days largely replaced the overhead game, giving football a superficial similarity to rugby. We can imagine how badly this similarity would have gone down in earlier years.

*

So much for the roots and context of Gaelic football. As for hurling, surely this is the greatest and most athletic of sports. Any commentary on hurling, thankfully, can draw on a deep well of wisdom: the words of the great GAA commentator Patrick D. Mehigan, to whom I referred in the last chapter, and who is better known by the nickname 'Carbery'. Carbery had been a famous athlete in the early years of the twentieth century, winning acclaim on the athletic field and playing hurling for Cork. He was also a noted naturalist, an expert on coursing, and responsible for the first running commentaries on hurling that were ever broadcast from Croke Park. It is safe to claim, I think, that Carbery can take the credit for spreading the popularity of Gaelic games in general – and hurling, of course, in particular – by a factor of several hundred per cent.

Writing long after the passions of the War of Independence had subsided, Carbery wrote truly of the sport of hurling and of the stadium at Croke Park, these two great GAA signature institutions:

> Hurling and Croke Park have changed out of all knowledge. Though still fast and fierce enough to please that war lust, which appears to be innate in all humans, in hurling the GAA have evolved a fine, manly open-air spectacle, clean, sportsman like and honest.

We will allow Carbery his use of hyperbole. And yet I must underscore the point that, while the game of hurling itself is just as he describes it, those who play it are not, perhaps, always quite so sporting. After all, let us not forget the arresting image conjured up by the phrase: 'He gave him the timber.' It is also worth noting that while some of Carbery's writing might not be exactly politically correct in today's terms, it does illustrate very well the cultural attitudes of the time under review.

Certainly he knew how to turn a phrase – and he was able to put his command of the natural world to excellent use. For example, he thought so highly of Jack 'Skinny' O'Meara of Toomevarra (whom he described as Tipperary's greatest goalkeeper) that he described in vivid terms how O'Meara kept up his training in the summer months 'standing in an open barn door and stopping the swallows'. This was a typical turn of phrase from a man who, when subject matter was scarce, used his knowledge of ornithology to write entertaining columns about the blackbirds in his garden. One of his sons later commented that those blackbirds paid for his and his siblings' education! It also demonstrates how speed – supernatural speed, as it sometimes appears – is the essence of the game of hurling.

But it is also the case that hurling – and its female form, camogie – was and remains one of the most skilful and potentially dangerous stick-based games in the world. It has to be learned young because the skill level involved is nearly impossible to acquire in adulthood. And so, while Carbery's depiction of hurling as being intrinsically 'clean' might on occasion prove debatable, he was entirely correct when he spoke of the sport's distinctly warlike aspect.

Hurling is a most ancient sport too, in this respect leaving its footballing cousin in the dust. For centuries it has figured in Irish folklore and legend and is clearly one of the identifying characteristics of Irish culture. One of the earliest mentions of the sport dates from myths of the Battle of Moytura, fought between the two Irish tribes of the Fir Bolgs and the Túatha Dé Danaan. By way of preparation for the battle, which is said to have resulted in great slaughter, the two sides staged a hurling match – and this too seems to have been a fairly savage affair, even before battle itself was joined:

> Rúad, with 27 sons of the courageous Mil, sped westwards to the end of Mag Nia to offer a hurling contest to the Túatha Dé Danaan. An equal number came out to meet them. The match began. They dealt many a blow on legs and arms till their bones were broken and bruised and they fell outstretched on the turf and the match ended.

Hurling also figures in the early Irish legal codes known as the Brehon Laws, and there were provisions for compensation for accidents and for deliberately caused injuries or deaths. By way of ensuring that these provisions were necessary, the ancient texts also refer to the fact that hurleys – the sticks themselves – were embossed with tin and brass rings.

The warlike character of the game is made known to every Irish schoolchild by means of the legend of how the boy Sétanta received the name Cú Chulainn, going on to become the great swashbuckling Irish hero. Sétanta killed a great hound by using his bronze hurl to drive his ball, also of bronze, into the hound's mouth. He is also said to have single-handedly out-hurled 150 boys of his own age who were being trained in martial arts.

Hurling is associated with warfare, then – and it's also associated with sex. According to legend, the saga of Diarmuid and Gráinne, one of the great love tales of Ireland, began at a hurling match. The High King of Ireland, Cormac MacArt, had promised three kisses (he clearly assumed they were his to promise) from any woman present, except his wife and daughter, to the man who would score the first goal of the match. Diarmuid scored – and kissed Cormac's daughter.

This Gráinne was no shrinking violet. She is said to have responded to her lover's advances with ardour that was greater than anything Diarmuid himself could muster: when water splashed on her leg, she chided Diarmuid, saying that the water was showing more initiative than he was. The resultant love affair gave rise to the story of the Pursuit of Diarmuid and Grainne, the Irish version of the Tristan and Isolde legend.

Carbery delighted in this romantic tradition of hurling – although he cloaked what he considered its excessive devotion to sex by emphasizing that the story of Diarmuid and Grainne led respectably to the altar. His 'The lass that loves a hurler' contains the following:

> *Her deep blue eyes and neck of snow,*
> *Her breasts like billow soft below,*
> *Her hips in easy numbers flow,*
> *Going to the well for water,*
> *She cheers our team, her eyes aflame!*
> *And after Sunday's final game,*
> *I'll meet her in a glen I'll name –*
> *And ask her to the Altar.*

A more martial view of hurling was well summarized by another outstanding GAA commentator, Seamus O'Ceallaigh, who wrote breathlessly:

> Hurling is an art. Without question the hurling game was zealously practiced by the ancient Celts to prepare their young manhood for the arts of war. Single combat and not mechanized or chemical skill then decided the fate of nations. Hurling developed a harmony of mind and body which drew out all the best qualities of the budding man, an erect stately carriage and commanding presence, a graceful swing of movement, firm, straight and powerful limbs inured to hardship [...] Hurling formed an essential

part of each youth's education [...] as no other game it made for balance and efficiency of every muscle and sinew, every organ and facility of body and mind. It taught reckless courage, initiative speed of thought and action. It encouraged collective effort mutual respect and gallant sportsmanship. When such writers and indeed many spectators and players went to a game they felt themselves in communion with the heroes of old, with an Ireland that once was.[6]

Hurling seems to have attracted the hostility of invaders early on. The Statutes of Kilkenny of 1367 – passed in an attempt to shore up crumbling English power in the colony of Ireland – forbade the playing of the game and directed the attention of the Anglo-Norman settler class towards what the authorities considered more beneficial pursuits: the Statutes proclaimed that:

It is ordained and established that the commons of the said lands of Ireland who are in divers marches of war use not henceforth the game which men call Hurling with great clubs and ball upon the ground but that they apply and customize themselves to use and draw bows and throw lances, and other *gentle* games that appertain to arms, whereby the Irish enemies may be better checked.

Men caught in the act of playing hurling were liable to imprisonment or fines – and yet pursuit of the game continued so enthusiastically that they had to be outlawed once more in the Galway Statute of 1527.

By the time Michael Cusack was striding the grassy spaces of the Phoenix Park, a version of the game was being played in the grounds of Trinity College Dublin. This form of the ancient game did not allow for overhead stick play and frowned on 'dangerous' play, such as hooking an opponent's stick or hard-charging. This Trinity version of hurling was played with a narrow boss or blade some 5 centimetres (2") thick. This ruled out overhead play, the skilful running with the ball on the boss of the hurl, and the tremendous long pucks of the traditional game.

And it did not please Cusack at all. He wanted to revive hurling along traditional lines, and deplored what he considered the effete pastimes of Trinity. And he also, in a more general way, wanted to restore an essential *order* to the playing both of hurling and to the evolution of Gaelic football.

The Famine, and the extraordinarily high rates of emigration that accompanied this cataclysm, had played havoc with sport, just as it had with other aspects of Irish life. All contact sports are, in my opinion, essentially substitutes for the bear-pit spectacles of the Colosseum. But hurling in particular, rather than being codified and developed as a popular spectator sport, had degenerated into a form that recalled faction fighting between parishes, rather than sporting activity. As a result, the English writer and commentator Arthur Young famously – and perhaps reasonably enough, given what he had witnessed during a tour of late eighteenth-century Ireland – dismissed the ancient sport as the 'cricket of savages'.

As for the individuals called upon to referee such early games: they had courage. Indeed, they had to possess courage, as they were not issued with whistles and had to try to control events on horseback, from the sidelines. Moreover, they could only intervene in the most serious altercations by riding amongst the players and separating them as best they could. As the games were normally played with twenty-seven players on each side, this was no easy task. In addition, aspects of the game such as the size of the goal posts, and the ball and stick – not to mention the minor consideration of timekeeping – varied widely from place to place.

Following the initial formation of the GAA, Michael Cusack played a major role in rectifying this state of affairs. He drew up the set of rules (given in the Appendix) which transformed hurling and, with occasional alterations and modifications, have governed the game to this day. Cusack's other great contribution to the sport involved settling it firmly into a parish, county and inter-county context. There could be no better way to ensuring grassroots strength and assuring a degree of popular loyalty: after all, the games were now associated with and identified with the very stuff of people's own lives – and, since each contest culminated in the spectacle of the All-Ireland, it brought a pleasant charge of drama to proceedings too. Order, meanwhile, was maintained and disputes resolved by an over-arching and authoritative Central Council.

*

Women's hurling – the sport of camogie – was codified and encouraged rather later than the men's game. A competitive women's match took place at Navan in 1904: and thenceforth the female, or modified, form of the game of hurling attracted a steady following – including the mandatory cohort of RIC observers.

As pointed out by Eoghan Corry, one of the best writers on GAA affairs, the development of the women's game should be seen as part of a larger movement at this time towards female emancipation. One of the first camogie teams emerged in 1904 – and it adopted a name which underlines Corry's essential point. This was the Newry team Fág an Bealach: this literally translates as *leave the way*, but actually means *get out of my way* – a motto used as a war chant by Irish regiments of the past.

Of course, whether emancipation has truly been achieved, even in today's sporting world, is a question raised by the very term *Ladies' Hurling*. This vexing term is still current today: for some reason, these two tougher-than-tough sports of hurling and rugby persist in referring not to *Women's* but to *Ladies'* forms of the sport. I believe that in the case of camogie, this may have something to do with the upper- and middle-class origins of the modern sport.

Camogie was supported initially by late nineteenth-century university women – including Máire Ní Chinnéide, Hanna Sheehy Skeffington, and Agnes O'Farrelly – who had an impact on Irish cultural and political life, as well as on sport itself. In addition, the new Camogie Association, founded in 1911 to give the then-flagging organization a second wind, appointed

Elizabeth, Countess of Fingall as its president – the idea being that installing a titled personage would give the game cachet in decision-making circles. And this appointment certainly helped to broaden the appeal of camogie in these critical early days.

Of course, the game also began increasingly to draw energy from the cultural ferment taking place all around it; it is worth noting, for example, that the development of camogie as a national sport also owes much to an inter-varsity competition organized by O'Farrelly, who lectured at University College Dublin. It is significant too that the development of camogie had a bearing on the GAA's 'ban' culture: many of the female leaders of the organization were of a mind to add women's hockey to the list of proscribed sports – and this indeed came to pass.

In terms of a specifically *female* cultural context, the women of the GAA could look to the contemporaneous female nationalist movement Inghinidhe na hÉireann – the Daughters of Ireland. The latter was founded by Maude Gonne, and it embraced both cultural and military activity, eventually becoming affiliated to Cumann na mBan and playing its part in the Irish Volunteer movement. Amongst Maude Gonne's supportive 'daughters' was Constance Markievicz, who would later become the first female member of parliament elected to Westminster – and who has, as we will see later, a GAA stadium in Sligo named in her honour.

The first female camogie club emerged from Dublin's Keating branch of the Gaelic League, which at this time was the largest in the organization. Some may raise an eyebrow at the fact that the country's first camogie club, founded in 1904, should have adopted the title of the Cú Chulainns. After all, this was a sport firmly rooted in the ideal of independent and emancipated womanhood – and the legendary Cú Chulainn in Irish folklore is the greatest symbol of male dominance: the archetypical warrior; and a harvester of women.

In hindsight, of course, this name is also symbolic of the 1916 revolution: a bronze statue of the hero stands in Dublin's General Post Office, depicting Cú Chulainn nearly dead, the body still upright, because the hero tied himself to a pillar with a raven perching on the shoulder signalling to his enemies that he was dead and that it was at last safe to approach. But it remains a fact that this was an odd choice of name: for in 1904, the women of the namesake camogie club could not have known how the cards of history would fall.

Though born of the middle classes, the founders of camogie as a national sport insisted on egalitarianism. In particular, they resisted efforts to have their games transferred from Sundays to Saturdays, arguing – of course, correctly – that this was a move aimed at preserving class divisions. Had camogie been played on Saturdays, such a change would have excluded women and girls who had to work on that day. So Sundays it was – for women as for men.

Later, during the revolutionary period, camogie players suffered in much the same way as hurling and Gaelic football players. That the authorities were fully aware of where the camogie players sympathies' lay, for example, may be gleaned from what might be termed an honourable mention of their activities in a Cork riot of 1917. This began after a camogie game, when the homeward-bound participants stopped at Cork Gaol to cheer a group of militant women prisoners and, apparently, to throw stones. A British military report on the incident stated the riot was caused 'by the camogie contingent'.

*

Handball – curiously for a sport said to have been Thomas Croke's favourite game – remained decidedly the poor relation of the GAA for the first three decades of the organization's existence. The sport's origins are lost in the mist of antiquity: it is known to have been played in the Basque regions of what are now Spain and France; in addition, the English game of 'fives' is also clearly connected to handball – and so it is a fair assumption that it evolved as a thoroughly and healthily demotic game, taking its influences where it would.

In his famous comic novel *At Swim-Two-Birds*, Flann O'Brien used handball to satirize the heroic exaggerations of the Gaelic Revivalists who sought to popularize their message by peopling the deep Irish past thickly with warrior kings and beautiful queens. In a famous passage, O'Brien uses handball to illustrate the attributes of those legendary Irish warriors, the Fianna:

> Three fifties of fosterlings could engage with handball against the wideness of his backside, which was wide enough to halt the march of warriors through a mountain pass.

The game certainly did not figure in the IRB's planning to the same extent as its fellow Gaelic sports – this despite the fact that handball alleys had been the haunt of many a United Irishman in the approach to the 1798 uprising. Another passage illustrates how the popular young United Irishman Michael MacRandall was seized in Co. Louth:

> He was arrested while playing handball in the village of Collon and shortly afterwards, hanged in the most public spot in Drogheda, opposite the Tholsel, on 22 June 1798, one hour after receiving his sentence. There was some delay in getting possession of his body, and his funeral took place from Pitcher Hill, Drogheda, to Kildemock, Ardee, arriving in early morning, the coffin being carried all that distance [25 kilometres] on the shoulders of his sympathizers, Peter Boylan, father of Michael, being one of them.

Clearly, hurling and football would always receive more attention than an inherently small-scale game like handball, in spite of the latter's grassroots popularity: such team sports could command crowds of a different order to a game played between a minimum of two and a maximum of four players. But other factors were at work too which reduced the prestige of handball in the eyes of the GAA – and not least of these was the popularity of handball among members of the Royal Irish Constabulary. The RIC encouraged the construction of handball alleys immediately adjacent to its stations and barracks – both for reasons of physical fitness and to cultivate a sense of camaraderie. Such a close association led to a tainting of handball in the eyes of many, and an association grew up between the game itself and the GAA 'ban' culture.

And there was another potent reason. Handball was associated with widespread gambling: and this fact did not sit well with many puritan-minded individuals at the top of the GAA. Prominent handball players across Ireland attracted large wagers from their followers, with bets of up to £300 being far from unusual. The celebrated eighteenth-century rake Buck Whaley had famously won a purse of one hundred gold sovereigns for fulfilling his boast that he would play handball against the walls of Jerusalem (some versions of this story had Whaley fetching up not in Jerusalem but Mecca – but this seems distinctly unlikely). Put simply, there was a reek of sin from the sport of handball that attracted some, but repelled others, and led to its marginalisation in the pantheon of Gaelic games.

Which was a shame – because it takes a rare combination of strength, stamina, and skill to play handball well. Top players do not strike the ball with their hands so much as catch it in flight and hurl it back against the wall. There are several authentic accounts of men in their forties playing and defeating much younger opponents: the most celebrated examples of these concerns a seventy-three-year-old man who played another man for a purse of £300 – and won.

The modern game is played on a court which is generally enclosed. It measures 18–19 metres (60–63 ft) feet in length, and 8.5–9 metres (28–30 ft) in width; its front wall is anything up to 9 metres (30ft) in height and the back wall may not be less than 2.7 metres (9 ft); with the sidewalls the height of the front. Earlier courts were constructed of stone and later concrete – but thick glass is often deployed today; and in general terms, indeed, contemporary courts are light years away in quality and sleekness from the courts of my youth. Those early courts, however, had the undoubted virtue of being thoroughly flexible; and were often pressed into service as cinema screens. I recall the court at Clogh in Co. Kilkenny as one such makeshift picture house: we thought nothing, in those innocent days, of watching Hollywood stars kiss on screen – with the imprint of muddy handballs clearly visible behind them on the alley wall.

Handball players are a hardy lot: they have to be. What is known as the Irish softball is made of rubber: it is a little over 5 centimetres (2") in width and weighs sixty-two grams (3 oz). It is supposed to have a rebound capacity of 2 metres (70") when dropped from a height of 2.5 metres (100") – and getting around a court in pursuit of such a projectile with such capacities is no mean feat! It is nothing, however, to the use of what is sometimes called the 'alley cracker': a thoroughly perilous hardball which resembles a golf ball without the indentations.

The GAA's initial neglect of handball did not go unremarked by all. Criticism of the organization's attitude to the sport can be summed up in a letter from a certain P. J. Cusack, who wrote to the *Irish Independent* on 4 December 1923 to complain that:

Since the foundation of the GAA forty years ago, I find nothing to show that the Association did anything to encourage handball. The handball history of those years is one of a sordid professionalism. One leading player challenged another for a stake anything from £10 and £100. The loser was invariable dissatisfied, unpleasant incidents frequently arose, and an acrimonious and unsportsmanlike press controversy ensued.

Twenty years ago, Oliver Drew in an interview published in the *Daily News*, New York, complained that the GAA were doing nothing to help the game in Ireland...

With the assistance of Eoin O'Duffy (as we will see later, the first head of the new Irish police force), the GAA moved to take handball under its wing. The sport was played in the Tailteann Games, convened in 1924 to showcase Irish sport and culture and to help heal the wounds of the Civil War; in the same year, the Handball Association became part of the GAA. The benefits of this change soon flowed: in particular, handball became a beneficiary of the GAA's influence within government, which saw the sport's financial returns removed from the taxation net. Handball continues as a popular sport in Ireland today: not as a vast popular game, but rather as a niche pastime – albeit one with a huge following among Irish emigrants in North America.

*

I want to end this chapter with a short excursion into matters literary – and to visit in particular a small village in south Tipperary, just on the Kilkenny border. I do this to demonstrate the importance of the parish in Gaelic games – and what the games meant to the people of any given parish.

The greatest parochial hero in Irish literature is Matt the Thrasher in Charles Kickham's novel *Knocknagow or, The Homes of Tipperary* (1879), which tells of the joys and sufferings of life in an Irish village. Reading its descriptions of the effects of emigration and the predations of landlords, one can well understand how a person might take up arms to help alleviate such sufferings. It seems to me that Kickham, himself a Fenian who had suffered the pain of exile and imprisonment, caught the spirit of rural Ireland in a manner never equalled by any other writer.

Knocknagow probably impacted on me to a greater degree than on most people of my generation because my Tipperary-born mother used to read extracts from the novel to myself and my younger brother and sister after our father died in 1948, thus linking a sense of bereavement to this early experience of access to Irish literature and history.

But Kickham's work found a place in many hearts: indeed, it has had a powerful impact on generations of Irish readers. Brian O'Higgins, a noted republican writer and editor who fought in the War of Independence, described the effect the characters in Kickham's work had on an Irish emigrant:

> *When I think of Matt the Thrasher's strength*
> *And Nora Leahy's grace,*
> *I love you Tipperary though*
> *I never saw your face.*

And indeed, the 'honour of the little parish' for several decades remained the motivation of generations of GAA players.

One of the most famous episodes in the book describes a hammer-throwing contest between Matt and the Captain. Matt hesitates to defeat the popular Captain who is regarded as a good man: however, as he prepares for the last throw, his eyes fall on the little whitewashed cottages of the village – of *his* village. He overcomes his reluctance to defeat the Captain and with his throw smashes all records saying to himself: 'for the honour of the old home'.

As a result, perhaps, of Matt the Thrasher's hammer-throwing effort, subsequent generations of GAA players were sent into battle by their coaches with fiery team talks and fists pounding benches with the abjuration ringing in their ears: 'Do it for the parish!' This heroic vision of Gaelic games was further disseminated by people such as Carbery who, when he went to a game of hurling, took Kickham's words with him. In a description of an All-Ireland hurling final between Kilkenny and Tipperary, played decades after one would have thought the passions of the War of Independence had subsided, he recalled feelingly how:

[...] splintering ash crashed round the Tipperary goalie Jimmy Marr, 'five feet nothing' of the best, coolest and most fearless stuff that ever crouched eagle eyed between hurling posts [...] full-blooded pulling of the ash. Fit bodies crashed together with resounding thud; Kilkenny 'black and amber' boys like wasps at a hive; heads went in where hurls should be. And what Thomas Davis called 'the matchless men of Tipperary' weathered the Autumn storm that battered down, but did not destroy, their plenteous harvest won with so much pain and care in Leinster's field last summer. Soon the sweeping ashen sides of these tall wiry Tipperary backs swept the field [...] Tipperary 5–6 Kilkenny 3–6.[7]

If hurling could bring out those emotions decades after the revolutionary era, one can well imagine its effect during the War of Independence. We will leave the last word to the (English) sportsman, cricketer and sportswriter C. B. Fry, who observed that hurling was 'the best training for hand-to-hand fighting between armies'. The experiences of the War of Independence, as we will see, bear out Fry's judgement. Let us now turn to this era – and in particular to the decade leading up to the great year of 1916 itself.

CHAPTER FOUR

A Strengthening Force

T HE GAELIC ATHLETIC ASSOCIATION'S ANNUAL CONVENTION of 1901 was an upbeat, confident affair. At this meeting, held in Thurles, a crop of driven, talented, focused young men emerged who would steer the association in the years to come – years that, though the membership of the GAA could not know it, would prove fraught and dangerous. Such was the steadiness of this steering, indeed, that fifteen years later the Kerry-born GAA luminary and IRB activist Thomas O'Sullivan could look back on the passage of time with considerable satisfaction.

Much had changed since Carbery described a pigeon-infested, ramshackle ground at Jones Road in inner-city Dublin. That ground was now renamed Croke Park: and while it still consisted of little more than two stands and turf banks, it was now the focus of much energy and activity. Moreover, this energy was rippling through the GAA at grassroots level too, in parishes and at county level up and down the land. The association was in rude health, with the result that O'Sullivan could note with pleasure that:

The foundation of the Association as we know it today, a well officered, intelligently governed and widely directed national organization with large resources at its command, was laid in 1901 [...] there was a large succession of young men to the governing body of the organization and their ability, earnestness, enthusiasm, and patriotism raised the whole character of the movement within a few short years.

It is nevertheless important at this stage to stress that the GAA gains were relative to its impoverished origins and circumstances. Essentially, the funds were not here to do all that the association wished to do, in terms of training, grounds, and infrastructure. The association had managed to extend its presence to every town and every townland – and yet facilities in many parts of the country were not all they might have been, and certainly not all the GAA wanted them to be. The *energy* was abundantly present, then – but other aspects of GAA life would sometimes have to wait.

The following extract illustrated vividly the difficult context against which GAA players habitually played. Let us not forget that, circumstances or no circumstances, these players were expected to give their all – and that they expected this of themselves too. And all this in the days before protein shakes and hot showers:

The match was played in the middle of the day at twelve o'clock and don't forget I was working in the bar business and had to be back at work at half-past-one. I was staying in digs at the time, and after I had my breakfast about 8.30 I went to Mass and then walked to Jones Road where the match was being played. We took the field at 12 o'clock and came off winners after as tough and hard a game as ever you looked at. When you played against those Tipperary fellows you knew all about it. Seasoned campaigners every one, and as hard as the anvils they hooped their hurleys on. I played on Jack Power at right half-forward. That was always my position. One of the vital scores of the match, a sizzling goal came from Brendan Considine who come on for us instead of Hugh Burke. Well, the final whistle saw us All-Ireland champions and saw me and a lot of the lads with the marks of battle fresh on us. Then we made a dash for the dressing room, tore into our clothes and away helter skelter to our jobs. I had eaten my breakfast at 8.30 that morning and all I had between that and seven o'clock was a drink of water. These were tough times, tough games and tough men that played them.[8]

By way of contrast, allow me to glance forward for a moment – to the era when, some fifty-odd years after O'Sullivan's upbeat assessment, I ran a rugby team in the *Irish Press*. The 'ban' was still in operation, meaning we could not be photographed or draw much attention to ourselves. Our rugby team had, one might say, a foot in several camps: one of our team, Sean Power, had won an All-Ireland hurling medal for Waterford; others had played at high level for their club and county. We played in what might be termed a 'business' league, and we played – just like the GAA – generally on a Sunday. Though not all Sundays: only when we could put together a passable team. Not an exalted league, then, by any means – and yet all the former GAA players on our team assured me that on average, the club facilities we enjoyed were far superior to those available to the GAA. And this at a time when many of the team were used to playing Gaelic games before crowds of 20,000 or more. It was an extraordinary state of affairs.

By this era, Croke Park had no more turf banks or the like. New stands had been constructed at Jones Road and the stadium could hold upwards of eighty thousand spectators at a push – and yet the impressive dimensions of 'Croker' and a few other stadiums were not reflected in the average facilities available at parish level. Sometimes our team would play Gaelic football matches – and at one such rural GAA ground, I enquired of an official of the opposing club: 'Where are the showers?' He pointed towards the sky and replied, 'See those big black clouds? When they come over you'll get plenty of showers!'

This was hardly a sustainable or acceptable state of affairs: and it is clear that what kept the GAA going during lean times – in periods when investment could not be passed vertically through the organization, and in periods before sponsorship and the sale of lucrative television rights swelled the coffers beyond the dreams of avarice – was pure goodwill. And specifically, goodwill distilled into the spirit of voluntarism that has always been the organization's spine and skeleton.

Voluntarism that has extended from the days of the Hayes Hotel meeting to the present moment. Voluntarism that takes the form of arranging matches, ferrying teams to and from them, collecting the money for travel and for club houses, and performing the myriad tasks that anyone familiar with organizing sport fixtures will understand – wearisome tasks, sometimes, and tedious tasks, and utterly *necessary* tasks.

*

The delegates at that Thurles convention of 1901 anticipated change, of course – indeed, how could they not? – but they could have no concept of how radical would be the changes witnessed in Ireland in the decades to come. Still, change must be anticipated and prepared for – and so the next generation was installed with this in mind. Of this generation, two major figures in particular stand out: the president of the organization, James Nowlan of Kilkenny and the general secretary, Luke O'Toole of Wicklow.

O'Toole was, needless to say, a committed nationalist and sports enthusiast; plus he was a businessman who owned two Dublin newsagents. Evidently, however, he preferred working with the GAA to running his own business: and so at the Thurles convention of 1901, at the age of twenty-seven, he campaigned for and secured the position he coveted, defeating Michael Cusack by nineteen votes to seventeen. (Thurles was one of the milestones along the road to ruin followed by Cusack in his protracted but ultimately futile attempt to regain his position in the organization he had helped to found.)

O'Toole was chosen in the hope that he would prove fleet of foot too: after all, his task was partly to steer a safe course between the Scylla of his role as general secretary of the GAA charged with running a purely sporting organization, and the Charybdis of a potentially vortex-like conflict between the IRB and the British government. And his spell as general secretary (a post he would hold until his untimely death in 1929) saw one significant change in the way that the GAA operated. He was the first holder of the post to receive a salary: the princely fee of £75 a year, plus a house adjacent to Croke Park – though given that he spent so much time travelling the country on GAA business, one wonders how much time he had to spend at home. His appointment as a salaried employee of the organization, however, certainly marks a significant step towards the sort of professionalisation that is a hallmark of the contemporary Gaelic Athletic Association.

It was the fate of Luke O'Toole to preside over some of the best and worst days of the GAA. He spearheaded reform of the organization's administration of its games, paid off its debts, and improved Croke Park's facilities to an extent that not even Carbery's pigeons would have recognized the place. No wonder, then, that Thomas O'Sullivan, a decade and more later, could look back on these years with such satisfaction, and laud O'Toole's tenure in such glowing terms.

O'Toole always put the requirements of the GAA front and centre – but, in an indication of the enduring politicization of the organization, there is every likelihood that he was a member of the IRB too. Certainly it is the case that he was the representative in Ireland of Clann na nGael, the successor organization in the United States to the Fenian Brotherhood. Indeed, he made little secret of this last affiliation. In one of his earliest addresses to a GAA annual convention (the convention of 1902, which was in fact held in the following year), he told the gathering that the Clann wanted 'every Gael in Ireland ready for the fray.'

He also proposed that the GAA be reorganized along Fenian lines: meaning, as readers will remember, that the leadership in each county would be organized in circles of six – although O'Toole was not proposing the sort of theoretical secrecy that governed IRB arrangements. This meant that, for example, the identity of James Nowlan, the new president of the GAA, was a widely known fact! – although it was less widely known that he was also a member of the Supreme Council of the IRB. Nowlan never recanted his belief in force as a means to securing political goals – and as we will shortly see, he was happy to mingle his GAA and IRB roles where necessary.

There was another side to the success of O'Toole, Nowlan and the new generation of ardent young nationalists who had taken the reins at the GAA. Although they did not come from the commanding heights of Irish society, they were a better educated generation than the one they supplanted. Whereas the backbone of the GAA in its first years had been drawn from what we might call the labouring and shop-assistant classes, the new men were of a different order: teachers, office clerks, and individuals with their feet on the lower rungs of the civil service. The GAA, in fact, was and is reminiscent of a great tree: and one can trace its development and the history of the society it grew in, by studying its rings and what was taking place when they were formed.

What was taking place in Ireland during the tenure of Luke O'Toole and James Nowlan, in these opening years of the twentieth century, was an event of great significance. This was the healing of the Parnellite split we looked at earlier in this book: the great rupture that had opened in the ranks of the Irish Parliamentary Party (and in the GAA to boot) following the fall of Parnell. Gradually, under the leadership (patient, plodding and honourable, though hardly electrifying) of John Redmond, this rupture had been healed. The world was changing: nationalists could now once more aspire to Home Rule eventually coming to pass in Ireland.

For the GAA, there was another side to this progress. Not alone did the economic and sporting culture flourish, so too did the 'ban' culture harden within the organization. The revival of a strong IRB influence within the GAA against a renewed climate of nationalist confidence and optimism in these years, led to a change in the official GAA mindset – one that might be reasonably compared to a ban of fraternization with a wartime enemy. Once more, 'foreign' games were frowned upon; once more, 'foreign' forms of cultural expression – up to and including such dances as the foxtrot and waltz – were seen as a violation of the nationalist rules. And once more, vigilantes were appointed to see that these rules were upheld. Membership of the association, and admittance to its games, was forbidden to British soldiers or members of the RIC. Furthermore, not alone was it denied to those who had taken an oath as a condition of service to the state – but the ban was extended to people who drew pensions from oath-bound employment.

Schools were written to, urging them to favour Gaelic games over foreign ones. In Dublin, such elite schools as Blackrock, Belvedere and Castleknock chose to stay with rugby. However, it is worth mentioning one school in south Co. Dublin which opted for Gaelic games: this was Presentation Brothers School in Glasthule, not far from the grounds of Cuala, which I mentioned at the outset. This decision must have had a bearing on Cuala's continued success in these years, although the school is closed now.

There were many consequences, then, to this spike in nationalist energy. As the GAA flourished, so too did the Gaelic League: de-Anglicisation, with all the energy, optimism and intolerance of youth, spread through the country. But there was one section of the population to whom this phenomenon was unwelcome – Ireland's Protestant population.

It is important to reiterate that the founders of the GAA were *not* hostile to Protestants. Croke, indeed, was quite explicit: he wanted to support Irish games but he wanted them open to all his fellow Irish citizens. He clashed on this very point with Michael Cusack – who was not anti-Protestant either, but whose calls for undivided loyalty to the organization was a response to the effort of the AAA to undermine and destroy GAA independence. Come to that, the IRB was by no means anti-Protestant either: its republican roots derived directly from such figures as Wolfe Tone and other Protestant leaders of Irish nationalism. But, human nature being what it is, as the IRB influence on the organization grew and nationalist sentiment hardened within the GAA, it was only natural that Protestant enthusiasm – which initially had been quite pronounced – began progressively to fall away. After all, many in the Protestant tradition venerated the crown, respected the RIC, and played cricket and rugby. In this context, the GAA must have seemed like the coldest of homes.

The result was lasting damage to the GAA's relationship with the Protestant community in Ireland. Put simply, the 'ban' policy, though perhaps natural enough, was poorly considered – and Ireland's Protestants formed collateral damage. The ripples from the ban radiated for years, with frequently absurd results: in 1938, for example, Douglas Hyde, the President of Ireland and a Protestant who had been a founder of the Gaelic League, was dropped as patron of the GAA because he attended a soccer match.

This sorry incident lay in the future. In these opening years of the century, however, the Protestant relationship with Ireland was placed under strain from another quarter. With Home Rule once more a looming issue in the Anglo-Irish relationship, an intervention by the British Conservative Party manipulated the Protestant position in a way that was both cynical and profoundly dangerous. Tory strategizing was used to damage Ireland, in a manner which would find no parallel in Anglo-Irish relationships for a century and more to come.

*

As Europe drifted perceptibly towards war, the skies were darkening in Ireland also, presaging a storm that had been brewing since 1886 when the leading Tory Randolph Churchill uttered the words which ensured that, as these words are written, six of Ireland's thirty-two counties remain part of the United Kingdom. They also ensured that, from 1886 onwards, rioting between Protestant and Catholic became a feature of life in the northeast of Ireland.

The words, which to this day retain their malignant effect on Irish life, were: 'Ulster will fight and Ulster will be right.' Churchill uttered them while launching a policy he described as 'playing the Orange card'. He had decided on this course when, as we have seen, the Liberal prime minister William Gladstone had brought forward a Home Rule Bill for Ireland: the opposition of Ulster Protestants would be harnessed, Churchill resolved, in order to stave off the prospect of Home Rule.

This era was over and Churchill dead and gone – but now Home Rule had returned as a realisable dream, and the Orange card continued to circulate. By 1912, indeed, its introduction appeared imminent: the twin elections of 1910 had swept away Prime Minister Herbert Asquith's Liberal majority in the House of Commons – and from now on, the Liberals would depend on Redmond's votes in order to govern. Once more, Home Rule was on the cards.

With this in mind, the Liberals in 1911 pushed through the Parliament Act which introduced a limitation on the ability of the Tory-dominated House of Lords to veto legislation – and with this Act, the ability of the Conservative Party to block

Home Rule was also at an end. Henceforth, the Tories would have to use extra-constitutional means to block Home Rule – and in so doing, to achieve their ultimate wish of destabilising and overthrowing the Liberal government of the United Kingdom. The foiling of Home Rule for Ireland was, after all, merely a means to a greater end – and the unionists of Ulster mere pawns in a greater Tory game.

In July 1912, the Tory leader Andrew Bonar Law urged Ulster unionists to resist Home Rule. At a rally at Blenheim Palace in Oxfordshire, he called on them to 'use all means in their power, including force' to achieve their ends, and observed in incendiary fashion that he could imagine 'no lengths of resistance to which Ulster can go in which I should not be prepared to support them.' One of the unintended consequences of this flagrantly anti-democratic policy was that in Germany, Kaiser Wilhelm II's advisers told him that Britain would be too preoccupied with the Irish issue and the threat of civil war to resist any German show of military might in Europe. The Kaiser accepted this fateful advice – with results which are only too well known.

Another result of the playing of the Orange card was, as we have seen, the formation of a militia – the Ulster Volunteer Force (UVF) – to resist Home Rule. Unionists flocked to join this force: there were over 200,000 signatories to the Ulster Covenant, which was dedicated to resisting Home Rule, and over 100,000 men joined the Volunteer Force itself; while Tory influence ensured that neither the navy, army nor civilian police interfered with the illegal landing, at the port of Larne in 1914, of German guns and ammunition bound for UVF stores.

It was natural, it was inevitable, that the formation of such a militia force in Ulster would create an equal and opposite response in other parts of Ireland. In his article 'The North Began' published in the Gaelic League newspaper *An Claidheamh Soluis* (Sword of Light) in November 1913, the Irish scholar Eoin MacNeill scorned the 'political histrionics' ongoing in Ulster, and suggested that an armed force should be created to defend the introduction of Home Rule should it be opposed. And where would the volunteers for such a militia be sourced? An early RIC report on the formation of the GAA provides the answer: 'The Gaelic Athletic Association', this report notes, 'could supply an abundance of first-class recruits.'[9]

This prophecy proved to be entirely correct – for MacNeill's idea met with enormous support from nationalists, including members of the GAA. The result was the formation of the Irish Volunteers, formed with the ostensible intention to 'secure and maintain the rights and liberties common to the whole people of Ireland', and whose numbers swelled rapidly towards the 175,000-mark. Few if any of these – and certainly not MacNeill, who was no Fenian supporter – realized that behind the scenes the IRB were infiltrating the Volunteers, just as they had infiltrated the Gaelic League and the GAA. For the fact was that the military council of the Brotherhood saw the formation of the Irish Volunteers as a tremendous opportunity.

As for the IRB-tinted GAA leadership and its attitude, we must assume that O'Toole and others used the principle of mental reservation to square these developments with the organization's 'no-politics' rule. In defiance of the GAA's own rules, for example, Nowlan spoke at a meeting of the Irish Volunteers convened in November 1913 at Dublin's Rotunda Rink, a temporary building in the city's Rotunda Gardens, capable of holding four thousand people. Nowlan's role at this meeting was to counsel GAA members to join the Volunteers, and to learn how to shoot straight. O'Toole did not go quite so far – but he did join his colleague in urging enrolment in this new militia.

The Irish Volunteers, however, would not stay united. Redmond insisted on controlling the organization – and when war came with Germany in the summer of 1914, he pledged the militia's support to the British war effort, reasoning that loyalty now would guarantee Home Rule later. He pledged this support publicly: first in the House of Commons, and then in a speech at Woodenbridge, Co. Wicklow, in September, in the course of which he urged the Irish Volunteers to join the war effort:

> The interests of Ireland—of the whole of Ireland—are at stake in this war. This war is undertaken in the defence of the highest principles of religion and morality and right, and it would be a disgrace for ever to our country and a reproach to her manhood and a denial of the lessons of her history if young Ireland confined their efforts to remaining at home to defend the shores of Ireland from an unlikely invasion, and to shrinking from the duty of proving on the field of battle that gallantry and courage which has distinguished our race all through its history.

I say to you, therefore, your duty is twofold. I am glad to see such magnificent material for soldiers around me, and I say to you: 'Go on drilling and make yourself efficient for the Work, and then account yourselves as men, not only for Ireland itself, but wherever the fighting line extends, in defence of right, of freedom, and religion in this war.' [10]

Such sentiments were too much for the IRB: and the Volunteer movement split – though into two unequal parts. It is estimated that in excess of 170,000 Irish Volunteers flocked to the British colours, and that only a rump of some 10–12,000 remained under a nominal control of Eoin MacNeill.

And so the road to 1916 was laid out.

*

I have written extensively elsewhere about the Easter Rising, the details of which fall outside the scope of this book. In terms of the GAA's role in the rebellion, it is evident that the organization was seen by the authorities as an accessory to the events of the Rising. As every GAA member knew, indeed, the authorities took pains to demonstrate this belief that the GAA was the enemy. Raids, disruption of matches, arrests, the overall violence of the period, drastically affected the organization's ability to carry out basic function such as staging games. Sir Matthew Nathan, the undersecretary in the British administration of Ireland, told the Royal Commission established to investigate the Rising that the GAA had 'always been anti-British'; and senior officials in the RIC claimed that extremists had control of both the GAA and the Gaelic League.

As for the statement of rebuttal issued by the GAA itself: this was strongly reminiscent of Croke's defence of the organization, after it had been attacked by Bishop Coffey of Kerry. Mental reservation was in full flow, as the GAA underscored that it was strictly non-political and non-sectarian, and that these points were woven into its constitution, its very fabric. Political questions could not be raised at its meetings, nor could its clubs or committees take part in political affairs. The statement conceded that its members were free to join any organization they chose: and that it was certainly the case, therefore, that some could have joined the Irish Volunteers. But, it claimed, the GAA had never been used 'in furtherance of the objects of the Irish Volunteers'.

This was quite a statement. It sidesteps, for example, the fact that James Nowlan had urged those present at the Rotunda meeting to join the Volunteers; and that Luke O'Toole had echoed this call. It seems to me that the statement recalls a French comment on the qualities required in war: *de l'audace, encore de l'audace, et toujours de l'audace*: audacity, more audacity, and ever more audacity. In quite barefaced terms, the GAA evaded discussion of small matters, such as its widespread custom of denying British soldiers and RIC personnel access to its meetings. And overall, it provided a sort of useful guidance list for players replying to accusatory referees with pained expressions of 'Not me, ref.'

And so: what *was* the GAA's role in the Easter Rising? In percentage terms – that is, in proportion to the total number of people who participated in the Rising – it was very considerable. But of course, not very many people did participate: a total of perhaps 1,500 Volunteers and three hundred members of James Connolly's Irish Citizen Army. The bulk of the Irish Volunteers had followed Redmond, and this included the bulk of GAA members too. So: small numbers overall, small numbers of GAA members – but a large proportion of total participants.

Paul Rouse of University College Dublin – himself a former GAA player, and also, at the time of writing, manager of the Offaly senior Gaelic football team – told the *Irish Times* (5 March 2016):

> There is stuff that has been written about the GAA and the revolution and there is this perception that the GAA was more involved than it actually was and that it was the only sporting organization involved in the revolution. This would have come as a surprise to the various soccer players like Oscar Traynor or rugby players like Kevin Barry. It's shown to be a nonsense. There were GAA members involved and the GAA was targeted on Bloody Sunday but the GAA involvement in 1916 was more as a ghostly presence.

In proportional terms, however, three hundred-odd GAA members out of fewer than two thousand participants surely constitutes more than a 'ghostly presence'. It is said that the Battle of Waterloo was won on the playing fields of Eton. If so, it is the case that the three hundred-plus GAA personnel who took part in the Rising, constituted a far higher percentage of participation than did the sprinkling of old Etonians who fought in the British armies at Waterloo. It is also the case that many more GAA members would have answered the call had not Eoin MacNeill issued instructions that fateful Easter for all Volunteers to stay at home – in effect stifling the Rising before it had properly begun.

I feel that it is also important to underscore the fact that individual GAA members of real calibre contributed to the Rising. Such individuals as Éamonn Ceannt, a signatory of the Proclamation; Michael O'Hanrahan, quartermaster of the Irish Volunteers; and Con Colbert, executed at Kilmainham Gaol; Harry Boland, chairman of the Dublin County Board; and Frank Burke, the epitome of a clean-living GAA man, and a winner of All-Ireland football and hurling medals. Other individuals would become future leaders of Ireland: William T. Cosgrave, who became in effect Ireland's first prime minister; Seán T. O'Kelly, who became Ireland's second president; and Thomas Ashe, who commanded the only successful Volunteer operation of the Rising – an attack on an RIC party at Ashbourne in Co. Meath. Indeed, Ashe's funeral, following his death while on hunger strike, was one of the largest ever seen in Ireland, and was accompanied by an escort of hurley-carrying Volunteers. We will look at this particular episode in more detail later in this book.

Other GAA Volunteers who took part in the Rising included Tom Ennis, later a general in the Irish army; and Cork's J. J.

Walsh, would later became Postmaster General of the Irish Free State government. And above all these, in status and prestige, comes another Corkonian: Michael Collins, who would later make an important unequivocal statement about the importance of the GAA to the revolutionaries.

However, probably the most telling detail of the relationship between the Rising and the GAA lies in the huge participation in the rebellion by Dublin GAA clubs. St Laurence O'Toole's GAA club alone supplied over seventy members to the Rising. As the Rising was largely confined to Dublin, one can of course only imagine the participation throughout the country by GAA clubs had things gone as the leaders hoped. But, by examining the preparatory work that took place in the province of Munster in general and in Co. Kerry in particular, one can gain a real insight into a possible alternative future.

In a real sense hopes for the success of the Rising had rested on the ability of GAA members in Kerry to bring ashore from the German vessel *Libau* – masquerading as the neutral Norwegian ship *Aud* – a vital supply of German arms for distribution throughout Munster. The IRB, Volunteers and GAA in the Kingdom can reasonably be thought of as three leaves of a shamrock. The Volunteers were largely controlled by the IRB: and the leading IRB man in the county was Austin Stack, who was also the county's most prominent Gaelic footballer, and one of Kerry GAA's most influential figures. The knowledgeable Anthony Gaughan, a biographer of Stack, notes that:

There were close links between the Volunteers and the GAA throughout Kerry and, by the end of 1914, the Volunteers in the county were organized along GAA lines. Just as each football and hurling club in the county sent delegates to an annual county convention of the Kerry GAA, so each Volunteer company in the county was represented – often by the same delegates – at the annual county convention of the Kerry Volunteers. Also, as in the case of the GAA, the county convention of the Volunteers elected a county board to run the affairs of the Volunteers in the county for the coming year.[11]

It is worth adding that in practice, neither the GAA nor the IRB was entirely happy with this closeness. For example, the prominent Volunteer officer J. J. 'Ginger' O'Connell complained that it sometimes happened that if a parade or a drill session conflicted with a GAA fixture, the match took preference over the parade. Perhaps such carping was inevitable when two separate organizations – one open, one secret – attempted to coexist. And perhaps this was also the reason for the Kerry bungling which took place in advance of the Rising itself.

This bungling had in fact commenced, not in Kerry but in Dublin, and not in the approach to Easter 1916 – but the previous November. The IRB had made arrangements for arms to be collected from a house in Dublin owned by Kerryman Michael Joseph O'Rahilly ('The O'Rahilly'), and then transported to Kingsbridge railway station for transportation to Kerry. Once in Kerry, these guns would be stored safely, ready to be used the following spring to protect the expected German arms landing at Fenit Pier on Tralee Bay. This dangerous movement of arms would take place under the cover provided by the excitement of Kerry being in the All-Ireland final: for the shipment would be moved in the very train that was to bring Kerry GAA supporters from Kingsbridge back to Tralee.

As recounted by Tadhg Kennedy, a member of the Kerry GAA Board and the Volunteers' principal intelligence officer in Kerry, the operation initially went well. On 7 November 1915, two cars duly turned up to drive the arms party to O'Rahilly's house. One car, however, contained a certain Tadhg Horgan who was very drunk: he had taken to the drink, not to quell fears arising from the small matter of transporting illegal weaponry across Dublin under the noses of the police, but rather because Kerry's All-Ireland dreams were suddenly in tatters – the Kingdom had been trounced by Wexford the previous day.

So drunk was the wretched Horgan, in fact, that his companions, led by Kerry IRB operative Tadhg Kennedy, felt unable to leave him on his own: Kennedy decided there was nothing for it but to put his drunken colleague in the back of one of the cars and carry on to O'Rahilly's house to complete the mission. Kennedy left Horgan sleeping in the car and entered the house to collect the weapons: but when he emerged he found that Horgan had woken up – and worse, had driven off in the car! Nevertheless, the resourceful Kennedy made the best of a farcical situation: he managed to pile the guns into the remaining car, get the car to Kingsbridge, and place the arms aboard the packed Tralee train – and all without being detected.

By way of commentary on how some Kerry citizens rate their footballing tradition compared to their revolutionary one, it might be noted that during the 1916 centenary celebrations an elderly Kerryman was so moved that he went public to correct a radio interview given by Tadhg Kennedy in 1948 about the Horgan incident. He was not concerned, as might have been expected, about the patriots of yore being traduced by allegations of drunkenness – but rather by the fact that in his interview, Kennedy had said that Horgan got drunk celebrating a Kerry victory. But no, Horgan was not celebrating, this modern Kerryman reminded us mournfully: he was drowning his sorrows because Kerry had *lost*.[12]

This important detail disposed of, let us continue with the saga of the arms landing. The IRB, in the person of Michael Collins, expended a great deal of useless and ultimately tragic effort to secure a wireless transmitter in Kerry in order to be able to make contact with the *Aud* and bring the arms shipments safely to Fenit pier. In a further stroke of bad luck, however, the car containing a group of wireless experts whom Collins had sent from Dublin, took a wrong turning and drove off Ballykissane pier at Killorglin, drowning three of its occupants. The deaths proved to be even more futile when it subsequently emerged that the *Aud* had no wireless aboard in any case. The ship subsequently cruised fruitlessly up and down the Kerry coast waiting for a signal from the shore that never came.

The IRB had initially informed the Germans that the arms were to be landed on a day between Thursday 20 April and Easter Sunday, 23 April. In the confused atmosphere that prevailed immediately before the Rising, however, this plan was changed, and the IRB sent Joseph Plunkett to Berlin to ask that the arms be landed instead precisely on Easter Sunday. But German efficiency meant that the *Aud* arrived on the Thursday, as initially planned – only to linger until its inevitable capture.

How a strange ship could cruise off the Kerry coast for a number of days without an allegedly expectant Volunteer commander being aware of its presence is one of the enduring mysteries of the Rising. In a fishing and maritime community, after all, even a strange currach attracts attention. In addition, in the course of researching this and other books, I have been informed by responsible people that many people on the Kerry coast in those days recalled sightings of the *Aud* cruising hopelessly offshore.

To me, the most telling detail to emerge from the sorry saga of the failed arms landing was a brief statement on the affair made by Tadhg Kennedy. He stated that from the window of a train he was able to see the *Aud* in the mouth of Tralee Bay.[13] But Kennedy did not at this time even know about the *Aud* and its role in this operation. His statement was one of those made in confidence under a thirty-year rule to the Irish Bureau of Military History in the aftermath of the Second World War. Kennedy did not elaborate on this reference, nor point the finger at anyone: but his recollection helps to throw a troubling light on the whole question of the arms issue.

How could a man like Kennedy – the rebels' principal intelligence officer in Kerry, and thus a pivotal figure – not have been made aware of the *Aud*'s approach? After all, for the ship's mission to be successful, its cargo would have had to be met on arrival by a cavalcade of cars and lorries to transport not merely twenty thousand rifles but the ammunition for them, plus the machine guns which were also aboard. Gathering such a convoy of vehicles, in time of war, and without the authorities' smelling a rat, would have been a huge operation which Kennedy would have to have known about – had it existed.

But speaking for myself at least, I can say that I never found anyone in Kerry who was aware of such a transport fleet being mobilized – and it seems clear that Stack sent no one out to sea to check on the *Aud* and its cargo. The ship's voyage ended on a note of drama: as the *Aud* was being escorted by Royal Navy ships into Queenstown, the crew scuttled the vessel rather than let it fall into British hands: and so 20,000 rifles and a quantity of machine guns went, not to the Volunteers and not to the British – but to the bottom of the Atlantic.

Meanwhile a German submarine had put Roger Casement – who had been in Berlin attempting to negotiate German support for the Rising – ashore on Banna Strand, near Tralee. He arrived in a small boat that capsized, leaving him to struggle ashore in the darkness, wet and dejected and with no thought in mind but to get word to the IRB leadership that the planned Rising should be called off. It was later revealed that the British knew all about the submarine's voyage: they did not, however, make the authorities in Dublin aware of the fact – because this might have led to the Germans being alerted to the fact that the British had broken the German code.

Casement was soon picked up – as was Stack, who walked into the RIC station where Casement was being held, ostensibly to find out what he could about Casement's position. He was promptly arrested, and incriminating documents were found on his person – this despite the fact that he had previously been warned by his deputy, Paddy Cahill, to make sure he had nothing on him when he went to the barracks.

As a result, there is a persistent belief that Stack deliberately held on to the documents to ensure his arrest and safe removal from the expected troubles. Over the years, these facts have contributed to rumour and suspicion that still circulate in Kerry. But despite these, Stack's memory is commemorated by having one of the best GAA clubs in the country named in his honour.

In general terms, the bungling and mishaps that characterized the planning of both the Kerry landings and other features of the 1916 Rising would have baleful after-effects. They would, for example, cause such prominent revolutionaries as Éamon de Valera and Cathal Brugha to distrust and dislike the IRB thereafter – and this in turn would lead to strain and tension between different factions within the Irish nationalist alliance. Let us now look at the post-Rising scene in Ireland, and the part the GAA played in the tempestuous years still to come.

The Republican University

T HE EXPERIENCE OF SERVING A PRISON SENTENCE IS
referred to by many in Irish republican circles as the
'Republican University'. With this in mind, it would be
fair to say that after the 1916 Rising, the Irish Republican
Brotherhood and the Gaelic Athletic Association emerged with
a shared degree from one of the most famous and certainly
most influential 'universities' of the twentieth century. For the
fact of the matter is that the environments within which those
imprisoned for their part in the Rising found themselves, were
controlled and dominated by the IRB.

Most of the outstanding leaders within these 'universities'
took their lead from Michael Collins, who now came to the
fore as a leader of Irish republicanism. His associates would
assume prominent roles in the dangerous wars that lay ahead;
and some of those that survived these experiences would secure
important positions in the first Irish governments to emerge
from the smoke and ruins of the revolutionary period.

The prison best remembered from this period was Frongoch,
located on the site of an old distillery near Bala in Gwynedd in

North Wales. The site had previously been used as a prisoner of war camp for Germans captured in the opening years of the First World War: following the 1916 Rising, these men were rapidly and unceremoniously dispersed to other locations, with Frongoch turned over now to specifically Irish prisoners. The camp encompassed a large field beside the river Tryweryn – and this proved to be a fortunate circumstance. For, as part of their vision of that new future Ireland, the republican prison leadership very deliberately encouraged participation in Gaelic football, in combination with a purposeful learning of the Irish language. The one served to keep these confined individuals physically fit, the other provided a necessary degree of mental stimulation – and in combination, they brought a distinctively Irish-themed philosophy to bear upon these otherwise gloomy environments of incarceration. And so it was on this Welsh turf that some memorable GAA encounters took place. Indeed, it would be true – literally and metaphorically – to say that on that field, both the IRB and the GAA were strengthened immeasurably.

Collins understood that there were other opportunities available in this ostensibly unpromising environment of imprisonment. In particular, he was able to turn to his advantage the fact that the indiscriminate round-ups in the immediate aftermath of the Rising had brought together thousands of young Irish men in the environs of Frongoch and other prisons. These internees would otherwise not have met; if they had not previously been subversively inclined, they certainly were now; if they had not previously felt a grievance towards the British, they most certainly did now; and in addition to all of this, their wider family circles now shared this grievance, thus spreading the spores of revolution across Ireland.

In the environment of Frongoch, such individuals soon fell under the spell of the IRB: and it is difficult to overestimate the importance of this new cadre in Ireland's subsequent history – in the War of Independence, the Civil War, and the establishment of the Irish Free State which followed these convulsions. As Sean O'Mahony notes: 'It is indisputable that all those Frongoch prisoners prominent in government and the security forces of the Free State Army were the key IRB men in the camp.'

In Ireland, meanwhile, Tom Clarke's widow Kathleen Clarke organized a fund to assist the prisoners and their families: and soon, people from all classes in Ireland were taking the opportunity to offer tangible support to the Frongoch internees. As the post-Rising pendulum swung, this fund became an invaluable source of financial sustenance – both to succour the prisoners' dependants in Ireland, and to provide gifts and support for the prisoners themselves. Amongst the items sent to Frongoch were Gaelic footballs – though (and perhaps understandably) the camp authorities were not willing to have hurley sticks enter Frongoch.

Inside, men of all backgrounds were being drilled in debate, public speaking, and other political skills – and a prophecy was being fulfilled. Ever since the establishment of the GAA, observers within the Royal Irish Constabulary were (as we have seen) apprehensively noting the organization's vast political potential. All that was required, these observers realized, was the right context, and a smart leader – and a wave of recruits to the republican cause would appear. Frongoch and the post-Rising wave of internment provided the context – and Michael Collins was the leader the movement needed.

Inside the fences of Frongoch itself, the inmates were being schooled in the virtues of physical force as a means to an end. In one prison debate, Richard Mulcahy – later chief of staff of the IRA and later still a mainstream politician and leader of Fine Gael – told his listeners that:

Freedom will never come without a revolution, but I fear Irish people are too soft for that. To have a real revolution, you must have bloody fierce-minded men who do not care a scrap for death or bloodshed. A real revolution is not a job for children, or for saints or scholars. In the course of revolution, any man, woman or child who is not with you is against you. Shoot them and be damned to them.

Out on the field, Collins himself emerged as the camp's best all-rounder. He won the hundred-yard sprint in 10.45 seconds ('Ya hoor, ya can't run,' he shouted as he passed M. W. O'Reilly) and then went on to win the long jump and triple jump for good measure. The authorities tried to make use of his athletic prowess, claiming in the House of Commons that contrary to what the prisoners were saying, the diet in Frongoch was in fact healthy and nourishing; and that such athletic prowess proved this fact.

The prison diet was in fact poor: but food parcels from home helped bring it up to scratch – and they provided the fuel to sustain two major GAA competitions at Frongoch. One, on the All-Ireland model, came down to a battle between Kerry and Louth, played by internees from the two counties. Kerry had a panel of thirty-nine internees held in the camp, Louth had thirty-eight. Kerry won by a single point.

These camp football games would appear to have drawn at least some inspiration from Mulcahy's dictum of revolutions being made 'by fierce and bloody men'. One of the most celebrated quotes made in and about Frongoch came from a British soldier who, watching a Gaelic football match, turned to his companion and commented: 'If they [the Irish] are like that at play, they must be bloody awful at war'. He was correct: subsequent history would show that for many a young GAA player held at Frongoch, a belief in physical force entered his being as fire enters iron.

At Christmas 1916, Frongoch was emptied and closed, and its internees were released and returned to Ireland. Their education had begun – and now the newly liberated Collins began in earnest the next phase in the revolution.

*

Through 1917 and 1918, the Sinn Féin party began growing in electoral strength in Ireland. The original Sinn Féin had been established in 1905 by Arthur Griffith, with the intention of promoting a new constitutional relationship between Britain and Ireland: this would echo the *Ausgleich*, the Compromise of 1867 which had established the dual monarchy of Austria and Hungary.

Immediately after the Rising, however, the British began referring to the event as the 'Sinn Féin Rebellion' – and this nomenclature rapidly became fact. Griffith had opposed Redmond's call to arms in 1914, and peeled away from the Volunteers – and now he consented to his party becoming the principal vehicle for anti-British sentiment and activity in Ireland. He himself remained committed to his ideal of a Dual Monarchy – so much so, indeed, that the swollen movement almost split at its annual congress in the autumn of 1917. But it reached its own form of compromise: nationhood for Ireland would come first, and the constitutional niceties could be settled once this nationhood had been achieved.

Behind the scenes, Collins was in charge – and Collins and his friend (and GAA stalwart) Harry Boland set about manipulating the selection of candidates for each election so that men of what was euphemistically termed a 'forward outlook' were selected over moderates in the Griffith mould. The relationship between Collins and Griffith, indeed, is of considerable interest. Collins was a long-time admirer of Griffith's writings and Griffith admired the younger man for his courage and energy – though he disliked Collins's conspiratorial side.

There are echoes here in the relationship between Collins and the GAA itself. Collins and Boland were, on one level, frank admirers of the organization as well as enthusiastic players and practical supporters – and yet they sought ceaselessly to manipulate the organization for their own political purposes. Boland, for example, was instrumental in the decision taken by the GAA in 1917 which focused on civil servants working within the British administration in Ireland: these individuals were barred from joining the organization if they had taken an oath of allegiance to the crown, Boland remarking that the Irish had always been able to distinguish 'between the garrison and the Gael'. Boland's move was clear and targeted: it placed such civil servants in an impossible position and caused difficulty to well-intentioned GAA fans and to the GAA itself – and it tightened the screws on the government itself and its ability to fully function, which of course was the whole point.

Michael Collins himself would later make his attitude to the GAA abundantly clear when Dublin and Kilkenny contested a provincial hurling final at Croke Park on 11 September 1921. His speech was reported in the *Freeman's Journal* the following day:

> He would just remind them that they represented the great factor in the life of Ireland that has always distinguished the Gael from the Gall:
>
> 'You are not only upholding the great game', he continued, 'but you are also upholding one of the most ancient and cherished traditions of Ireland. If it were not for the GAA, when it stood for Ireland, England in her great war would have annexed much of the finest bone and muscle that were saved to Ireland. The great part that it has played in the revival movement is known to every one of us. The Gaelic

League came afterwards and several organizations doing noble and useful work as national servitors: but the GAA was the pioneer body in the defence of the national interest.

Now that we are coming into our own again the GAA must be a more serviceable factor in upbuilding the muscular prowess and consolidating the national spirit. He would like specially to point out that recently the college of Ireland were showing a proper interest in the games, that were racy of the soil of Ireland, and he was glad to know that the people of Ireland appreciated these colleges and schools. Some colleges have yet to come into line, but he had no doubt the popular desire would prevail in these also.

In using the phrase 'racy of the soil', Collins was gesturing at what was already a deep nationalist past: these words had been the epigraph of the *Nation*, the radical newspaper published in the 1840s against the tumultuous backdrop of Daniel O'Connell's campaigns. Collins's sentiments would not, perhaps, have been those of some of the more cautious members of the GAA who still remembered the cautious and determinedly non-political path walked by some of the organization's early members.

But Collins had his finger on the pulse of the newly radicalized foot-soldiers of the GAA: and his views found an echo in the hearts and minds of the ardent youth who now made up the bulk of GAA membership. Statistically, of course, one might claim – correctly – that a majority of the GAA's membership were not in the IRA, or the IRB, and would take no part in any of the military-style encounters of these years. But this point is irrelevant, because this is not how a guerrilla organization functions. What it requires for its survival are gifts such as the blind eye, and the unacknowledged medical treatment. The bed for the night, the necessary hot meal, the quiet loan of a car (or more often, in this period, a pony and trap, or a bicycle).

And above all – omertà. No loose talk, no giving of information to the authorities. And the fact is that GAA members and supporters provided all of these gifts, and more, in great and unacknowledged quantities. And in addition to all this, the openly acknowledged gifts, the greatest of which was the flow of money and materials from GAA members and their families to the National Fund and the Prisoners' Dependents Fund which functioned essentially as safety nets, as forms of social security offered to hard-pressed individuals.

*

The first death amongst crown forces in the aftermath of 1916 was significant both in itself, and in its potent symbolism. On 10 June 1917, RIC Inspector John Mills of Co. Westmeath was in charge of a police operation at Beresford Place in Dublin's north inner city. Mills was tasked with breaking up a Sinn Féin meeting taking place outside the Irish Citizen Army's former headquarters, which had been destroyed during the week of the Rising. As George Plunkett and Cathal Brugha – the main speakers at the event – were led away by the police, Mills was hit on the back of the head with a hurley wielded by nineteen-year-old Edward Murray.

Mills was taken to Jervis Street hospital, where he died the following day. Murray escaped into the crowd: it seems evident that he had not intended to kill Mills – for he afterwards suffered a breakdown, during which he was cared for by Patrick Pearse's mother Margaret. She regarded Mills's death as murder: nevertheless, she shielded Murray until Collins succeeded in smuggling him out of the country. Murray ended up in the United States, where he lived until his return to Ireland in 1922.

This was just one incident in what was a stormy year in Ireland. With war in Europe still raging, the threat of conscription hung over the land – and the zeal of those who had followed Redmond in 1914 had long since faded. A national sense of defiance took hold: under the terms of the Defence of the Realm Act, the flying of the tricolour was an offence; and now gaols across Ireland filled up as all over the country young men defiantly waved flags under the noses of the police. There was a strong sense of camaraderie: when a group of young men in Co. Sligo, for example, were sent to gaol for flag-waving, their neighbours showed their sympathy by delivering to their families a year's supply of turf.

The GAA became involved in one of the most public events of the year: the release of Éamon de Valera from Lewes prison in Sussex, and his victory in a by-election in Co. Clare a month later. This was a significant moment: for de Valera stood as a Sinn Féin candidate – and he roundly defeated an Irish Parliamentary Party candidate, demonstrating to a watching Ireland that the establishment party was now in the process of being eclipsed by the reborn Sinn Féin movement.

Against this backdrop of swift political change, GAA figures were moving to make a public link between the organization and the new radical politics now taking hold in Ireland. Dick Fitzgerald, who had been released earlier from Frongoch, trained the hitherto lacklustre Clare Gaelic football team that now moved from obscurity to stardom, beating Cork in the Munster final. The various stages of the competition were marked along the way by overtly political gestures: players gathered before matches under banners proclaiming 'Up de Valera'; and Harry Boland took to marching at the head of pre-match parades waving a Sinn Féin flag. Clare Volunteers made a practice of marching publicly in military formation and holding hurleys, thus further identifying the GAA with the growing struggle.

The GAA was also involved in September of that year in the funeral of Thomas Ashe, which became a profoundly politicized event. Ashe was a teacher from Lispole, Co. Kerry: he was a tireless GAA supporter, an avid player of Gaelic football, and an organizer of GAA clubs across north Co. Dublin and south Co. Meath, in districts where cricket had previously enjoyed an enthusiastic following.

Ashe had also taken part in one of the few successful military operations outside Dublin during the 1916 Rising: a successful ambush on an RIC contingent in Ashbourne in

Co. Meath. He had an eye for strategy: at Frongoch, he was one of the influences that helped to move Michael Collins's military philosophy from the 'static warfare' of 1916 – the seizure of buildings which could be retaken with relative ease by a better armed and numerically superior enemy – towards such classic guerrilla tactics as flying columns and the simple device of using bicycles to slip unseen from one place to another. Ashe, indeed, had used bicycles to good effect in Meath during the Rising, dominating a large area of countryside and inflicting significant casualties on RIC patrols. He had been sentenced to death for these activities: this was commuted to life imprisonment as the outcry grew against the post-Rising executions that had already taken place; and so he had found himself in gaol instead.

After his release and return to Ireland, Ashe resumed his IRB activities: and in August 1917 he was charged with making seditious speeches and sentenced to hard labour. In gaol he and a group of other prisoners claimed political status, and went on hunger strike. The prisoners were force-fed – but an inexperienced doctor botched the procedure on Ashe, and bruised and lacerated his face and throat. Ashe died on 25 September.

The funeral of Thomas Ashe at Glasnevin Cemetery was one of the largest ever seen in Dublin. It was estimated that some 15,000 people participated in the procession to Glasnevin from City Hall in central Dublin, where Ashe's body had lain in state. Volunteers openly carrying rifles marched at the head of the procession. Some two hundred priests marched behind them; and hurley-carrying members of the GAA were prominently involved. Dressed in Volunteer uniform, Michael Collins delivered an oration at the grave.

On 19 November, there was considerably less publicity for another highly significant event involving Michael Collins – this time at Croke Park. This was the first Volunteers' Convention to be held since the Easter Rising. The delegates sat about on bales of hay as de Valera, who had earlier been elected as president of Sinn Féin, also became president of the Volunteers. The meeting in effect moved to put the Volunteer movement on a war footing, setting up a military structure of brigades, battalions, companies and so on. Collins himself was elected director of organization. His cadre of Frongoch associates was by now a ruling circle within the IRB.

While open drilling by Volunteers at Croke Park was not permitted, it is evident that some of those in high places within the GAA condoned the use of its facilities in more discreet ways. The leading Tipperary Volunteer Edward McGrath has described an important secret meeting he attended with Collins and Richard Mulcahy, who were debating the organization of the Volunteers into a fighting force.[14] Collins favouring local officers taking initiatives as opportunity offered, while Mulcahy favouring what McGrath termed a more 'red tape' approach. Significantly, this meeting was held in Luke O'Toole's house on the grounds of Croke Park itself. In addition, both Collins and Boland are known to have slept at the house while on the run and to have kept fit by using the stadium pitch itself to practise their hurling skills.

In late 1917, the military operation at Dublin Castle had been reorganized so that only officials of proven unionist sympathies were left in positions of authority. Ireland was placed under military rule, and now preparations began to enforce conscription in Ireland. In 1918, Sir John French was appointed Lord Lieutenant. He offered what he took to be a simple solution for enforcing conscription: 'I should notify a date before which recruits must offer themselves in the various districts. If they do not come, we will fetch them.'

Sir John was not allowed to put his not-so-bright idea into operation. In London, the prime minister David Lloyd George proposed that the pill be sweetened by introducing conscription in tandem with Home Rule – but in Ireland, Sinn Féin was successfully mobilizing opposition to conscription, regardless of the context of its proposed introduction. This opposition can best be encapsulated, perhaps, by describing the raid that took place at the local RIC barracks in the parish of Ballymacelligott, near Tralee in north Co. Kerry, on 13 April 1918.

*

In hindsight, the Ballymacelligott raid was an opening salvo of sorts in the War of Independence that would soon explode in earnest: in my view, certainly, it ought to be seen as equal in its intent and consequences to the more famous raid at Soloheadbeg in Co. Tipperary that took place some months later. The incident at Ballymacelligott was planned and carried out by members of the local GAA club – but it did differ from the later Tipperary raid in that the RIC shot first and killed their Volunteer attackers.

The Ballymacelligott raid was not sanctioned by the Volunteers' command in Dublin. It was led by local GAA man Tom McEllistrim, who had played a part in the abortive story of the *Aud*, and who had been sent to Frongoch for his pains. McEllistrim played on the Kerry team in the Welsh 'All-Ireland': now, released and back in his native Kerry, his intention was to organize a barracks raid in order to steal arms, the better to counter the looming threat of conscription. Poor scouting, however, led to the raiders being surprised by a returning RIC patrol – who fired on the raiders, killing two of them.

On 14 June, McEllistrim and John Cronin attempted to take revenge on the two RIC men who had shot their comrades: the policeman had been summoned to Tralee to give evidence at the town courthouse. McEllistrim once more failed in his objectives: one policeman was slightly injured, the other escaped unharmed – but the joint incidents foreshadowed many more calamities that would befall this district of north Kerry in the course of the war.

While one comes across much talk of IRA discipline, training, parades and so on, it is important to note that individuals such as McEllistrim learned their trade on the job. In Co. Kerry as in other parts of the country, IRA units were formed amongst men who put down their hurleys and picked up their guns. And there were consequences as result of an occasionally lackadaisical and unprofessional way of doing things.

McEllistrim, Cronin and their men, for example, were very nearly captured *en masse* as a result of a drinking session – which McEllistrim himself had opposed. However, his men called for a vote, and McEllistrim was overruled, with the result that the IRA unit enjoyed a convivial night attending first a shebeen (an unlicensed public house) and then a party in a friendly farmhouse in nearby Ballyfinnane. The house was surrounded by a party of soldiers under the command of the redoubtable John MacKinnon, an Auxiliaries commander who was much feared in and around Tralee – and who was intent on capturing McEllistrim and Cronin. The IRA party, however, received some warning, and managed to beat a hasty exit, leaving just one of their party (drunk and out for the count) behind.

After the party had left the scene, the drunk woke up and began staggering about the farmyard. A quick-witted daughter of the house saved his life by telling the soldiers that he suffered from mental illness and was often to be seen shambling and incoherent – but the drunk was so indignant at being left behind that he subsequently joined another IRA unit. McEllistrim and Cronin quarrelled over this foolish incident – though they later patched up their differences.

Such episodes are significant in many ways. They remind us of a pre-existing hinterland in existence around Soloheadbeg and other famous raids; and of the frequently dangerous spadework undertaken by individual GAA members in these years. But the details of shebeens and drunkenness illustrates a certain shoddiness at work: and underscore the sense that many such otherwise courageous individuals were, if not exactly self-indulgent, then certainly not always and everywhere wholly professional in their conduct. This was not always – for all the mythology of the fearsome military machine ostensibly put together by Michael Collins – a thoroughly well-oiled outfit.

*

As opposition mounted in Ireland, and in the face of such alarming events, the conscription proposal was delayed again and again; it had still not been enforced by November 1918, when the armistice at last brought the First World War to a close.

A few months before the Armistice, on 14 August 1918, an event had taken place that would later become known as 'Gaelic Sunday' – and that marked the GAA's most public demonstration of identification with the rising tide of public disaffection in Ireland. For some months, GAA sporting activities had been increasingly targeted for disruption by the authorities in all parts of the country. At the same time, serious effort had been made to interfere with the organization's revenue stream through the imposition of an entertainment tax.

At its annual congress in 1917, the GAA had resolved to resist this tax, promising to hold a special convention to discuss ways of defying the authorities in the event of its imposition. When an effort was made by the authorities to force the Dublin County Board to pay the tax, this convention duly passed a resolution stating that no member of the organization, never mind any club or committee, should pay any tax.

Relationships between the police and GAA deteriorated. Police and military personnel attacked both spectators and players at matches at Ballymena in Co. Antrim and Banagher in Co. Offaly. In Tralee, Kerry club players were attacked by the RIC, backed up by soldiers wielding fixed bayonets. Even boys playing Gaelic football in Dublin's Phoenix Park were taken into custody.

As tensions rose, the GAA leaders realized they had to make a stand. They despatched a deputation to Dublin Castle – but to no avail: the GAA representatives were informed that the organization was subject to a proclamation issued earlier in the month by Lieutenant General Frederick Shaw, commander in chief of the British forces in Ireland, which banned 'the holding or taking part in any meetings, assemblies or processions within the whole of Ireland'. The GAA was told at the Dublin Castle meeting that its members could not hold any matches unless a permit was first applied for and secured.

The GAA central council reacted swiftly, ordering all clubs not to apply for a permit, and making it clear that it would suspend any club that did so. 4 August was selected as a 'day of defiance', in the course of which 'unlicensed' football and hurling matches were to be played all over the country. As the days ticked down to Gaelic Sunday, the government realized the potential for widespread violence – and chose to back down: the authorities at Dublin Castle issued a circular stating that Gaelic games were *not* subject to Shaw's proclamation; and that the previous widespread interference with GAA matches had occurred because the police had 'unfortunately misunderstood their instructions'! The fact that the police, under instruction from the authorities, had been 'misunderstanding their instructions' almost from the day the GAA was born, was not mentioned.

Despite the Castle's climbdown, the GAA decided to go ahead with Gaelic Sunday as a useful demonstration of the organization's strength. Highly politicized figures such as Collins and Boland took part in the organization of the activities, as did senior Volunteer officers throughout the country. Collins and Boland, indeed, participated fully: they took part in a hurling match at St Margaret's in north Co. Dublin.

An extract from the *Freeman's Journal* described Gaelic Sunday in the following terms:

FIXTURES BROUGHT OFF WITHOUT A HITCH

Gaelic Sunday, organized by the Gaelic Athletic Association, was observed throughout the country yesterday with great success. Every football and hurling team in the country took part in a match, and in all some 54,000 players were engaged. As a result of the withdrawal of the prohibition against Gaelic games enforced for the past couple of weeks by police and military, there was no interference with the matches, which were carried out with perfect order in the presence of large numbers of spectators. Every town and district had its own venue, and all the matches started simultaneously at three o'clock (old time). The progress of the play was everywhere followed with enthusiasm, and the occasion provided a unique display of the popularity of Gaelic games.

The proceeding of the day, the good order among the crowds, the perfection of the organization, and the magnificent response made by every team and club throughout the country, constituted at once a vindication of the Gaelic Athletic Association and its objects, and a demonstration of the popular hold which Gaelic games have on the interest and sympathy of Irish people.[15]

It was certainly a day of considerable activity, with some 1500 football, hurling and camogie matches played across the country. The number of participating athletes was huge and the volume of spectators even greater. The only police and army personnel seen at the matches were paying spectators; and the only casualties of the day were a group of children in Dublin who had their names taken for selling flags on the street. The principal source of interruption was the weather: downpours of rain caused most fixtures in Co. Kerry to be interrupted; the only exception was that held in Kilgarvan, where the redoubtable local GAA stalwart Dick Fitzgerald refereed the game, and insisted on it being played to the bitter end – rain or no rain!

Subsequently, historians have differed as to whether Gaelic Sunday was to be viewed as a demonstration in support of political aims, or purely as an impressive sporting spectacle. The day could be seen, it is true, as the winning of a battle in which the *enemy* had not joined. But even such doughty individuals as Dick Fitzgerald did not stand out in a Kerry downpour for purely sporting reasons. It seems evident to me that Gaelic Sunday cannot be viewed merely as a sporting event.

No: this was an initial demonstration on the playing fields of a phenomenon that would be witnessed in the polling booths a few months later. As the GAA moved, so would Catholic Ireland follow, for a seismic political shift was occurring in which the GAA was playing a leading role. Tommy Moore, a player with the Dublin GAA club Faughs, described the spectacle of Gaelic Sunday in terms that would now be regarded as unfashionable – but which nonetheless accurately record the feelings and the rhetoric of the rank-and-file GAA membership of the period:

> From Jones Road to the craggy hillsides of the Kingdom, the day was fought and won in fields no bigger than backyards, in stony pastures and on rolling plains, on the banks of rivers and on village greens, and in the official venues of the Gaels wherever posts could be struck up and spaces cleared, the descendants of Fionn and the Fianna routed the seal of servitude. In one never-to-be-forgotten tournament, we crossed our hurleys with the lion's claw and emerged victorious.

And indeed, Moore was witnessing a sea change that had already taken place. Ireland was swinging decisively now towards Sinn Féin. In the general election of December 1918, called in the immediate aftermath of the Armistice, the public demonstrated its gratitude for having escaped the curse of conscription by decimating the ranks of the old Irish Parliamentary Party and returning Sinn Féin as the largest party in the country, with seventy-three seats. Among the new members of parliament was Constance Markievicz, the first woman ever elected to Westminster.

Gaelic Sunday had been a curtain-raiser to the seismic events of that general election: it had shown the power and influence of a national mood in action – and the GAA had in the process demonstrated its own power too. For better or for worse, the fate of the organization was now bound up with national politics, as the story of Ireland entered a dangerous phase. I want to look now at how slowly, over the course of several years, matters began to spin out of control in Ireland – with, for the GAA and its followers, truly devastating results.

CHAPTER SIX

'Countless Shapes of Death'

O N 9 NOVEMBER 1920, IN THE COURSE OF A SPEECH delivered at Guildhall in the City of London, British prime minister David Lloyd George openly admitted that British policy in Ireland was now 'to take murder by the throat'. Of course, there was nothing surprising about such a declaration – at any rate, not to the Irish, who were by now well aware that this was indeed *de facto* British government policy in Ireland.

Indeed, it had previously been spelt out for all to see and hear in an address given by Lieutenant-Colonel Gerald Bryce Smyth to a group of RIC men at Listowel barracks in Co. Kerry, on 19 June. Smyth was a native of the strongly Unionist district of Banbridge in Co. Down, and District Commissioner of the RIC for Munster. On that day in Listowel, he told his audience:

We must take the offensive and beat Sinn Féin at its own game. Martial law, applying to all Ireland, is to come into operation immediately. In fact, we are to have our scheme of amalgamation completed on 21 June. I am promised as many troops from England as required. Thousands are coming daily. [...] If a police barracks is burned, or if the barracks already occupied is not suitable, then the best house in the locality is to be commandeered, the occupants thrown out into the gutter. Let them lie there, the more the merrier. Police and Military will patrol the country at least five times a week. They are not to confine themselves to the main roads, but make across the country, lie in ambush and when civilians are seen approaching, shout 'up hands'.

Should the order not be obeyed at once, shoot and shoot to kill. If the persons approaching carry their hands in their pockets, or are in any way suspicious-looking, shoot them down. You may make mistakes occasionally, and innocent persons may be shot, but that cannot be helped, and you are bound to get the right person sometime.

The more you shoot the better I shall like you and I assure you that no policeman will get into trouble for shooting a man.

The speech caused consternation: one RIC constable, Jeremiah Mee, placed his gun on the table, and called Smyth a murderer; and fourteen RIC constables resigned there and then from the force.

What were Smyth's motives for such an incendiary speech? He was well aware of the electrifying context of the Ireland of the time – and his words derive directly from this context. For the IRA was targeting RIC personnel mercilessly – and effectively: these were cruel and brutal times – and it is necessary to emphasize this cruelty and brutality, for such details explain why the GAA would become, notoriously, the victim of state terrorism.

Indeed, the organization found itself participating in a sort of hellish blood wedding, as its sporting traditions, its IRB influences, the specific political context of the day, and the extreme actions of the British state met and exploded on the pitch and in the stands of Croke Park on 21 November 1920, as Dublin was playing Tipperary in a Gaelic football game. The events of this day have passed into Irish history as the first 'Bloody Sunday'. The day has created such a deep impression on the Irish psyche, indeed, that as this was being written, a GAA enthusiast paid €7,500 for an entrance ticket issued for that fateful game of Gaelic football.

Let us look at this specific context, then: at this large and bloody canvas – and let us begin by stepping back in time, to explore the chain of events that led to that fateful day at Croke Park.

*

It is generally accepted that the War of Independence began in Ireland on 21 January 1919. On that day, a group of Volunteers – acting without official sanction – shot dead two RIC men at Soloheadbeg, Co. Tipperary, as they guarded a cartload of gelignite. On the same day, the provisional Irish parliament convened in Dublin: this first Dáil Éireann consisted of those seventy-three Sinn Féin members of parliament elected at the recent election of December 1918. These new parliamentarians now abstained from taking their seats at Westminster, and met instead in solemn session in the Mansion House. Or rather, some of them did: twenty-seven, to be precise, for many other members were in prison.

This new Dáil was both a practical and powerfully symbolic assertion of Irish independence. Its members formally agreed a Declaration of Independence, a new constitution, and a socialist-tinged Democratic Programme: all eye-catching measures; and indeed, the Mansion House meeting attracted a good deal of attention, both national and international. It was at this time that the term Irish Republican Army (IRA) first came into common usage – little wonder, therefore, that this January day, between the events that took place in Dublin and those that took place in Tipperary, tends to be remembered as a pivotal one in Irish history.

It *was* pivotal – but it was only one of many such days throughout 1919 and 1920. The political temperature rose steadily: the Dáil met again in April; and over the course of months, the paraphernalia of a new parallel state was set in place. The so-called Dáil courts were established: these would have the joint role of undermining the British rule of law in Ireland, and increasing the legitimacy of the parallel state by being seen to be an at least reasonably effective legal and social tool, thus claiming the loyalty of the public. By August, the symbolic and practical power of the Dáil could no longer be ignored by the British authorities, who moved to declare it illegal.

Simultaneously, the situation of Ireland became of greater interest internationally – especially and crucially in the

United States. De Valera, rearrested in 1918 and imprisoned in England, escaped from Lincoln gaol in February 1919, in a plan masterminded by Collins. By June, de Valera was in New York – and he would remain in the United States until the end of 1920. This mission was useful, in that it raised the profile of Ireland in the US and gained the support of the American public in general and of Irish-Americans in particular to the cause; it also raised a good deal of money, and increased diplomatic pressure on the British authorities.

Back in Ireland, while there was no declared war, undeclared conflict gradually gained ground across the country. On 30 July, the first officially sanctioned killing of an RIC officer took place in Dublin: Detective Sergeant Patrick Smyth was shot and killed in the district of Drumcondra. On 8 September, drunken British soldiers ransacked the centre of Fermoy in Co. Cork: further attacks during the week were repelled by local residents. In early November, the shape of a possible future settlement in Ireland became apparent: in London, Lloyd George proposed the establishment of two Home Rule parliaments in Ireland – one in Belfast and one in Dublin.

But on 19 December, a daring raid in Dublin showed the potential of the IRA to strike at the very heart of the British administration: a cavalcade carrying the viceroy, John French, to his residence in the Phoenix Park was attacked: the raid failed, and one IRA man was killed – but French, though wounded, escaped with his life. And these a mere selection of a multitude of incidents taking place in the course of the year.

1920 was even more dangerous and violent. It kicked off with a GAA-infused murder: the assassination of RIC District Inspector Tobias O'Sullivan at Listowel in January. The killer in this instance was Con Brosnan, a controversial future Kerry captain and prominent member of the local GAA club. Brosnan was subsequently arrested, and in July 1921 was deported to England.

The temperature of country at this time, indeed, may be measured usefully by reading the memoir of Seamus Malone, one of the most important IRA leaders of the period. Malone is said to have been Michael Collins's favourite spy and his memoir *Blood on the Flag* gives a chillingly vivid picture of the background against which Smyth's speech at Listowel was made.

To give one example: Malone describes an attack on Kilmallock barracks in Co. Limerick in May 1920, a month before the Listowel speech. Kilmallock had a reputation as a strongly fortified barracks – the strongest such in the country. Clearly not strong enough though, for Malone's account shows how the IRA attacked during the night, and succeeded in setting the barracks alight. It was a bloody business: Malone wrote that: 'People have no idea how many of the police were burnt in the barracks. [...] there were sixteen policemen at home on the evening before the attack' – but only eight were accounted for. Afterwards at least eight women travelled from Britain in search of their husbands.

Spates of killings and counter-killings, abductions, and the burning of property afflicted town and country alike. The

RIC were gradually driven from their barracks; ultimately, they were able to venture into the countryside only in large patrols, or while under the protection of British troops. Here and there an occasional horrific deed stood out starkly: for instance, the shooting dead in November of the pregnant Eileen Quinn as she stood on a Co. Galway street with a child in her arms.

Early in the year, the plan for two parliaments in Ireland moved further ahead, with the publication of the British government's Home Rule Bill. Ulster Unionists consented to the bill a month later; a few days later, on 20 March, Tómas Mac Curtain, the Sinn Féin Lord Mayor of Cork, was murdered in his home by RIC officers – and a few days after that, the first of the so-called Black and Tans arrived in Ireland from Britain. These were members of a British-recruited *de facto* militia, raised with the express intention of stamping out unrest in Ireland; they were given their name from the colours of their improvised uniform.

The period of the Black and Tan presence in Ireland – the so-called 'Tan war' – had the effect of raising the temperature still further. The Black and Tans were, in effect, an ill-disciplined and violent rabble: they would be joined in August by the Auxiliary Division of the RIC; and during the period of these militias' service in the Irish war, they were responsible for many notorious attacks on civilians, businesses and property. In mid-September, a Black and Tan raid on the town of Balbriggan in Co. Dublin destroyed more than fifty properties in the town; and this would be followed by an even greater assault in December on the commercial centre of Cork, which left parts of the city in flames.

In addition to all this, unrest and violence was spiralling out of control in what would soon become the new entity of Northern Ireland. Here, Protestant mobs, together with state-sponsored underground death squads drawn from the Ulster Volunteer Force, murdered dozens of Catholics and drove thousands from their homes and places of work in Derry, Belfast and elsewhere. The island of Ireland appeared to be a confused, bloody political mess: but underneath the killings, the burnings, the reprisals, there were two very clear-cut visions of the political future at war with each other.

One was a republican desire for Irish independence which by now had completely outstripped the once acceptable idea of a limited form of Home Rule. The other was an imperialistic policy of divide-and-conquer which was taking itself all too literally by proposing the division of Ireland into two entities. Indeed, it is worth noting that the upsurge of violence in the northeast of Ireland must be seen against this context: Unionists were attempting to clear territory, by force and violence, of nationalist residents in a form of ethnic cleansing; nationalists, seeing the future of this part of Ulster all too clearly, were fighting to stave it off by whatever means they had to hand.

In the rest of Ireland too, violence continued unabated. In Co. Kerry in early November, IRA action and police reaction brought extraordinary havoc and violence to the town of Tralee. The Lord Mayor of Cork, Terence Mac Swiney, who had died while on hunger strike, was buried on 31 October; vast crowds turned out for the funeral. The following day, the young IRA volunteer Kevin Barry was hanged in Dublin for his part in a raid that saw three British soldiers killed. There began a wave of killing and counter-killing in Kerry: on 1 November, civilians were fired upon at they existed Mass in Tralee; and in the days that followed, the town shut down. A curfew was imposed by the Black and Tans, and citizens that stirred out of doors were shot. The siege continued until it was lifted on 9 November by order of Dublin Castle.

The French journalist Jean de Marsillac (whose very presence in the town is indicative of overseas interest in Irish affairs at this time) wrote in *Le Journal* that 'The town was as deserted and doleful as if the Angel of Death has passed through it. Not a living soul in the streets. All the shops shut and the bolts hastily fastened. All work was suspended, even the local newspapers. [...] I do not remember, even during the war, having seen a people so profoundly terrified as those of the little town of Tralee. The civil authorities are powerless; that there is literally nobody in the world to whom one can appeal, and from whom one can demand protection.'

A bloody mess, then – and all the bloodier as a result of the British government's determination to 'take murder by the throat'. And so this was the frightful background against which Lloyd George delivered his Guildhall speech – and this was the context against which Smyth (with the Black and Tans' commander standing alongside, and nodding his agreement) had delivered his Listowel speech some months previously.

Smyth would be dead within the month, shot by the IRA in Cork, but his words had fallen on fertile ground.

*

There had been peace talks – tentative, secretive – in progress throughout the latter half of 1920: but both sides had too much to lose for these negotiations to proceed. Instead, the violence continued to escalate, building to a shocking climax in November of that year – and with the GAA literally in the firing line.

Early on the morning of Sunday 21 November 1920, a group of highly trained IRA operatives under the command of Michael Collins, moved to destroy the 'Cairo Gang': the British intelligence network in Dublin named for the Cairo Café in the city where meetings were held and information collated. The Cairo Gang had been making steady inroads into IRA intelligence circles, and Collins judged that it must be eliminated before more damage was caused.

I have written in detail of this episode in my book *The Twelve Apostles* – and so at this time, suffice it to say that in a series of early morning raids, Collins's so-called 'Squad' fanned out across central Dublin; by the time the raids ended, thirteen of their targets had been killed.[16] Collins had a list of thirty-five names to be eliminated: many were not where it was assumed they would be, and so these individuals escaped with their lives – but just the same, British intelligence activities in Ireland were crippled that day.

For reasons best known to themselves, some revisionist historians have attempted to downplay the importance of this strike at British intelligence operations. For example, the Trinity College Dublin academic Anne Dolan[17] and other like-minded historians have cited opponents of Collins in questioning the significance of the operation and the behaviour of those who carried it out. However, Oscar Traynor – who succeeded Dick McKee as commander of the IRA's Dublin Brigade after McKee was captured and tortured to death in Dublin Castle on the morning of Bloody Sunday – has left a different evaluation.

It is important to note that Traynor was not a particular admirer of Collins: indeed, in the future, he would command the anti-Collins forces in Dublin during the Civil War. But in relation to the raids, Traynor was unequivocal – they were needed, and they were essential. 'It was discovered', Traynor noted, 'that a particular type of trained intelligence officer was being established in the city. It was discovered that these individuals were living as civilians and resident in and around the same areas, mainly Upper and Lower Mount Street and the adjacent Squares.' Traynor confirmed that this unit had been responsible for a series of damaging blows to the IRA and stated that 'it was decided to take action against these individuals.'[18]

On the morning of the raids, the news spread – and now British officials poured into Dublin Castle, seeking shelter and demanding reprisals. The perfect target for British retribution, it turned out, lay just a few miles away.

*

It is important to note that, even if Collins's 'Squad' had not had a busy morning in Dublin, that day's game between Tipperary and Dublin at Croke Park would have been viewed by the authorities as a GAA-inspired provocation. Indeed, it *was* a provocation – doubly so: firstly, Tipperary was provoking Dublin in the time-honoured way of all fine sporting rivalries – and secondly, the GAA itself was provoking the authorities.

The game had been heralded by an announcement in the press on 1 November as a challenge match in aid of the Prisoners' Dependents' Fund, and the advertisement had been signed by the captain and secretary of the Tipperary team, who proclaimed that: 'We understand that Tipperary's superiority over Dublin is being questioned by Dublin. We therefore challenge Dublin to a match on the first available date at any venue and for any objective.'

On one level, then, this was pure sporting talk – the sort of language deployed in any sport when the intention is to drum up support for a fixture. But we must reflect that this advertisement had been placed in the middle of a war – and a war which, moreover, had already seen significant violence in both Co. Dublin and Co. Tipperary. Tipperary had been the scene of the Soloheadbeg raid – as well as of ferocious reprisal and counter-reprisal in the months that followed. Similarly, Dublin needed no lessons in political and military violence.

And so this hype was potentially dangerous – and everyone knew it, or should have known it. Tom Ryan, who was at this time both a leader in the IRA's Third Tipperary Brigade, and a member of the Tipperary team, later recalled observing British newspaper reports claiming that Tipperary assassins would be involved in the game. And all this, without taking into account the political dimensions of the game's charitable purposes. And so we have to wonder: in this specific dangerous context, ought the GAA to have pressed on with that day's game?[19]

But the GAA *did* press on. It had withstood official pressures on Gaelic Sunday and would withstand pressure on this day, too. And it had a specific beneficiary in mind: the game would benefit a certain member of the Volunteers and of the IRA in Dublin's Second Battalion. This anonymous young man was injured in a fight involving GAA stewards and a bookmakers' gang in the north Dublin district of Clontarf. Charity was not to be promised, and then withdrawn. Such was the GAA line.

On the night before the game, rumours spread in IRA and GAA circles that something dramatic was about to take place in Dublin. Ryan, indeed, promptly volunteered to take part in whatever this episode might be – but his offer was turned down. Collins put the word out that trouble was indeed brewing: and many individuals that night took steps to bolster their personal security.

When the news of the overnight assassinations broke, a mood of apprehension gripped the city. Priests at Sunday masses in Dublin advised that worshippers remain indoors for the rest of the day; and it became so difficult to find individuals willing to deliver despatches that, at the risk of his life, Michael Collins himself went around the city dropping off messages. Looking back on the events of that terrible day, Jack Shouldice – who was in charge of Croke Park gate receipts – uttered what is surely the most memorable understatement of the entire Anglo-Irish war: 'We were rather unfortunate in the date selected.' Never were truer words spoken.

After analysing the accounts of the onslaught on the British intelligence network, Collins sent an assistant, Joe O'Reilly, to Croke Park to warn Luke O'Toole and the other officials to call off the game: a reprisal raid, reported Collins, should be expected. The IRA's Dublin Brigade, Second Battalion, which had arranged to provide stewards for the event, reacted to the news of the shootings by standing down its men. And yet, despite the warnings and the lack of stewarding at Croke Park, the GAA decided that the show must go on.

Shouldice took part in the discussions, and has left a record of what happened.[20] According to his account, money does not appear to have figured in the decision to allow the game to go ahead. The main overriding problem, according to Shouldice, was the age-old issue grappled with by successive GAA leaders: how best to maintain the public image of the GAA as a sporting organization – and *not* a political group guided by revolutionaries prepared to use violence.

The consensus, according to Shouldice, was that the GAA could not allow itself to be associated in the public mind with the violence of that morning in Dublin – and therefore, it could simply *not* call off the game. GAA leaders were perfectly aware that violence might be visited upon Croke Park that day. But, Shouldice reported, the GAA reasoned that:

If we called it off, the GAA would appear to be identified
with what happened the previous night at Mount Street
[and other locales]. Raids anyhow were common but we
never anticipated such a <u>bloody</u> raid. [Shouldice's emphasis]
But, anxious about the outcome, we decided to carry on.

Shouldice was well informed on the interaction between the
authorities and the GAA. He was an officer of the IRA himself
and had played a significant part in organizing the show of
mingled politics and sporting power that was Gaelic Sunday
in 1918. Yet his evaluation of the raids that had taken place
in advance of that fateful day in Dublin appears well wide of
the mark. Raids had been so extensive, and martial law was
in force in so many parts of the country, that the Croke Park
fixture was one of the few to be played in the country that day.

Above all, forecasting some sort of tolerable, acceptable level
of violence in the face of the brutal state policy of 'frightfulness',
seems unreal at this remove. Account must of course be taken
of the pressures to which the Croke Park leaders were subject
that fateful morning – and yet, it seems that these men may have
judged ill. Readers will remember how an admiring observer of
Luke O'Toole's career judged that one of O'Toole's outstanding
attributes was this: that he always placed the interests of the
GAA before any other consideration. Can we speculate that he
put the GAA first in this situation too?

For the fact is that in November 1920, O'Toole's beloved
organization was nearly bankrupt. In fact, on the day before the
game, a cabinet meeting of the Dáil considered an application

from the GAA for a loan. The Association had greatly improved the facilities at Croke Park, but naturally these improvements had to be fully paid for – and on the morning of Bloody Sunday, the GAA was in debt to the tune of £1700. In the conditions of the time, and amid a widespread cancellation of fixtures which effected revenues, this was a very serious matter indeed.

As it turned out, the GAA loan application was approved; Collins was, after all, a fan of the organization. The Dáil agreed to pay off the organization's debt, and approved a loan of £6000, at a rate of five per cent interest. But the GAA could not have been certain of such a positive outcome as that Sunday morning dawned in Dublin: there was thus a powerful financial incentive to permit the game to go ahead. And this, when it cannot possibly be gainsaid that the game would be played amid a climate of danger – I would say, in fact, of *extreme* danger.

*

On the pitch at Croke Park that day, the afternoon began undramatically, with the replay of an intermediate curtain-raising game between Dunleary Commercials and Éireann's Hope; Dunleary Commercials won.

Behind the scenes, meanwhile, the Croke Park authorities were taking stock. Another message was received at the stadium, warning that a raid was no longer a mere possibility; it was now the case that a raid was in preparation.

A member of the Dublin Metropolitan Police (DMP) stationed in Dublin Castle, had been horrified to find that a

1. Michael Cusack: first secretary of the GAA. 'The shining blackthorn, firmly grasped in his right hand is raised and with a smile of real joy, he crashed it against the hurley of a waiting player and half shouts, half sings in his big husky voice, "That's the *ceol* (music) that stirs the heart!"'

2. Archbishop Thomas Croke: 'we are daily importing from England not only her manufactured goods... but, together with her fashions, her accent, her vicious literature, her music, [...] her games also and her pastimes to the utter discredit of our own grand national sports.'

3. Thomas Ashe: Gaelic footballer and tireless GAA organizer. His funeral, following his death in prison in September 1917, was a highly politicized affair. Among the vast crowd that accompanied Ashe's body to Glasnevin cemetery were hurley-carrying members of the GAA.

4. Members of the Irish Volunteers drill with hurley sticks instead of rifles in 1914 – common practice at a time when guns were in short supply.

5. Gaelic footballers in Stafford Goal, 1916. The immediate aftermath of the Rising brought together thousands of young Irishmen in Frongoch, Stafford and other British prisons.

6. Eamon de Valera, president of the nascent Irish Republic, throws in to start the Wexford v Tipperary football match in aid of the Irish Republican Prisoners' Dependents Fund at Croke Park, 6 April 1919.

7. Dan Breen throws in at Croke Park, 1922. Breen's ambush at Soloheadbeg on 21 January 1919 – which coincided with the first meeting of the Dáil – marked the start of the War of Independence.

8. Harry Boland TD at Croke Park, 1919. Active in GAA circles as a young man, Boland refereed the 1914 All-Ireland Senior Football Final between Kerry and Wexford.

9 and 10. The football teams that took part in the 'Great Challenge Match' on Bloody Sunday, 21 November 1920: Tipperary (above) and Dublin (below).

11. A ticket for a Gaelic football match that would end in mayhem and the murder of innocents.

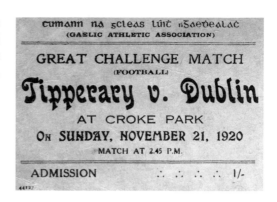

12. 'Jesus, Mary and Joseph, I'm done for.' Michael Hogan, Tipperary footballer and victim of a British bullet, 21 November 1920. Hogan died in the arms of his Tipperary team-mate Tommy Ryan.

13. Weapons allegedly found at Croke Park, 21 November 1920.

14. Michael Collins shakes hands with Alderman James Nowlan, IRB man and the GAA's longest-serving president, before the Leinster hurling final at Croke Park, 11 September 1921.

15. Michael Collins throws in the *sliotar* (ball), 11 September 1921. Dublin prevailed over Kilkenny in the provincial final.

16. The women who founded Cumann na mBan in Tralee, Co. Kerry, were ardent GAA supporters. Aggie Sheehy, seated on the far left, was a sister of John Joe Sheehy, IRA commander and captain of the Kerry team that won the All-Ireland Senior Football Championship in 1926 and 1930. Brigid 'Bunty' Barrett, seated on the extreme right, was a sister of another All-Ireland-winning Kerry captain and IRA commander, Joe Barrett.

17. The first meeting of the standing committee of the Irish handball association (IAHA), 1923. Jack Shouldice (back row, second right) argued it was impractical to cancel the Bloody Sunday football match. Eamon Broy (front row, right) replaced General Eoin O'Duffy (front row, left) as commissioner of *An Garda Síochána* in the 1930s.

18. Action from Ireland v America at Croke Park, during the 1928
Tailteann Games. The Games were conceived by J. J. Walsh as a showcase
for Irish arts, culture and sports.

19. Members of the Kerry hurling team that defeated Waterford in 1926 – and
a remarkable coming together of republicans and Gardaí just two-and-a-half
years after IRA prisoners were released from Free State gaols in 1923–4. All-
Ireland winner and IRA commander Joe Barrett is standing on the far left in
the back row. Humphrey Murphy (standing, fifth from left) was the principal
IRA commander in Kerry during the Civil War. Also in the picture are IRA
members 'Pluggy' Moriarty (back row, fourth from left), John Joe Sheehy
(back row, seventh from left), Jacky Ryan, Johnny O'Riordan, Jim Sheehan,
Gerald Landers and Jerry Hanafin. The individuals holding hurling sticks in
the front row include Garda Kennedy and Garda Hawkins.

reprisal party composed jointly of members of the Black and Tans and the Auxiliaries was being organized at the Castle. The DMP sergeant, though no friend of the IRA or even Sinn Féin, was horrified: and he immediately made his way to the home of an acquaintance, one Thomas Kilcoyne, who was suspected of having IRA connections.

The suspicions were correct: Kilcoyne was in fact a member of the Dublin Brigade Second Battalion; and upon hearing this alarming intelligence, he went immediately to his battalion commander, Sean Russell. Russell was no shrinking violet: he would in fact become one of the most intractable republicans of the first half of the twentieth century. In later years, he would mastermind an IRA bombing campaign in Britain at the outbreak of the Second World War; he died during the war aboard a German submarine returning him to Ireland in the vain hope of triggering a revolution that might somehow hinder Britain's war effort.

Russell counselled that the game be abandoned – but the morning's decision held. Senator Harry Colley described what happened:

On Bloody Sunday, we cancelled the mobilization of the Second Battalion men to act as stewards at Croke Park. At about 2.30, I happened to have occasion to go to the Battalion O.C. Sean Russell. [...] When I arrived, I found Tom Kilcoyne O.C. B. Company [of the IRA] already there. Sean came out immediately and said, 'You come on too Harry, I'll tell you what it's about on the way.'

Russell said that Tom Kilcoyne had brought word that the Auxiliary and Military were already mobilized and under orders to proceed to Croke Park to mow down the people. The information it seems had come from a Sergeant of the D.M.P. who, while not in any way in sympathy with us, had been so horrified when he discovered what was about to happen that he thought it his duty to get word to us to see if the calamity could be avoided.[21]

Colley recollected that Russell 'appealed to those officials to close the gates and stop any people from entering Croke Park. He pointed out what an appalling thing it would be if the enemy opened fire with machine guns on that crowd.' In reply, O'Toole and Shouldice 'pointed out the difficulty of getting the people out now, that they would probably demand their money back, and that if an announcement was publicly made it might lead to panic and death in another form. They pointed out also that the match was a benefit one for a member of Russell's own battalion who had been badly injured a few months earlier when acting as a steward for the GAA in the fracas with bookies' touts.' The IRA party responded that this could not be helped: and that the match should be held at a later date.

According to Colley, the IRA trio left with the understanding that no further admissions to the grounds would be allowed. As they walked away, however, Colley remembered that the IRA stewards had been pulled out that morning. They decided that they should attempt to try to prevent fresh spectators entering the grounds. They approached a turnstile-keeper and, noted Colley: 'We told the man on the stile there was the arrangement we had made and that he would be receiving orders not to allow any more people into the grounds. He stopped letting people through at our request and went to verify the IRA man's message.' While he was away, the crowd at the gate swelled and was 'getting very impatient as the match was due to start. It did start at that moment and the man on the turnstile came back, swearing at us and proceeded to let the crowd in.' The IRA trio left, recalled Colley, 'the whole three of us very downhearted'.

Colley went to his mother's house in nearby Clonliffe Road: here, a meal was prepared, but he was too agitated to eat it. A little later, he heard the sound of nearby gunfire – and shortly after the noise ceased, he saw crowds of panicked spectators, some of them covered in blood, surging past the house. One of them, Colley saw, was a member of Collins's 'Squad' who had taken part in the attack on the British agents earlier that day. The man was wounded: Colley now brought him into the house where he was treated by his sister, a member of Cumann na mBan. Later a dead man was found at the back gate of the Colley house on Clonliffe Road – one fatality among many.

Inside the stadium, there were witnesses too. The Tipperary player Tom Ryan was about to take a free kick when the apprehension outside the ground gave way to horror within.[22] The match had been in progress for about ten minutes when a plane flew over the stadium and fired a Verey light. Then there was a burst of machine-gun and rifle fire, and the crowd at once began a stampede.

Most of the players made for the sidelines: but Ryan and five others, all of them members of the IRA, remembered their training and threw themselves flat. Six players who were active Volunteers out of a total of thirty – and this in itself gives an insight into the GAA contribution to the War of Independence.

One of the players was Johnny McDonnell, the Dublin goalkeeper who had taken part in the assassinations that morning. Another was the legendary Frank Burke, a dual All-Ireland winner at both hurling and football, and a former pupil of Patrick Pearse who had fought in 1916 with fellow students in Pearse's company.[23] Burke would later become the custodian of Pearse's political legacy, becoming first a teacher and then headmaster at St Enda's, the school founded by Pearse.

Ryan had the Irish tricolour emblazoned on his shorts and stockings – and soon he realized that he was dangerously conspicuous. Burke too realized this: and as he was borne along by panicked spectators, he appealed in vain for someone to lend him an overcoat. Ryan too, could have done with clothing of any sort, for he was stripped naked after attempting an escape from the stadium, and was brought back to join a group lined up against a wall before a firing party of troops. The group fully expected to be shot. They were told that if anyone fired on the troops, two of the Irish prisoners would be shot in exchange. Many of the troops who took part in the shooting were clearly drunk; Ryan, however, was lucky enough to come under the command of a British officer whom he later described as a 'decent man' with military decorations on his chest. This individual said that

'There's been enough killing for today' – and ultimately he permitted Ryan and the others to leave the scene unscathed, although their belongings were ransacked and cigarettes, money and watches were taken.

Ryan described how he managed, in the aftermath of that traumatic day, to make his way back to Tipperary. First, he sought shelter in a friend's house near Seville Place in Dublin's docklands. In those days, many Dublin houses in poorer areas either had a piggery attached, or a shed used to stable a pony or horse used for cabbying or milk delivery – and as a consequence, many back yards contained manure heaps. During the night, a house a few doors down from Ryan's refuge was broken into by British forces, and the owner taken out and shot.

Hearing the firing, Ryan and two companions dashed out into the yard and hid themselves in the manure heap. The raiders did not come into the yard, and eventually withdrew from the area altogether. Next day, Ryan and his friends were stranded in Dublin: penniless, and without food or any means of getting back to Tipperary. But a former British officer named Jack Kavanagh came to their assistance. He gave them £50: and at length all three men reached home in safety. Ryan would respond to Bloody Sunday by becoming a full-time – and very formidable – IRA operative.

Ryan's personal experiences on that awful day in November, were only the tip of an emotional iceberg of death and desolation – and though it is painful to trace the events of the day in greater detail, it is absolutely necessary to do so.

*

Eyewitnesses stated – universally – that the firing at Croke Park that day was carried out by members of the Black and Tans. Official accounts declare that no Black and Tan personnel were present; and inquests were told that most of the bullet casings recovered were RIC issue. But nobody disputes that around 3.15pm, the military party began firing on the defenceless crowd, deploying both machine-gun and rifle fire. There was no attempt made to halt the game so that a search for weapons might take place – this being, the authorities later claimed, the reason for the raid on Croke Park. A spurious claim, of course: the true reason for the raid was to carry out a massacre – and a massacre was indeed carried out.

Different slivers of horror, preserved in eyewitness accounts, retain the power to shock:

A ten-year-old boy fatally shot off the branches of a tree overlooking the ground. A man impaled on barbed wire on top of a high wall, trampled on as spectators rushed to jump some twenty feet to what they hoped was safety. A young woman shot dead as she stood beside the man she had planned to marry three days later. Apple-sellers' carts overturned and their vendors trampled underfoot. On the pitch, a priest clubbed unconscious with a rifle butt as he knelt to give the last rites, the Sacramental wafer blown across the turf.[24]

Outside the ground, the exits were choked. Men and women fainted and screamed as they were confronted by lines of military personnel with rifles at the present. As the people somehow forced their way out of the grounds and ran down the adjoining laneways, they were pursued and fired upon. Inside the stadium, a famous Irish cleric of the period, Monsignor Pádraig de Brun, absorbed the scene after the first burst of firing had subsided:

> There was a momentary pause and there ensued the wildest panic, the spectators on the north side raced towards the railway, those on the south went on headlong flight towards the main exit. Occupiers of touchline seats ran onto the field and threw themselves flat on the ground. While they lay there, another wave of fugitives passed over them.

Brown made it to the safety of a dressing room: later, he described taking up a position near the door and thus being able to breathe more freely than those behind him. His training in the classics, he said, returned to him as he looked across the pitch: for these sights reminded him of descriptions he had read of the slaughter that ensued when the Greek warriors emerged from their wooden horse inside the walls of Troy: *crudelis ubique luctus, ubique pavor et plurima mortis imago* – 'everywhere is relentless grief, everywhere panic and countless shapes of death'.

On the pitch itself, Frank Burke had been marking a Tipperary player named Mick Hogan. Hogan's tale offers another insight into the mingled histories of the GAA and Irish nationalism: for he had come to Dublin not merely to play in the game but to deliver IRA despatches from Tipperary which he carried in his shoes. The two men had been watching the plane pass overhead when the play switched to their side of the field and both went for the ball – and Burke describes vividly the dreadful circumstances by which the present Hogan Stand received its name:

At that moment the shooting started. As the play was mostly near the now Hogan Stand entrance, the majority of the players were over that end and immediately made for the dressing rooms. There was nobody remaining in the Park at that time but myself, Mick Hogan and Stephen Sinnott. […] We ran but we didn't know where we were going. Confused, we ran to the centre of the field. We could see the bullets hitting the wall at the railway end […] we realized they were shooting at somebody in the crowd. The three of us threw ourselves on the ground. Hogan was on the right-hand side; I was in the centre and Stephen Sinnott on the left. And we started creeping from the centre of the field towards the goalposts […] then I turned sideways and started rolling. Mentally making an Act of Contrition, I was wondering what was going to happen next. Eventually, through creeping and rolling, we got to the racetrack, they used to have a cycle track around the grounds in those days. Hogan said 'We lie in here close and we might get some protection.' We lay close to the edge of the field and all the time they were firing. They were only about four or five yards away. Then I heard Hogan cry out: 'I'm shot,' and immediately the crowd started running over towards Hill 16.'

A Cumann na mBan member present on the scene later offered further dreadful testimony of the violence visited on Hogan: Catherine Byrne described 'the body being shot again and then kicked by a Black and Tan'.[25] Ryan heard Hogan cry out, 'Jesus, Mary and Joseph, I'm done for.' Ryan picked him up, but Hogan died in his arms.

One could, of course, validly end this account of that searing Sunday in 1920 by reporting the death toll. In all, twelve people were shot and killed, and another died of wounds a few weeks later. But the most eloquent testimony comes from the silent turf of Croke Park itself. By the time a reporter from the *Freeman's Journal* arrived at the stadium the following day, Luke O'Toole had engaged a man to undertake the task – ghastly but necessary – of retrieving human bone fragments from the grass. The newspaper report was used many years later in *The Bloodied Field*, Michael Foley's superb reconstruction of the events of that day:

> A mist spread like a veil over the field, softening the outlines of the pools of blood and the bullet holes in the wall, hiding the walking sticks and fragments of human bones scattered all over the pitch. A trail of blood streaked the ground outside [Luke] O'Toole's own house where a wounded woman had been carried. Blood stains marked the ground where the bodies had lain. A small group had gathered to pray at the

spot where Mick Hogan had been killed. The pitch was still covered in hats, umbrellas [...] the ground was torn up and rutted. The walls at the Clonliffe Road end were chipped by bullets and ricochets. There was blood on the walls where people had climbed to safety and the streets around the park were bloodstained. Croke Park had ceased to be the site of a playing field and had become a national shrine.

Such was the outcome of the British government having murder by the throat. And with Lloyd George's comment in mind – a comment, let us not forget, that was delivered less than a fortnight before Bloody Sunday – let us turn to how the cabinet reacted to the news of the day's massacre.

*

The authorities were supplied with a report prepared for Sir Hamar Greenwood, chief secretary for Ireland. Sir Hamar began with the news of that Sunday morning's 'Squad' assassinations in central Dublin, remarking that: '[T]he motive for these terrible crimes is hard to explain, but the fact that several of the murdered officers were engaged on work commissioned with the preparation for cases for Court Martial suggests an endeavour on the part of desperate criminals to strike back at the men who were thought to be specially concerned in bringing them to justice.' Sir Hamar was being a little disingenuous: certainly he made no mention of the dead men being members of a British-commanded and British-controlled undercover hit squad.

As for the events at Croke Park: these, the report claimed, occurred during a search operation intended to capture:

Men belonging to the Tipperary Units of the Irish Republican Army [...] most desperate characters in that organization. The police were fired on by armed Sinn Féin pickets at the entrance to the field [...] the police returned the fire [...] there is no doubt that some of the most desperate criminals in Ireland were amongst the spectators. The responsibility for the loss of innocent lives must rest with those men, and not with the police or military who were forced to fire in self-defence and used no unnecessary violence. A civilian and a boy of ten were shot in the streets of Dublin [...] and three prisoners who were being detained in a guard room at the entrance to Dublin Castle were shot while trying to escape.'

Winston Churchill subsequently embroidered this account by stating at another cabinet meeting that no reprisals had taken place after the killings on the morning of Bloody Sunday.

The British government was obliged to be seen to act. A plethora of inquiries was established and a flood of statements issued, all aimed at creating an authorized and heavily sanitized version of the history of that day. The formal investigation went so far – but no further, ruling that:

[A]ll the above wounds were inflicted on the deceased persons [who] were spectators at a football match, the said crowd being raided at the time by a mixed force of RIC, auxiliary police and military. The court find that the firing was started by civilians unknown, either as a warning or with the intention of creating panic.

The court find further that the injuries on the deceased persons were inflicted by rifle or revolver fire, fired by members of the RIC from the Canal Bridge and the Canal Bridge gates of Croke Park football ground, and by civilians in the football ground; that some of the RIC fired over the heads of the crowd and the others fired into the crowd at certain persons who they believed were attempting to evade arrest.

Further that the firing by the RIC was carried out without orders and was in excess of what was necessitated by the situation.

The court further find that that no firing was carried out by the auxiliary police or by the military except that the military in an armoured car fired a burst of fire into the air to stop the crowd from breaking through.

We must acknowledge that all not British eyewitnesses were willing to go along with this scrubbed version of history. Brigadier General Frank Crozier, who was in overall charge of the Auxiliary Division in Ireland, was outraged when a subordinate reported to him what had happened during the afternoon. He directed the officer to put down what he saw in writing. The account by Major E. L. Mills was as follows:

Shooting at Croke Park 21/11/1920
Report from Major E. L. Mills
To Adjutant, Auxiliary Division RIC, Beggars Bush
Barracks, Dublin

A 1.30 pm 21st ins. I was detailed to take the charge of a mixed force of RIC and Auxiliary Division to hold up and search people at CROKE PARK.

I arranged with Major Dudley, DSO, MC, who was in charge of a party of 100 of RIC to split up the two forces so that there would be an equal number posted at the four gates of the ground to search people as they came out.

The method to be adopted was that as soon as possible they were to make the onlookers file out of the ground. I was ordered to leave the barracks at 3.20pm and arrived at the gate at Russell Street at about 3.35pm.

I was travelling in a car in rear of the RIC leading the Auxiliaries. As we approached the railway bridge in Russell Street near the SW corner of the ground, I saw men in the tender in front of me trying to get out of their car and heard some of them shouting about an ambush. Seeing as they were getting excited I stopped my car, jumped out and went to see what was the matter. At this moment I heard a considerable amount of rifle fire. As no shots were coming from the football field and all the RIC Constables seemed excited and out of hand, I rushed along and stopped the firing with the assistance of Major Fillery who was in the car with me. There was still firing going on in the football ground. I ran down into the ground and shouted to all the armed men to stop firing at once and eventually the firing ceased.

The crowd by this time was in a state of panic.

After considerable trouble we got the people into a more or less of a queue and they filed out as they were searched.

I went around the gate and saw two children being carried out apparently dead. I found a female who had been trampled to death, and also a man who had apparently died the same way. I saw a few wounded men and I got some sense into the crowd. I got the DMP [Dublin Metropolitan Police] to get ambulances for the wounded. We found no arms on any of the people attending the match. After the ground had been cleared and all the buildings had been searched, I returned to the barracks. I did not see any need for any firing at all and the indiscriminate firing absolutely spoiled any chance of getting hold of any people in possession of arms.

The men of the Auxiliary Division did not fire.

The casualties I personally saw were 6 dead and 4 wounded, two of the dead were apparently trampled to death.

Signed

EL Mills

Major, 1st DI

Adjutant Auxiliary Division

RIC

Beggars Bush Barracks

Dublin

But Mills and Crozier were wasting their time. The complaints of a couple of officers about what was in effect government policy: these were easily brushed aside and ignored. The formal state inquiries did what they supposed to do: they drew attention away from the shootings, and they deflected public attention – by focusing on allegedly truthful accounts from the troops who alleged that they only commenced firing after gunmen had opened fire on them first.

A number of small arms were found in the stands at Croke Park subsequent to the killings: these had presumably been jettisoned by IRA men who had been watching the match. Several members of Collins's 'Squad' were amongst the spectators: but no evidence has ever been produced to show that those guns had been used to fire on the troops that afternoon.

As for Crozier himself: he had made himself unpopular by standing down men under his control who had been found guilty of breaches of military discipline; and he found himself undermined when these troops were reinstated behind his back. Ultimately, he resigned in disillusionment at the system he had devoted a considerable career to upholding; he would become a dedicated pacifist.

The war would continue – and so would the GAA. *Its* immediate reaction to the tragedy was muted: two weeks after Bloody Sunday, the Dublin County Board meeting at its O'Connell Street premises passed a vote of condolence for the victims and their families – but the organization's Annual Congress Report for the year made no mention at all of Bloody Sunday. All GAA fixtures scheduled in Dublin for the weeks after the slaughter were cancelled: quickly, however, the timetables were scheduled, and once more the games began.

CHAPTER SEVEN

A Border War

O N 16 DECEMBER 1920 – LESS THAN A MONTH AFTER THE killings at Croke Park – the *Cork Examiner* reported an item of news.

DIED SAVING A YOUNG MAN: Our Dunmanway Correspondent wired last evening – I regret exceedingly to report the death of our beloved P. P., Canon Magner, at the hands of some auxiliary police, recently come to Dunmanway, and a young man, which occurred this afternoon on the Ballineen road, outside Dunmanway. The town in horrified, and the deepest mourning and resentment are displayed.

It would appear that Canon Magner was taking his customary walk when he came upon the scene while they were shooting somebody.

He intervened and suffered death in consequence, as was characteristic of his charity and benevolence.

Thomas Magner had in fact been chatting with two acquaintances by the roadside, when a group of Auxiliaries arrived on the scene. One of the team shot a member of the group, a young man named Timothy Crowley, without warning – and when the horrified priest protested, he too was shot dead. It has been claimed that the cleric himself was in fact the main target of the group, because he had failed to toll his church bell for Armistice Day, despite having received a note signed 'Black and Tans', telling him to do so. The killer received due process: which is to say, he was duly convicted of the killing – and duly released on grounds of mental illness.

At the same time, prominent GAA individuals found themselves involved in exceedingly grisly deeds. Eddie Crowley, secretary of Rathmore GAA Club, and unrelated to Timothy Crowley. was arrested in November 1920 on suspicion of being involved in a failed attempt to ambush a Black and Tan patrol – but, luckily for himself, was released after interrogation. During his incarceration, however, he discovered that local man Thomas O'Sullivan, who was eighty years old and blind, was acting as an informant for the Black and Tans. When Crowley revealed O'Sullivan's activities, the Rathmore IRA not only killed O'Sullivan – but used him as bait, by bringing the Tans to the road where his body had been deposited. Five members of the Black and Tans died in the resultant ambush.

I mention such passages in history because they indicate that the ghastly tenor of Irish life at this time continued in the aftermath of Croke Park much as it had before – and that everyone was involved, including GAA members and priests alike.

Martial law had been declared in most parts of Munster in the days leading up to Magner's death; this would be extended to the entire southern half of the country in the days after his death. On 30 December, the British authorities formally sanctioned a policy of 'official reprisals': a modern version of the Biblical 'eye for an eye' dictum: and as the fateful year of 1921 dawned, there was no indication that the hellish situation in Ireland would ever settle into a state resembling peace.

If we look at 1921, indeed, we can see that nothing very much *did* change – on the surface, at any rate – for a long time. It is instructive to look once again at the situation in Co. Kerry in this period: a glance indicates both the chaos and violence that was now becoming routine across Ireland; and demonstrates too the stake held by individual GAA members in the gathering struggle for Irish independence. Once again, Tom McEllistrom of Ballymacelligott, Co. Kerry, steps into the story, for he went on to play a prominent part in one of the most significant events of the War of Independence.

This was the so-called Headford Ambush of 21 March 1921: an attack on a train carrying British troops as it passed Headford Junction near Killarney. This engagement lasted nearly an hour: nine British soldiers were killed in the firefight, together with two IRA men and three civilians. The raid was organized by two prominent GAA players, Humphrey Murphy and John Joe Rice, who had recently assumed prominent roles in the Kerry IRA; and one of the IRA volunteers killed at Headford, Jim Bailey, was also a prominent member of the GAA.

Yet another GAA man would become a 'collateral' casualty of the engagement: prominent hurler William McCarthy of Lixnaw GAA club was arrested by the Black and Tans following

Headford – and was shot (it was claimed) while attempting to escape. A huge crowd attended McCarthy's funeral in Tralee; and his death was avenged by an IRA hit team which included yet more GAA stars. These were Joe Barrett, Gerry 'Pluggy' Moriarty and John Joe Sheehy, all of whom were, or would become, famous club and county players.

*

A couple of months before the end of the War of Independence, the Ballymacelligott district again figured in a famous assignation – and now Major John MacKinnon reappears, just in time to receive his just deserts. Readers will recall encountering the formidable MacKinnon in Chapter Five: he was a commander of the Auxiliaries in North Kerry; and while he was certainly admired in some quarters for his courage, he was abhorred in equal measure for his ruthlessness. He was noted for driving around in an open car with a machine gun on his knees: his hope was to observe his enemies, and be in a position to engage them – and among his most prominent enemies in the north Kerry region were McEllistrim and Cronin.

Certainly, MacKinnon appears never to have been idle: and it was one particular incident that would in the end prove his death knell. He had captured two Ballymacelligott Volunteers on the night of Christmas Eve, 1920: John Leen and Mossy Reidy, both of whom were unarmed, and both of whom were shot out of hand. The local IRA swore vengeance – and vengeance was duly exacted at Oakpark golf club near Tralee.

MacKinnon was in the habit of playing golf on this course. On 15 April 1921, he was on the third green when the local Boherbee column of the IRA struck. Kerry Gaelic football star John O'Riordan, of John Mitchel's GAA club, was stationed in a tree above the green: he alerted a waiting marksman Connie Healy (another outstanding Gaelic footballer), who waited for a shot at MacKinnon. This was difficult: for sightlines were poor, and his quarry was wearing body armour, to boot. Following an excruciating wait, however, O'Riordan let out a wolf-whistle, MacKinnon's head jerked upwards in surprise – and Healy fired the fatal shot.

The hated MacKinnon was dead: but it seems that he was nothing if not focused on the task in hand – even *in extremis*. Folklore has it that, as he lay dying, MacKinnon managed to gasp out a final message: 'Get Mac and Cronin, burn Ballymac'. His words were immediately translated into action: over a dozen houses in the Ballymacelligott district were burned, and the creamery was torched too, thus destroying at a stroke a central element in the local economy. British propaganda afterwards spoke of the 'Battle of Ballymacelligott': and a famous set of pictures was issued to the press showing Auxiliaries holding up an IRA suspect, while in the background dead bodies lay, casualties of this 'battle'. In fact, it was nothing of the kind. An alert Sinn Féiner studied the photos, and discovered that the pictures were staged: the 'battleground' was in fact on the Vico Road at Dalkey – only a couple of hundred yards from the swimming place where Paddy Darcy, the founder of Cuala, had related to me his sanguinary encounter with the nun! The resultant publicity reflected very badly on the British, both in Ireland and internationally.

As we can see from this snapshot of the war years in Co. Kerry, few places in Ireland better illustrate the correlation between GAA members and IRA personnel.

*

I have charted in greater detail elsewhere the course of the War of Independence, the details of the Anglo-Irish Treaty, and the bloodletting of the Civil War: and I shall not attempt to do the same in these pages.[26] Instead, I want to look at one of the incidents from these years in which the GAA had a stake.

The organization was unwittingly involved in one of the most extraordinary and bloody chapters of this violent period. This was the so-called 'Monaghan Footballers' incident of 1922 – which, albeit indirectly, probably triggered more deaths than Bloody Sunday, and which for a time came close to wrecking the Treaty settlement itself.

Before examining the episode in more detail, and assessing its effect on the GAA, it is necessary to establish the intricate context of this incident. It seems evident that it was the influence of Michael Collins's IRB network in Irish nationalist circles of power, that led to the acceptance and eventual ratification of the Treaty by the Dáil in January 1922 – this following lengthy and exhausting negotiations over the preceding weeks.

Inevitably, then, the GAA would also accept the Treaty: such was the extent of IRB influence within the organization that any other outcome would have been unthinkable. This was in spite of the fervent opposition in sections of the GAA – and especially among members in Counties Kerry and Cork. The public too was minded to accept the Treaty: for a period of relative tranquillity while negotiations were ongoing had reminded Irish citizens what peace could be like.

Naturally, there were disagreeable aspects to the Treaty, and everyone was aware of the fact. The partition of the country was not to the taste of all – and nor in particular was the required oath of allegiance to the British crown, to be sworn by Irish parliamentarians. But the failure of the Treaty and a move instead to what the British had threatened would be 'total war' could not be stomached: the Treaty must be ratified and implemented.

Ireland south of this newly minted border now held the status of Dominion – the same status held by Canada and Australia, Newfoundland, New Zealand and South Africa. This new Irish Free State had its own army, police force, civil service, and independent parliament (the formality of the Oath notwithstanding). In addition, Dublin secured control of customs and taxation in its territory. The settlement secured by the Treaty was, in other words, light years ahead of the original proposed Home Rule deal; and it was quite enough to satisfy most – though not, of course, all.

In the new Protestant-dominated Northern Ireland, a different reality ruled the day. In this infant state – lying north of a border that had been drawn up with demographics in mind, to secure a Protestant majority for (it was assumed) all time – pogrom and sectarian violence were facts of life. The minority Catholic population were now confronted with an unpleasant reality. If they wished to remain in their homes and communities, they would be obliged to be governed by what the first Northern prime minister James Craig accurately described as a 'Protestant Parliament for a Protestant people'.

This was a tricky backdrop against which Collins was forced to manoeuvre. He desperately needed the support of Northern republicans in particular – that is, those most affected by partition in the border country – to get the Treaty accepted. It is important to remember that Collins and many others viewed the Treaty as a mere stepping stone: a stage on the road to full Irish unity and independence. His decision to sign the Treaty stemmed from pure pragmatism: peace must be delivered and the Free State secured politically and militarily, before the next steps could be ventured.

And much work would have to be done in economic terms to secure this Free State: the damage sustained by years of violence and disorder would take time to be set right. Northern Ireland would have to wait – but, Collins advised, it would not have to wait for very long. And so, in public Collins defended the provisions of the Treaty, in the face of bitter condemnation from his opponents.

In private, however, Collins was already looking to the future – and developing a battery of policies designed to destabilize the sectarian state north of the border. For example, in response to pogroms carried out against the Catholic population of Belfast, he organized a boycott of Belfast goods – this in addition to an undeclared policy of non-recognition of the Northern government. He also arranged – apparently without the knowledge of his cabinet colleagues – for Free State funds to flow north of the border to pay the salaries of Catholic teachers. The objective of this move was to encourage them to teach the Irish language and Irish history; and in general look to Dublin and not Belfast as the legitimate seat of government.

Strategically and politically, the Ulster county of Monaghan played a vital role in Collins's thinking. The county was surrounded on three sides by a new international frontier: it was cut off now from its natural hinterlands, thus affecting trade and, in a more general way, everyday life. In addition, some members of Monaghan's large Protestant population had enrolled in the Ulster Special Constabulary – the so-called 'B Specials', Northern Ireland's new and deeply unsavoury police reservist corps. This development only added to existing sectarian tensions in the area.

Monaghan was also the base of Eoin O'Duffy, who would later become notorious as a frontman of the quasi-fascist 'Blueshirt' movement in 1930s Ireland. For now, O'Duffy was a leading GAA figure in Ulster, holding senior provincial posts in the organization. He was also a leader of the local IRA; and he was very close to Collins, who saw O'Duffy as his natural successor. This was by no means an opinion shared by all of his cabinet colleagues: they regarded this Monaghan figure as something of an extremist and disliked the influence he wielded over Collins.

It was believed, for example – and with justice, I think – that O'Duffy had influenced Collins into taking a harsher line with the Northern Ireland government than his cabinet colleagues were comfortable with; it was feared that if O'Duffy had his way, the Free State army might ultimately be ordered to invade the North. Despite the varying interpretations as to his worth, however, it is certainly the case that O'Duffy, during most of the revolutionary period, was unquestionably a highly significant figure both in the IRA and in the GAA.

Eoin O'Duffy had been the youngest of seven children born into a farming family in the Monaghan countryside near Castleblayney. The family had only modest assets – but brains and work set him on his way: and eventually he won a clerkship in Monaghan County Council, where he studied surveying and engineering. His personality and opinions cannot be separated from his Monaghan upbringing: he had grown up in a part of the world where Protestants – and in particular the Presbyterian Church – had extensive property holdings and controlled employment opportunities; and this awareness affected his outlook thereafter.

Take his 'give them the lead' speech, which had been delivered from a platform in Co. Armagh in 1921, as the partition of the country was unfolding inexorably. Collins had suggested extending the hand of friendship to Protestants in the new Northern Ireland – but reports of O'Duffy's reply contained the following:

They were told that it was not right to use force against people of the North. That was so they did not like to use force against them: they did not want to give medicine to other people that they would not like to have themselves. Ireland was a nation, nobody ever said Ulster was a nation. He would be the last in the world to recommend force against the people of Belfast. If they were for Ireland then they would extend a hand of welcome to them as they had done in the past, but if they decided they were against Ireland and against their fellow countrymen they would have to take suitable action. [I]f necessary, they would have to use the lead against them.

And O'Duffy had already proved that he meant what he said. In January 1921, an incident had occurred which raised tensions on the border: George Lester, a prominent Orangeman in the Catholic-dominated Co. Fermanagh border village of Roslea, stopped and roughed up two Catholic boys whom he accused of carrying messages for the IRA. As a consequence, Lester was shot on the direct orders of O'Duffy himself. Lester recovered – but the B Specials retaliated by attacking Catholic interests in Roslea, firing on houses in the village and attempting to burn them while their occupants were inside. In the aftermath of these events, O'Duffy demanded and got a free hand from Collins.

I want to emphasize at this point that it was not any part of the philosophy of the IRA or Sinn Féin that Protestants should be shot simply for being Protestant. James McGuill, who was an IRB operative in Co. Louth during the War of Independence, has described how he quashed an attempt by Catholic ex-service personnel in Dundalk to burn Protestant businesses in retaliation for what was being done to Catholics across the border. He told the men:

> I took very firm action with the deputation. I informed them that the IRA would not tolerate any such reprisals and as I was responsible for all the citizens in the town and of their property; any attempt made to carry out the proposal they made to me would be drastically dealt with and that I would give orders to have any person found guilty of such attempts shot.[27]

Exaggerated claims to the contrary have from time to time been made by unionist apologists – but the fact is that the killing of Protestants in the border area came as a response to the sectarian nature of the conflict there, and was a direct response to sectarian actions.

But it is certainly the case that O'Duffy's reprisals and the counter-reprisals which inevitably followed, were grisly in the extreme. Members of the IRA, for example, had dug holes in a road in order to plant mines: but they were interrupted and fled, leaving the holes vacant. The B Specials filled them in by shooting suspected IRA men and dropping the bodies into the holes. IRA retaliation included the shooting of a woman amongst the group of Protestant farmers.[28]

After Collins's assassination in Co. Cork in August 1922, O'Duffy was appointed, as we have seen, to head the new unarmed police force, An Garda Síochána. O'Duffy used his position as commissioner to bolster both the strength of

Monaghan football and the GAA in general. He saw to it, for example, that members of the police who were Monaghan-born and skilled at football were transferred to their native county from other parts of the country in order to raise the standards of Monaghan county football. He also encouraged his officers to build handball alleys to both spread the game of handball and promote athleticism amongst the police.

O'Duffy, then, was a Monaghan man first and foremost; he was also clearly a gifted organizer who had honed his skills over many years – first in the GAA and then in the Volunteers, which he joined immediately after his first meeting with Collins. But he was also a keen grudge-holder – and this unpleasant streak in his personality found expression in his targeting of members of the Ancient Order of Hibernians (AOH) in his patch.

The AOH was a Catholic organization which had emerged in Ireland in the nineteenth century: its initial objectives were to defend Catholic property – especially Catholic churches – from attack or assault in troubled times; later, it evolved into an organization that opposed Orange Order activity in Ulster; while in a more general sense it worked towards the preservation of a Catholic ethos and the defence of Catholic culture. It had previously enjoyed a close relationship with Redmond's Irish Parliamentary Party – and as such, there was bad blood between the AOH, on the one side, and a general enemy consisting of the Volunteers, Sinn Féin and the IRA, on the other.

There was certainly no love between the AOH and Eoin O'Duffy – and this enmity was manifested in no uncertain terms in two incidents in Co. Monaghan. In November 1920 and again in March and April 1921, a total of three young members of the AOH – Michael O'Brien, Francis McPhillips and Arthur Treanor – were shot dead on O'Duffy's orders, apparently as a warning to others. Their crime had been to supply low-grade intelligence to their Protestant neighbours, who were members of the B Specials. O'Duffy himself was said to have participated in the shooting of O'Brien.

These shootings were *specifically* related to this flow of information – but O'Duffy was also keen in more *general* terms to target the AOH and instil fear in its members. With this in mind, some 210 AOH halls along the border were burned and destroyed before Collins put a stop to the practice.

There was another reason for O'Duffy's focus on the Ancient Order of Hibernians. His decision to kill the three young members of the AOH for passing information to B Specials, was also part of a bloody IRA reaction to a set of sectarian killings in the Monaghan area – killings in which O'Duffy, and Monaghan county GAA footballers, were directly involved.

*

The tale of the Monaghan footballers may be said to have begun in Derry in early December 1921 – just four days before the Anglo-Irish Treaty was signed in London on 6 December. On 2 December, IRA command sanctioned the attempt at a prison escape from the city gaol in Derry. Collins's only stipulation was that no violence be used in the attempt – which was, we must remember, made at a particularly febrile moment in the story of Irish politics. The Irish border had been established already: the Northern Ireland parliament was in session at Stormont; Northern Ireland existed as a legal entity – and the border snaked through the countryside just a mile or two beyond the walls of Derry's gaol.

Against this tense background, then, the prison break went ahead, with the aid of a little chloroform apparently supplied by a sympathetic nurse in the infirmary. It was also assisted by a warder named Patrick Leonard who, in addition to being allied with the prisoners, was also a friend of one of two warders attacked and chloroformed. Unfortunately, the escapees knew nothing about the possible effects of chloroform: the two warders died; and the hapless Leonard, together with two of the prisoners, was arrested and sentenced to be hanged. For watching republicans, this was intolerable.

The sentence was due to be carried out in February. That tense December and January, Collins – who, let us not forget, needed the support of republicans in the border area in order to secure the Treaty vote – sanctioned a series of desperate measures. Some of these measures were secret and silent, others were all too visible. In the secret category, he selected two of his most ferocious gunmen, Joe Dolan and Charlie Byrne, to go to England to shoot the hangmen who were to carry out the Derry executions. It was intended that the IRA in Liverpool would guide the two killers to the homes of the hangmen.

Dolan and his party arrived in a snowy Rochdale, the home of John Ellis, one of the hangman charged with the task. He was first brought to a pub which specialized in execution memorabilia: the place was festooned with ropes used in hangings, pictures of hangings, and so on. In these bizarre surroundings, Dolan studied Ellis's photograph so as to be sure he would recognize his quarry; and from here he proceeded to the Ellis family home.

Ellis's wife opened the door. Dolan refused to accept her word that her husband had already departed for Ireland: instead, he terrorized the woman into silence, and fruitlessly searched the house. The Liverpool IRA accompanying party prudently evaporated into the night: and Dolan himself, once he was convinced that Ellis was gone, endured a particularly uncomfortable rail journey to Manchester. His train was halted by snowdrifts; and Dolan sat and sweated for over an hour, fearing the train was about to be boarded by police.

Byrne had an equally fruitless journey. The car taking him to his target in Manchester broke down: then, his spooked IRA cover party, who refused to join him in staging a hold-up and seizing another vehicle, gave Byrne no other option but to abandon *his* mission also. When the two would-be executioners returned to Dublin, they found that the two licensed executioners had already arrived in Derry.

Onto this tense stage stepped the men of Monaghan Gaelic football team. On Saturday 11 January 1922, a convoy of six cars left Monaghan bound for Derry, where the Ulster provincial football final was to be held the following day. They were captained by Dan Hogan, who was now a major general in the newly formed Free State army. Hogan had become friendly with O'Duffy, both as a GAA man and an IRA officer; he was also a brother of Michael Hogan, shot dead on the playing field of Croke Park on Bloody Sunday just over a year previously. He had also been a feared commander of the Fifth Northern Division of the IRA; it was said that the loss of his brother affected his ruthless approach to his enemies.

Hogan's convoy was heavily armed – and was duly stopped at a checkpoint in Dromore, Co. Tyrone. He and his men were all found to be carrying weapons when apprehended: they argued that under the terms of the Treaty, which had passed the Dáil only a few days earlier (but still required ratification at the polls), they were fully entitled to their guns. The personnel on the checkpoint were not convinced – and the party was arrested. It is said that authorities thought (correctly) that the GAA men in Hogan's entourage were en route to Derry not principally to play a football game – but rather to rescue the condemned prisoners in Derry gaol, using the crowds attending the game as a cover. They were imprisoned, thus placing an entire GAA team at the epicentre of a political crisis.

The repercussion of the arrest of the Monaghan footballers was spelled out in an extraordinary letter from Eoin O'Duffy to Collins. It first came to my attention while I was researching some fairly chaotic state papers in Dublin Castle for my biography of Michael Collins (1988). I can safely say that I was almost bowled over – not merely by the contents of the letter, but by the fact that a highly placed person like O'Duffy would risk capturing in print such potentially explosive plans.

Let us remind ourselves of the context. Sectarian tensions were now at their height, resulting in some appalling deeds;

and Collins and Sir James Craig were conducting delicate negotiations, not merely aimed at stopping sectarian attacks, but at negotiating the future shape of the border. Neither leader was exactly dealing from the top of the pack: Craig was determined to resist Collins's maps showing where the border was *supposed* to run, while simultaneously he was arming his B Specials. Some of his newly formed Royal Ulster Constabulary, meanwhile, were engaged not in policing but in directing murder gangs; and Craig had failed to stop the expulsion of Catholics from their employment in Belfast amidst a hail of shipyard rivets known as 'Belfast confetti'.

Collins, on the other hand, was doing all he could to destabilize the new Northern Ireland statelet – partly out of a sense of outrage at what was being done to Catholics, but also in a desperate attempt to heal the breach with the increasingly militant anti-Treaty section of the IRA by being seen to establish a united front on the North.

In this hellish atmosphere, on *official Free State Army notepaper,* O'Duffy wrote to Collins concerning an offer made by Craig to solve the problem of the Derry prisoners, and hence that of the Monaghan footballers: the prisoners were to apply for bail; and Craig would instruct the attorney general not to oppose this application. This, of course, meant recognizing the Northern Ireland courts, and so *ipso facto* the new Northern Ireland state – which the new Free State government was trying not to do.

Accordingly O'Duffy wrote to Collins, saying crisply that 'Sir James's suggestion will not do'. He went on:

I have information from many sources this morning that there is grave consternation in the Counties of Monaghan, Cavan, Fermanagh and Tyrone over the continued detention by the A Specials of Commandant Hogan, and the officers of the Fifth Northern Division, they demand authority from me to take immediate action to bring public opinion to bear on the situation.

You understand that I have arranged for the kidnapping of 100 prominent Orangemen in counties Fermanagh and Tyrone. This was to take place last Tuesday, the 24th inst., but on account of the agreement arrived at between Sir James Craig and yourself I postponed action until Tuesday 23rd inst., and failing to hear from you to the contrary will commence at 7 o'clock tomorrow evening.

The North and South Monaghan Comhairle Ceantair jointly demand the boycott not be lifted in Co. Monaghan until the men, that did so much to secure the present measure of freedom, be released from the custody of pogromists. I am anxious to reply to my Monaghan friends tonight. I should add that there are 54 affiliated clubs in Co. Monaghan and each of them are sending two delegates to the Árd Fhéis [of Sinn Féin]; this means 108 votes from Monaghan for the Treaty.

Collins agreed – in the circumstances, he presumably felt that he had no option but to agree – and the result was extraordinary: on 7 February 1922, forty-two prominent Orangemen in Counties Fermanagh, Derry and Tyrone were kidnapped and held as hostages against the lives of the condemned Derry prisoners.

The IRA, meanwhile, awaited its chance – and it soon came. On Saturday 11 February, a party of B Specials was travelling by train from Newtownards in Co. Down west to Enniskillen in Co. Fermanagh. The railway line had to cross the newly installed border, slicing through Monaghan territory en route to Enniskillen. At Clones station, the B Specials were to change trains – and the IRA members were waiting. Their intention was to kidnap, not kill – but at the sight of the ambush, one young B Special began to shoot, and IRA volunteer Matt Fitzpatrick fell dead. The rest of the IRA party now opened fire: five B Specials were killed; some of the others fled across the nearby border; the remainder were taken away.

Violence now reached unparalleled heights in Northern Ireland. The Treaty itself did not merely tremble – it swung dangerously in a gale of violence. And yet – realpolitik emerged victorious. Lloyd George was not prepared to see the Treaty go down. Northern Ireland prime minister James Craig was pressurized into reprieving the Derry prisoners and releasing the Monaghan footballers. The Orange hostages were subsequently released too.

It is almost impossible not to imagine what might have happened had just some of these events gone the other way: had those prisoners been hanged in Derry; had the prominent Orangemen come to grief – or had just one of the Monaghan county Gaelic players been injured or killed. The Treaty might not have been ratified – for this was, after all, O'Duffy's unconcealed threat. Free State forces might have crossed the border in force; these might have engaged the British military in Northern Ireland. The shape of today's Ireland might be entirely different.

And all on account of a convoy of GAA members, driving in dangerous times between Monaghan and Derry. How history can turn decisively on a pivot.

*

I want to end this chapter by glancing at the terrible months of civil conflict that tore through the Free State in the period following the signing of the Treaty. The short and intense Civil War was as bitter and fratricidal as such wars will always be: and the GAA did well to remain an undivided body through the course of the conflict. It was impossible, of course, for the organization to remain utterly aloof from the bitter disagreements raging across the country, at town and county and parish level: indeed, it is a reflection of the GAA's position as a national barometer that it was intensely aware of these bitter disagreements, and aware too of its larger – or, one might say, higher – mission in remaining united in anticipation of better days.

Diplomacy was always called for. At the height of the Civil War, the Cork County Board passed a motion calling for GAA intervention as a peacemaker between the two sides. Counties Cork and Kerry saw some of the worst of the fighting, so such a resolution was no surprise. The Central Council appointed a committee to investigate the prospects of success for the proposed intervention: in the end, however, it was decided that, in view of passions involved, the GAA could not hope to bring hostilities to an end; the positive action that the GAA could take was to ban the distribution of political literature at its grounds.

And for all the talk of unity, there *were* divisions – but only one actual split. In 1922, the Clare County Board was particularly incensed at the execution of two of its hurlers – Con McMahon and Patrick Hennessy – for IRA activities. These executions caused a rift in the Clare GAA, which resulted in a creation, for two years, of a parallel organization in the county. This was serious enough – though not so serious as to destroy the GAA. Had a more prominent county – Cork, for example, or Kerry – split from the organization, the GAA could have been fatally wounded; and the fact that no such major split occurred speaks volumes for the unifying spirit of the organization overall.

The ceasefire, when it at length arrived in April 1923, saw large numbers of anti-Treaty prisoners of war held for some four months in internment camps. These were eventually released as a result of efforts behind the scenes by the prominent GAA member J. J. Walsh. His initiative was to build bridges in a riven society by holding a sports- and culture-based festival in Ireland, to be known as the Tailteann Games. The name was taken from an ancient Gaelic festival held to honour the dead – though it seems clear that Walsh also drew inspiration from the modern Olympics movement, which was gaining a head of steam at around the same time. The Games would,

Walsh proposed, embrace modern Gaelic games – but also activities from swimming to sailing to athletics to chess; a parallel programme of cultural events would take place, with writing, painting, theatre and crafts exhibitions taking place. W. B. Yeats, Augusta Gregory and Oliver St John Gogarty were amongst the many artists, poets and playwrights who weighed in behind the idea.

The GAA deserves credit for both helping to organize the inaugural games and providing Croke Park as the festival's main centre. The Games took place during the month of August 1924: and while they cannot be claimed as a complete success (the losers in the Civil War urged a boycott, and the Games came to be seen as a Cumann na nGaedheal project), they did have the effect of helping to knit the bones broken during the conflict. The main point of significance, however, is that the government released the Civil War internees in time for the games; indeed, a Kerry team took part – although Kerry had seen some of the most vicious Civil War bloodletting.

The release of the prisoners also led to one of the most remarkable series of events in GAA history: a series of matches between ex-internees from various counties and the Kerry county team. Kerry won overall: for the monotonous months in the internment camps, with nothing to do except play football, had resulted in skills being honed whereby Kerry achieved dominance in the game unequalled, at that time, by other counties. Indeed, the fact of the matter is that Kerry county teams became heavily reliant on the skills of these former internees.

I want to end this glance into the immediate aftermath of the Civil War by honouring a remarkable gesture which took place on the pitch at Croke Park in April 1924, with Kerry facing Cavan in the All-Ireland semi-final. As the Kerry team ran out onto the pitch, they went first to the spot where a Tipperary footballer had fallen in November 1920 – and knelt for a moment in a prayer to the memory of Michael Hogan. To paraphrase Rupert Brooke, 'There is a spot in Croke Park and in the collective memory of the GAA and the War of Independence that is forever Tipperary.'

CHAPTER EIGHT

North of the Border

To this point, I have chronicled the story of the
Gaelic Athletic Association in its earliest days: its birth
in the fiery years of the Gaelic Revival, and its adolescence, if
you will, during the violence and bloodshed that preceded the
creation of the Irish Free State. These years tell a considerable
story in themselves: but it seemed to me that I would be remiss
were I simply to end this tale at the conclusion of the Civil War
in Ireland – especially when the story so evidently runs into an
equally troubled period later in the twentieth century.

With this in mind, then, I want to continue to look north
– and focus in the following chapters of this book on the
later history of the GAA in Northern Ireland. The story of
the Monaghan footballers was played out against a violent
backdrop: and this later story is also told against a context
equally traumatic, equally violent – in many ways, indeed,
even more horrifying than anything that had gone before.
The Troubles lasted such a long time, after all: the death toll
was so high; and the situation in Northern Ireland has not yet
reached any sort of satisfactory conclusion. And the GAA was

there, witnessing all events. This, too, is a story that deserves
to be told.

*

The times had changed, of course: we are now stepping forward
four decades into the future – but it is interesting to note that
many of the patterns of politics in Ireland remained essentially
the same. As we will see, violence was once again sparked
by an unscrupulous playing of the Orange card for naked
political advantage; and once again, this violence was totally
unnecessary and sparked by political ambition – ambition
which had nothing whatever to do with Ireland or the GAA,
but which ultimately convulsed both. And the great irony: the
cycle of violence began with a simple handshake, with a gesture
of goodwill and rapprochement between North and South –
with a symbolic move which a profoundly unscrupulous man
seized upon to further his own career.

The gesture in question occurred on 14 January 1965 when
the taoiseach of the day, Seán Lemass, drove north of the
border to shake hands with his Northern Ireland counterpart,
Terence O'Neill. Lemass had now been prime minister for six
years: and his tenure had already been marked by considerable
economic and social reform: de Valera's dogmatic principles
of economic protectionism and social conservatism were
being replaced by free-market economics; the government was
investing heavily in education; and the Republic was opening
up slowly to Europe and the world.

O'Neill, meanwhile, had replaced the hard-line and inflexible Basil Brooke as prime minister of Northern Ireland in 1963: and while it would not be true to say that the winds of change were blowing through the Northern statelet, it could be said (if I may mix my metaphors) that the door to the profound Northern deep-freeze was being opened with a creak. O'Neill was patrician in background, but was recognized as something of a political liberal – and a reformer, albeit a tentative one. Certainly it is the case that both men were willing to at least attempt to mend the broken bridges between the two parts of Ireland, and their officials – including Lemass's deeply influential economics adviser T. K. Whitaker – had worked hard to ensure that such a symbolically significant meeting could take place.

Terence O'Neill himself told me a story which illustrates the context of the meeting. Following that first meeting at Stormont, he and Lemass were chatting in the unexalted milieu of a Stormont lavatory. They discussed how the day had gone: and Lemass, who was thinking apprehensively of the republican diehards waiting and watching at home, observed to O'Neill that nobody should think that this would now all be plain sailing! – not south of the border at any rate. 'You know', he said wryly, 'I'll get into terrible trouble over this.' But O'Neill knew that, no matter how bad the situation might be for Lemass in Dublin, it would always be infinitely worse for O'Neill himself in Belfast. And so: 'No,' he told Lemass as they stood at that Stormont urinal, '*I'll* be the one who gets into trouble.'

And O'Neill was right. A few snowballs had been thrown at Lemass's car as he drove into Stormont that January day: and these made as little impact on the political scene in the Republic as they did on Lemass's car. But both Lemass and O'Neill understood their longer-term impact: for these snowballs had been thrown by a fundamentalist preacher named Ian Kyle Paisley – who would prove to be a thoroughly baleful presence on the Northern Ireland political scene for decades to come.

This Ian Paisley was already, in 1965, an established figure in Northern Ireland. He had been making a name for himself since the 1950s – and more recently, in the 1964 general election, he had generated headlines in the North by leading hooligan parades in Belfast aimed at forcing the Royal Ulster Constabulary (RUC) to take down a small Tricolour which (if one looked closely enough and succeeded in penetrating into the solidly nationalist and Catholic Falls district of West Belfast) was to be found in the dingy window of republican election candidate Liam 'Billy' McMillen.

The simple fact was that McMillen's flag was indeed illegally displayed: under the legislation then obtaining in Northern Ireland, the flying of the Tricolour was illegal – and Paisley knew it. Here was an opportunity for popular agitation – and the incident of Billy McMillen's illegal window display would lead to a wave of car burnings and petrol bombings in Belfast. RUC personnel, using sledgehammers to crack a nut, smashed down McMillen's door and removed the Tricolour: the incident led to riots – and we can see in hindsight that the embers of the Troubles first sparked to life here, in the autumn of 1964.

These events were significant – and they were understood as such in Northern Ireland. But I want to emphasize that they aroused little interest south of the border. In this sense, it can be seen that the partition of the country had *worked*. Two very different states had been created on the island of Ireland. The entity south of the border had been paternalistic, priest-ridden, economically stagnant, and burdened by staggering levels of unemployment and immigration. The accession of Lemass, as I have mentioned, was instrumental in bringing about a much-delayed change of climate; in addition, the conclusions of the Second Vatican Council of 1962–5 had a liberating effect on Catholicism worldwide, and in Ireland not least; and other outside influences such as the presidency of John Fitzgerald Kennedy in the United States, and the emergence of the European Economic Community also acted to stimulate new political thinking. The Republic was on the cusp of change.

But in the North, in sharp contrast, the old slogans were alive and well. 'Not an inch' and 'No surrender' still acted as unofficial mottos for the government on the hill at Stormont. Northern Ireland remained a Protestant land for a Protestant people – and in the process it had evolved (if 'evolved' is indeed the appropriate word) into one of the most mean-spirited and unjust societies in Western Europe. Northern Catholics received the sanctions of the law, but not its protections. A property vote applied in local government elections ensured that as Protestants had more votes, they were allocated more council houses – plus more municipal and state employment. Catholics tended either to sign on the dole or to emigrate in search of greener pastures; and those that remained were more likely than not to live in substandard and chronically overcrowded housing.

Yet even in this benighted society, change could be detected. When education reforms were introduced in 1944 by a British government intent on a radical and progressive transformation of education in the post-war world, among the more potent measures was the delivery of free secondary education for every child – thus changing the future for a generation of working-class children. The law applied in England and Wales – but an equivalent bill enacted in 1947 extended the law to Northern Ireland, with effects that would take their time to feed into a frozen society, but that would eventually have revolutionary effects.

By the early 1960s, a new generation of university-educated Catholics and nationalists had emerged onto the scene in Northern Ireland. As was the case with their counterparts in the Republic, they were mindful of changes taking place in the outside world – and were influenced in particular by the civil rights movement gathering energy in the United States. Irish nationalists were also aware that fifty years had passed since the Easter Rising: marches were held, and commemorations staged along the border.

It was against this backdrop of a tentatively changing climate and society that Paisley operated, drawing on the fear of change now beginning to manifest inside defensive Protestant communities. As O'Neill remarked to me, 'The trouble is that [Paisley] does all this with the Book [the Bible] in his hand. The

Book is very important up here.' O'Neill was correct: the Bible was important – indeed, in many ways this remains the case – and Paisley knew this better than anyone. For decades, he would advance on power with – as the record of his scandal-ridden Democratic Unionist Party demonstrates – a Bible in his hand, ready to be thumped against any surface which presented itself.

And there would be many such surfaces.

In this context of steadily developing pressure for change and reform, indeed, Paisley's incendiary words found many eager listeners – and the result would be to push Northern Ireland over the edge. This would take some time: that meeting between Lemass and O'Neill seemed to gesture at a brighter future in Ireland – but the passing of several years brought a change, not for the better, but very definitely for the worst.

*

Many years after that winter meeting at Stormont, in the august surroundings of the Palace of Westminster, I had a discussion with the former Labour prime minister James Callaghan. He reflected on how he, Denis Healey and other luminaries of Harold Wilson's Labour government had met at an opulent Piccadilly restaurant in London to decide whether to send British troops into Northern Ireland. It was now the summer of 1969: and civil unrest and violence was growing on the streets of Belfast and Derry. British politicians are not known for their insights into Irish history and politics – but Callaghan and his colleagues had enough sense to see that the problem was not so much sending the troops *in*, but rather how to get them *out* again. But he could never have foreseen how matters would develop in Northern Ireland, nor how long the troops would remain there.

A variety of force had by now been unleashed in Northern Ireland. Sustained pressure by Paisley and his allies had led to the fall of Terence O'Neill, amid the gradual splintering of Unionist politics; before three years had passed, O'Neill's successor James Chichester-Clark would follow him out of the exit; and soon, the edifice of the Northern Ireland government itself would crumble.

Meanwhile the republican genie had burst from its bottle – and now the debate between the philosophy's two wings had once again emerged as a live issue. Should the aims of republicanism be achieved by constitutional means alone, or by armed force? Should an Irish Republican Army resume its existence, and should it be armed? The IRA, of course, had never gone away. During the Second World War, to be sure, de Valera had effectively crushed the organization in the Republic – in the aftermath of partition its main theatre of operations – by means of internments and executions. Indeed, one of the few remaining signs of republican influence was the renaming of a Kerry GAA club after The O'Rahilly, who had been killed in the 1916 Rising. The club was renamed Kerins O'Rahilly's, thus also honouring Charlie Kerins, the IRA chief of staff who had been hanged by de Valera following the murder of a detective.

In the 1950s, an attempt to revive the movement in the Republic collapsed after an ineffectual attempt at a military border campaign aimed at putting pressure on the Northern Ireland government. This campaign had been led from the Republic by a new generation of young IRA volunteers. It amounted to very little: a series of ineffectual raids on barracks and customs posts along the border, as part of a campaign which was soon snuffed out. North of the border, the security apparatus was so strong that almost nothing happened: Belfast and Derry remained quiet, and would remain quiet for a decade to come. The IRA was, if not exactly dead, then nearing death.

But now, as the 1960s approached their tense and smoke-filled end in Northern Ireland, Derry and Belfast were stirring – and the IRA was unquiet too. It was time to square up once more to that fundamental division in the movement. Since issuing a formal ceasefire in 1962, the IRA – led from Dublin by a house painter named Cathal Goulding – had opted for constitutionalism, and had decided that republican candidates should stand for election, with the promise that they would take their seats in the abhorred 'partition parliaments' of Belfast, London and Dublin. Abstentionism had been a central tenet of republican policy – and now it had been abandoned.

This change created severe strains in the movement – but no split: under Goulding, the movement held to a socialist and peaceful path. Instead, a newer generation of republican sympathizers south of the border became active in (for example) the trade union movement, as well as taking up potentially influential positions in such state bodies as RTE and the Revenue Commissioners. But the awakening of unrest and violence in the North, coming as it did on the heels of an awakening of nationalist sentiment, brought this process of what we might term 'constitutionalism' to a shuddering halt.

The history of one Belfast district off the Falls Road exemplifies what took place more widely in those violent times in the North. The district is Clonard, which is associated with Clonard monastery – and which is also known as 'Little India', on account of the area's street names. There is a Cawnpore Street, a Cashmere Street, a Bombay Street and so on – all remembering the period of the British imperial rule in India. In the summer of 1969, this small district was the focus of considerable violence, as loyalist paramilitaries and thugs made concerted efforts to burn Catholic families from their homes – and to burn the Catholic monastery into the bargain. The letters 'IRA' appeared on many a Clonard gable wall in those days – but now loyalists jeered that the acronym in fact stood for another slogan: 'Irish Ran Away'.

But the Irish had *not* run away. These loyalist thugs burned Bombay Street – but they failed in their efforts to clear Clonard of Catholics. They were defeated, in fact, by low-tech methods, in the form of hails of stones: local youth – including the Fianna, or republican boy scouts – had been organized by a young local republican leader named Gerry Adams into stone-throwing cadres, who became known as the Cashmere Fusiliers. But the very fact that these fusiliers had been necessary in the first place caused consternation and anger: for surely, it was reasoned, the loyalist thugs should have been met by the force of the law, and by the forces of the state itself – not by crowds of stone-throwing youths. And if the state was unwilling to assist them, then the people of Clonard should have had access to their own guns, their own weapons. So the argument went. But there were no guns: there were no weapons at all, except for stones. The IRA had no weapons, and it had embraced constitutional means. The blunt fact was that the organization was powerless to defend these communities.

I recall that, in the aftermath of the burnings, I was shown around Clonard by Liam Hannaway, who was Gerry Adams's uncle. Hannaway showed me how he had used one of the total of six guns available to Belfast republicans at that time. The weapon in question was a Wild West-style Colt .45 – not merely old, but featuring a defective chamber that had to be turned manually after each bullet was fired. Not much use, surely – but by running from one street corner to another, firing a shot and then retreating, the efforts of Hannaway and those of a handful of companions, combined with the efforts of the waves of stone throwers, saved the district until the introduction of British soldiers by the Labour government at last brought a measure of order.

A measure of order – and yet peace was by no means conceivable. In January 1970, faced with the stark facts which flowed from a policy of constitutionalism in a violent world, the republican movement split into two wings: Goulding's constitutional section became known as the Official IRA, dedicated to a socialist future achieved by peaceful means; while a new Provisional IRA was born, deriving its name from the 'provisional' government of Ireland proclaimed by Pearse and others in 1916. The Provisionals were willing and able to take up arms: their intent was readily understood by any observer of Irish republicanism, and it can be crystallized into one pithy phrase:

Get the British out of occupied Ireland.

The Provisional had many willing recruits – but at first, a dearth of arms; and while they recruited and drilled, most of the violence of the period came from the loyalist side. The first RUC member to be killed in the Troubles, for example, was Constable Victor Arbuckle, done to death by loyalist hooligans during a riot on the Shankill Road in October 1969. The first British soldier to die was Gunner Robert Curtis, killed by the IRA in February 1971.

Regardless of the prevalence of *loyalist* violence, however, the British government channelled the greater part of its resources into combating *republican* opponents – this partly on account of the advice and intelligence provided by the authorities at Stormont, and partly the result of traditional allegiances and instincts. British officers, indeed, recorded their bewilderment at being stoned by Protestant mobs waving Union Jacks and proclaiming themselves to be loyalist (loyal to whom?), but their military and political masters refused to open a second front against Ulster loyalism – this for fear of being shot in the back as they turned to confront their ostensible (Catholic) opponents.

Unionist influence and military strategy combined to produce one of the great policy blunders of the Troubles. This was the policy of internment without trial, introduced in August 1971 by the Stormont government and approved by Westminster.

The policy ought perhaps to be called 'internment of Catholics without trial': for in spite of the levels of loyalist violence in this period, Catholics and Catholics alone were imprisoned by the authorities, while known loyalists were left entirely alone. Over three hundred civilians were interned in the first wave of the policy: they were imprisoned at the former RAF base at Long Kesh in Co. Down; ultimately, close to two thousand civilians would be locked up without trial.

The policy was lamentably counter-productive. It merely served to swell the numbers of young volunteers joining the IRA: and led directly to one of the great traumas of Northern Ireland history – the hunger strikes of 1980–81. This crisis arose out of the decision to confer special category status on interned political prisoners. Until 1976 such inmates 'enjoyed' *de facto* prisoner of war status. They communicated with the authorities only through their own representatives, did not undertake prison work or wear prison uniforms, did not have to mingle with loyalist prisoners, and in many cases devoted themselves principally to acquiring an education.

In other words, Long Kesh evolved – as had Frongoch before it – into a republican university. To many unionists and politicians on the Tory right, however, this was not a university at all, but rather a 'Sandhurst of terror' – and such individuals wished to change the environment of Long Kesh and to strip its inmates of their special status. This was merely one element in a proposed plan which would see Northern Ireland's nationalist population targeted by all the tools of the state, as a means of destroying its political spirit.

In proposing such policies, the British government was reverting to the policies of the earlier Tan war. The IRA was not to be depicted as a guerrilla organization but rather as a criminal operation. Two other policies were introduced at the same time: 'normalization' meant that bomb damage was repaired as rapidly as possible after the rubble ceased falling, in order to give Northern Ireland the guise of a normal society; 'Ulsterization', meanwhile, essentially meant that local people – that is, local and mainly Protestant members of the RUC and the Ulster Defence Regiment – were increasingly expected to do the actual fighting. As these abnormal normalization and Ulsterization policies were rolled out, it became politically impossible to continue enabling the IRA to run its own university close to Belfast.

From 1976 the British began building cellular buildings on the Long Kesh site. Because of their H-shaped design, these buildings became known as the H Blocks. To bolster the criminalisation process, meanwhile, a further legal measure was introduced: the so-called Diplock Courts conducted non-jury trials which accepted the uncorroborated statements of police witnesses as evidence. Conviction rates accordingly rose rapidly, and the new H Blocks began to fill – and this led to what became known as the 'dirty protest'.

The spark was lit by Kieran Nugent, the first prisoner gaoled under the system: he refused to wear the prison uniform, remarking that the prison authorities would have instead to 'nail it to my back'.[29] The success of the conveyor belt system of conviction and imprisonment meant that there would be many more Kieran Nugents – for what neither the authorities nor the republican movement itself realized was that the apparent success of the policy contained within it the seeds of its own destruction. So many families became affected by what was going on in Long Kesh that the protest eventually would affect not merely Northern Ireland society, but that of the Republic. In addition, the wider nationalist public in the North could readily empathize with the prisoners: Northern Catholics had been born and raised within a political order founded on the basis of discrimination and injustice – and they saw within the walls of Long Kesh a new order that was but a more extreme version of what had gone before.

Both inside and outside the gaol, emotions grew as the prisoners were punished for refusing to wear the prison uniform: they were confined to their cells from which all bedding was removed during the day; and they were naked except for their blankets. From this condition the term 'on the blanket' became a potent rallying cry. In addition, the blanket protest was amplified by what became known as the 'dirty protest'. The normal prison routine involved 'slops out and breakfast in': the warders removed the prisoners' commodes with their night soil, as they handed over the morning's food. The prisoners claimed that as tensions grew, and warders and prisoners came into increasingly violent conflict, the warders began to kick over the slop buckets instead of removing them – and so to get rid of the excreta, the prisoners began throwing it out of the cell windows. The warders began throwing it back in again, and so began what might be termed the 'battle of the bowels'.

I was the first journalist to be allowed to visit the H Blocks during the dirty protest, and I recorded this memory of what I found:

The door was opened: the Governor asked me to wait a moment, stepped inside and said a word to the two occupants. All I could catch was the admonition 'no conversation': as if to underline this, two enormous warders, either of whom would dwarf me (and I am not a small man), entered the cell and stood behind the cell's occupants. They were then aged twenty-one and twenty-two, as I afterwards learned, serving ten and twelve years respectively. When the cell door opened, they both looked frightened and looked anxiously at us for a moment. They were pallid and naked except for a blanket draped over their shoulders. They stood silently, fear hardening into defiance, I felt, as we looked at the cell. It was covered in excrement, almost to the ceiling on all four walls. In one corner there was a pile of rotting, blue-moulded food and excrement and the two boys had evidently been using bits of their foam rubber mattress to add to the decor as we entered. There wasn't much of a smell but the light was dim and the atmosphere profoundly disturbing and depressing. I felt helpless and angry as I stood and looked at these appalling and disgraceful conditions, prevented by bureaucracy and by history from talking to two of my fellow human beings who had brought themselves and been brought to this condition of self-abnegation.[30]

It is not necessary to labour the effect on the families and friends of protesting prisoners of the repulsive drama played out at Long Kesh. Anger and anxiety translated into mass protests – and yet where it should have counted most, the protest achieved nothing. Margaret Thatcher was not for turning.

I want to emphasize here that, had very simple measures been implemented, there would never have been any trouble inside the H Blocks. And the examples were there for all to see. In the Republic, most IRA prisoners were held at the high-security prison at Portlaoise – and here, prisoner issues were resolved by means of a simple expedient: conceding to their demands without appearing to do so. IRA prisoners were segregated from other inmates and permitted to concentrate on furthering their education. They wore their own clothes; and parcels and visits flowed. The concession of the 'Portlaoise formula', in other words, would have solved the Long Kesh situation overnight – but when I put this suggestion to Michael Alison, the prisons minister at the Northern Ireland Office, and a reasonable person, he shook his head and replied, 'There's a lady in the case, you know.' Margaret Thatcher wanted a win, not a solution.

The protest spread to the women's prison at Armagh, which I also visited. Off-duty warders were targeted by the IRA, protesting civilians took to the streets barefooted and wearing blankets in the depths of winter – but Thatcher stuck to the criminalization policy. The dirty protest was at length called off – and instead a hunger strike began, which continued until Christmas 1980. I visited the prisoners' leader Brendan Hughes: my visit was undertaken at the request of Taoiseach

Charles Haughey; I was also in touch with Redemptorist priest Brendan Meagher, who was acting as an intermediary between prisoners and the authorities.

Meagher feared that the end of the strike was no breakthrough, but merely the beginning of something even worse. The prisoners had been led to believe that if they abandoned their protest, civilian-type clothing would be permitted – and that this might be a first step to greater concessions, including the renewal of special category status, in due course. And Meagher was correct in his pessimism: the British had won the day – but only the day. Inside the gaol, a new prisoners' leader was elected. His name was Bobby Sands – and Sands now began another hunger strike, the horror of which would grip the world. This strike began in March 1981, and continued until October – and resulted in the deaths of ten prisoners. As these men died one by one, Ireland was gripped by emotions on a scale not witnessed in the country since the days of the War of Independence.

In effect, the hunger strikes proved to be the North's 1916. Their impact transformed Northern Ireland politics: now, Sinn Féin embraced constitutionalism and emerged as a rapidly growing political movement. And, by choosing this constitutional path, the party took the road that would lead, in due course, to the Good Friday Agreement and to Sinn Fein itself becoming a potent political force – not only in Northern Ireland, but south of the border too.

Ever since the creation of Northern Ireland in 1921, Britain's error – its crime – had been to ignore the essentially vicious character of the entity it had been instrumental in bringing into being. Its original sin had been to enable the unionists of Northern Ireland to develop an apartheid state within the United Kingdom, thus denying a large section of those ruled from Belfast the fundamental rights to which they would have been unquestionably entitled had they lived in Bradford or Brighton or Bristol.

Now, a slow process of reform began – a process which would conclude with the passing of the Good Friday Agreement a quarter of a century later. This was no smooth process: again and again it was interrupted by events on the ground in Northern Ireland itself, and by the shifting currents of London politics. But, while the arc of the moral universe is long, it does indeed bend towards justice: the Good Friday Agreement, while it was far from perfect, was necessary; and while it has been attacked recently by unprincipled figures on the right of the Conservatives, and imperilled by Brexit, it must endure, as a stepping stone towards the future.

I make no excuses for such a long preamble – for if one fact is clear about the history of Ireland in the twentieth century, it is this: that the facts about Northern Ireland have been ignored, set aside and otherwise discarded at every opportunity – with the result that the details necessary to understand this corner of our islands have not always been neatly to hand. Now that I have provided some necessary context, then, let us look at how the GAA operated – and survived – through the maelstrom of these years in this place.

CHAPTER NINE

A Long War

T HE GAELIC ATHLETIC ASSOCIATION *DID* SURVIVE IN THE uncongenial environment of Northern Ireland, and it *did* continue to operate – but the Troubles in Northern Ireland led to a series of atrocities being visited on the organization and upon its supporters. There had, as we have seen, been a consistent vein of Protestant distaste for the organization since its very earliest days – the result of the tradition of the 'Sunday game', which violated strict notions of the sanctity of the Sabbath. Similarly, many Protestants disliked the drunkenness and violence which tended to accompany GAA matches; and disliked too the strong connections between the organization and the Catholic Church. These chilly attitudes were to be perceived across Ireland as a whole – but the imposition of the border placed the GAA in Northern Ireland in an even more challenging position.

That it was able to put down deep roots in such ostensibly infertile Northern soil, indeed, was largely owing to good fortune – in particular good management, which enabled the organization north of the border to husband its resources, and operate with the tact and diplomacy necessary in an essentially hostile environment. We have already seen, of course, that there were inherent limitations in what the GAA could hope to achieve, regardless of how nimbly it conducted itself: the episode of the Monaghan footballers speaks volumes about its room for manoeuvre, and the perils that presented themselves at every turn. The bottom line was this: regardless of how it operated, the GAA would always be seen by many unionist civilians and politicians as the IRA at play. Nothing would change this, and the GAA leadership knew it.

It seems to me that GAA played a most significant role in the effort to at least keep Ireland *culturally* whole in the aftermath of partition. As three Ulster counties – Cavan, Monaghan and Donegal – were now in the Republic, games played by those teams within a partitioned context maintained a link with the six Ulster counties north of the border; and the impact of such sustained contact and fellowship cannot be underestimated. When Northern Ireland was created, many Northern nationalists believed that partition simply could not last: and they continued to work as the previous generation had done towards the fulfilment of their vision of a Ireland that would be Gaelic in work, in leisure and in games – and all this in the face of the frosty disapproval of their Protestant neighbours, to whom Ulster was a British province, now and for ever. This sense of unionist exasperation was only heightened in the immediate post-partition era by the circumstance which saw Cavan emerge as the most successful team in Ulster. The county continuously sent teams and crowds of – in many quarters, wholly unwanted – supporters from the south to win sporting titles on what the unionists saw as British soil.

There were, of course, many practical difficulties – the most pressing being a lack of hard cash available to the GAA north of the border. Nevertheless, funds were found and investment made – most visibly in the form of new stadiums built at Breffni Park in Cavan (1923) and Corrigan Park in Belfast (1927). Ulster's largest and most significant stadium of all was at length also constructed at Belfast – and was named for Roger Casement, who had been executed for his part in the 1916 Rising. Casement Park was formally opened in 1953 on a tide of emotion. For years in advance of the opening, the GAA had been raising money for the ground's construction by running a pools operation – and when it was finally completed, it was blessed by the Catholic Cardinal of All Ireland, John D'Alton, who scattered soil taken for the occasion from Semple Park in Thurles.

Which brings us to the issue that led to the shedding of a great deal of innocent GAA blood during the Troubles: when one person's terrorist is another person's freedom fighter. To Irish nationalists, north and south alike, Casement was a humanitarian, a hero whose life was unjustly taken from him because he loved Ireland. To loyalists and unionists, on the other hand, Casement was a traitor pure and simple. For many Northern nationalists, who could not offer their allegiance to the Stormont parliament, Casement Park represented a bastion, a refuge, a reaffirmation of their identity. Unionist attitudes, on the other hand, have made Casement Park a source of controversy and division almost from the laying of the foundation stone to (as we will see) the time of writing.

It is worth stating yet again, however, that unionist fears of Casement Park and the GAA in general were largely baseless, for none of the GAA clubs and playing fields that developed in Northern Ireland in the period leading up to the Troubles were IRA training grounds. There simply was no IRA to train! But none of that mattered: it was the symbolism that counted. In particular, the use of the Irish language and the symbol of the hurley were enough in unionist eyes to confer IRA membership on GAA players.

As time went on, however, the GAA began – ironically – to receive British state funding: and this flow of money, combined with its own fundraising efforts, meant that the organization in Northern Ireland eventually became a force to be reckoned with. Ulster counties began to leave a mark on national competition: Down, and later Derry, Armagh and Tyrone, began winning All-Ireland football titles – accomplishments which to unionists were something of a curate's egg. They could not help but feel a tentative welling of pride in seeing teams from their own counties appear on television before vast crowds at Croke Park, and sweep all before them. But inevitably, these images also carried with them troubling visions of an Ireland that was already united on the pitch

When the Troubles erupted and Northern nationalists began to be killed in numbers, the GAA reacted sharply and with anger. In the aftermath of Bloody Sunday in Derry, the

GAA national president Pádraig Ó'Fainín issued the following statement which was read at all inter-county GAA games:

The Gaelic Athletic Association had its Bloody Sunday in Croke Park in November 1920, when British soldiers indulged in a rampage of murder against unarmed spectators and Gaelic Footballers. Derry's Bogside had its Bloody Sunday on 30 January, 1972 when British soldiers swept the streets with gunfire to teach the Irish another lesson. The sympathy of the Association goes out to the bereaved, and unqualified support is pledged to the cause for which innocent people, engaged in peaceful protest, died. But as Bloody Sunday 1920 shocked the world and strengthened the will of the Irish people to fashion their own destiny, so must it be, also, following the bloody massacre of 1972. These deaths will not have been in vain. Britain through this latest barbaric act of its soldiers stands indicted before the bar of world opinion. Most specifically, the British Government stands so indicted before God and man. Bloody Sunday 1972 has drawn the Irish people together. The point of no return has been reached and passed. That is the victory of those who were so cruelly and callously done to death on the streets of Derry. The Gaelic Athletic Association, already committed to a policy of organized relief of distress in the Six-County area, will re-double its efforts to ensure that the hardship resulting from all repressive measures of a discredited regime will not be permitted to weaken the will of brave people to press on to complete victory. The Association, as always, takes its place in pursuit of the national ideal – a free 32-County Ireland.

The emotion and passion of Ó'Fainín's statement – which was, ironically, so much more forthright than the somewhat muted response of the GAA to the original Bloody Sunday in 1920 – found a response in the Northern GAA that would, throughout the course of the Troubles, never completely die away. In the Republic – where, as I have mentioned, partition truly had worked, and where a Catholic society for a Catholic people had grown up – the outrage which followed Bloody Sunday faded relatively quickly: here, the GAA would continue through the period of the Troubles to view the unrest in the North from the position of a sympathetic, but essentially *uninvolved* sporting organization. In the North, such detachment was impossible, in both practical and moral terms – and the organization north of the border would have to deal with almost daily military and political issues.

At this point, I want to pause for a moment to comment on two decidedly over-simplified definitions of the 'Ulster problem'. One is the claim of the Ulster unionist, the descendants of settlers enforced on the native population in the seventeenth century: that Ulster is British, and that those seen to quarrel with this statement are by definition *traitors*. The other vision is that of the traditional republican: that there is no fundamental difference between the Northern Ireland Protestant and his or her Catholic neighbour; and that once the British depart, Ireland will be well.

Militant Ulster loyalists have taken considerable pains to disabuse republicans of this latter notion – and one of their principal methods of doing this was by killing members of the GAA. In this, as the records show, they were supported amply by the security forces, who gradually came to see the GAA as the enemy, and GAA clubs as hotbeds of republican sentiment. And so the GAA frequently came to be targeted, often with fatal results.

The persistently 'them' and 'us' nature of Northern society translated very readily indeed into sport. In general terms, the Protestant population of Northern Ireland focused its sporting energies principally on soccer, and to a lesser degree on cricket and rugby – which is of course ironic, given that both these sports are played on an all-island basis.[31] Northern Catholics too were enamoured with soccer – to a degree, indeed, that should have made it more difficult for the GAA to make progress in the twentieth century. But here, as in every other aspect of life in Northern Ireland, sectarianism intervened, driving Catholics to look to soccer south of the border, and to the GAA north of the border.

Around the time of partition, one national body governed Irish soccer. This was the Irish Football Association (IFA), headquartered in Belfast. But clear evidence of discrimination against players south of the border, eventually forced a split. In the years between 1882 and 1921, for example, players from Leinster soccer clubs won just 75 caps, while those from Ulster clubs won 798 for the Irish national team – and almost ninety per cent of the international matches played in Ireland were held in Belfast.[32] This resulted, inevitably, in a split: in

1921, the separate Football Association of Ireland (FAI) was established in Dublin.

For several decades thereafter, a bizarre situation existed: the island of Ireland fielded two soccer teams, each styling themselves 'Ireland'. During this period, the wealthier Northern team drew several players from the South – but this talent drain did not further cross-border friendship; and at length, the world governing body of football was obliged to put an end to a farcical situation. In 1953, FIFA decreed that henceforth each association could draw only from its own geographical area; and that there should be two teams, the Republic of Ireland and Northern Ireland.

This localism furthered Northern Ireland soccer's dependence on Protestantism for support. It also helped to increase the GAA's standing amongst Northern Catholics – as both a true All-Ireland body, *and* a prime manifestation of their identity. During the 1960s and 1970s, All-Ireland football finals at Croke Park involving Northern teams drew crowds of up to 90,000 spectators. In vain did a Belfast Protestant named George Best – the greatest soccer player that the island of Ireland has ever produced – attempt during the 1970s to create the united Ireland team that many of his fellow players in Manchester United and other English soccer clubs wanted to see. Soccer, unlike Gaelic games, cricket, rugby and other games, would continue to be played as a partitioned sport.

Instead, soccer in Northern Ireland continued to be a bastion of Protestant sectarianism. This situation was most vividly captured on the world's television screen at a time when the Troubles appeared to be moving towards an endgame. In November 1993, with Northern Ireland and the Republic of Ireland drawn in the same World Cup qualifying group, the two teams met in Belfast. Northern Ireland had already been eliminated from the competition; the Republic needed a draw or a win to go through to the finals in the United States. Much, then, was at stake – and for many Northern Ireland supporters, the game afforded an opportunity to deliver an unforgettable blow to the enemy team. In addition, the previous month had seen twenty-seven Troubles-related killings in Northern Ireland – the worst toll in some years.

The game at Windsor Park, then, was played against a backdrop of considerable tension – and the result was a deeply unpleasant spectacle: later, the manager of the Republic of Ireland team, the Englishman Jack Charlton, observed that he had 'never seen a more hostile atmosphere'. In the words of the Republic's Alan McLoughlin, 'I could hear it and feel it right behind me. You didn't dare look around and make eye contact. The venom in their eyes shocked me.'

The fraught history of Northern Ireland sport is such that not even the coming of the Good Friday Agreement could be said to have strengthened and normalized the position of soccer between the two communities. In fact, the Agreement might be said to have further encouraged the flow of players south of the border. But fair's fair: at the time of writing, it is a pleasure to recognize the efforts of an outstanding Northern Ireland team manager. Michael O'Neill must be credited with hauling his team out of the doldrums and bringing it a considerable measure of international success.[33]

*

We swore by King William there'd never be seen
An All-Irish Parliament at College Green,
So at Stormont we're nailing the flag to the mast:
May the Lord in His mercy be kind to Belfast.

O the bricks they will bleed and the rain it will weep,
And the damp Lagan fog lull the city to sleep;
It's to hell with the future and live on the past:
May the Lord in His mercy be kind to Belfast.

As we shall see, the GAA recorded a remarkable growth in strength throughout the Troubles – but this was not always accompanied by displays of kindness to Belfast. This is best epitomized, maybe, by the travails that befell Kickham's GAA club. Readers will remember my earlier mention of Charles Kickham: author, leading light of the IRB and creator of *Knocknagow*. By the time the Troubles erupted in Northern Ireland in 1969, Kickham was not much recalled in Irish history: his name, indeed, was only remembered as a result of the GAA, for several local clubs were named in his honour. These clubs were scattered throughout the country: in Co. Louth, in Kickham's native Co. Tipperary – and in the nationalist enclave of Ardoyne in North Belfast.

A sense of what the 'Kickhams' of Ardoyne endured and suffered in the course of the Troubles may be discerned from a vignette remembered by its coach Pat Murphy. 'One of our lads', recalls Murphy, 'plonked himself down on the bench, and a keg-bomb rolled out from under the bench. It caused a bit of a scattering.'[34] At the time, the 'lad' was about sixteen years old. One has to dig behind the smiling faces in a photograph of a group of other similarly youthful Kickham players in 1969, in order to learn something of the reality of what befell individual members of the GAA in this period.

The lads in the picture are smiling because they have just won that year's Antrim county championship. In a fine piece of investigative journalism for Melbourne's *Age* newspaper, Andra Jackson highlighted this team photograph, before going on to explore the future lives of these young players.[35] Two of the sixteen-year-olds would later be murdered – including Raymond Mooney, then thirty-three years old, who was gunned down by the Protestant Action Force in 1986 as he locked up the local church after a meeting. Others were victims of attempted murder; their families were similarly targeted. Two of the players lost their fathers, and another two their brothers – in each case murdered by loyalists. The brother of another player survived a murder bid. One was burnt out of his home by loyalists. Another left the club after loyalist death threats.

Other fatalities associated with the Kickham's club included Frank Carr, aged fifty-two, who was the South Antrim county secretary. He had been on his way to a Kickham's hurling match one night in 1972. His car was found burnt out; his body was in the boot, with a bullet wound to the head. Carr had taken a short cut through a loyalist area and had been stopped at a checkpoint. His friends believe that the security forces at the checkpoint noted the hurleys in his car – a clear indicator of his identity as a Catholic.

A second fatality was Ted McQuaid, aged twenty-five, chairman of Kickham's, and a senior football and hurling player. As McQuaid waited for a lift outside a party in the area in 1976, a taxi drove past, turned around and pulled alongside, and a gunman jumped out and pumped bullets into him. Another Kickham's fatality was footballer Seamus Morris, aged seventeen. He was making deliveries locally when gunmen opened up from a passing car in 1988. Not all of these individuals were killed simply because they were Kickham members. But the GAA represented an identifiable enemy – the Ulster Freedom Fighters militia publicly stated as much – and its members were recognizable and reachable targets.

All the foregoing atrocities are of course documented in histories of the period – but where the 'Kickhams' in particular are concerned, a remarkable cinematic record also exists. *The Kickhams* (1993) was produced by Brendan Byrne, who had himself played for the club. The film traces how Kickhams managed to sustain its activities throughout and in spite of the Troubles, and in the teeth of an endless list of atrocities; and as one views this film, it is impossible not to draw a parallel with the experience of the GAA in general in the course of the War of Independence.

The club, it becomes clear, survived due to a dogged determination to resist external pressures; to keep playing its sports; and to keep a specific identity alive in the teeth of those determined to – literally – kill it. And killing, let us never forget, was literally the objective both of Protestant paramilitaries, and on occasion, and unforgivably, that of the security forces themselves. Both loyalist terrorists and members of the security forces shot and killed individual GAA members; club premises were attacked and burned. Kickham's and other clubs were driven off the fields where they had traditionally played, because these grounds were located in Protestant areas, and were simply too dangerous to use.

This led to urgent practical difficulties. During the Troubles, some seventy per cent of all leisure centres were in Protestant areas, and in order to get access to training facilities, Kickhams officials invented a bogus club named the Crumlin Defenders – as Protestant-sounding a name as one can imagine. When the leisure centre authorities discovered the club's true identity, however, the 'Kickhams' had to flee once more. The club used buses to get around: while these offered some protection, they were also sometimes stoned; and club members were routinely warned not to appear on the street carrying a hurley, not to wear club colours, and not to don the colours of the Glaswegian soccer club Celtic FC. And, while the GAA ban on 'foreign' games and on British security forces membership were progressively removed from 1971 onwards, whatever *rapprochement* these ecumenical measures might have achieved were lost in the fallout from the Troubles.

The St Enda's GAA club, founded in the Glengormley area of North Belfast in the 1950s, holds the unenviable distinction of being one of the most bombed clubs in Northern Ireland. The recorded attacks on the club are in the high teens, and several of the club's players and administrators were murdered. As in the case of Kickham's, a photograph on a club wall sets the scene. The year is 1975, and the photograph shows a group of Enda's players who have just won an Under-12 competition; the letters 'RIP' sit alongside the images of two of these youths. Years after their photograph was taken, their membership of the GAA cost the lives of Liam Canning (in 1981) and Gerry Devlin (in 1997).

The most high-profile assassination associated with the club was that of club president Seán Fox. Fox had first attracted loyalist and police attention at a Sunday function in the club, which featured the customary raising of the Tricolour and the broadcasting of a recording of the Irish national anthem over the sound system. As the flag fluttered to the top of the pole, however, the sound system broke down. Fox broke the ensuing silence by stepping forward and lustily singing the anthem himself. A short while later, the police arrived to say there had been complaints about the anthem and the flying of the flag from adjoining Protestant neighbours. In 1993, Fox was tortured in his home, a short distance from St Enda's, before being shot dead.

The targeting of GAA players was not restricted to clubs and their officials in the Belfast area. Rather, this lethal practice was province-wide, and was carried on from a relatively early period of the Troubles. One of the most notorious cases occurred in 1972.

Louis Leonard was a well-known GAA figure in the Fermanagh area, and a star player for St Patrick's GAA club at Donagh, in the southeast of the county. On a day in 1972, Leonard was found shot dead in the fridge of his butcher's shop in the village. Leonard had died at the hands of loyalist paramilitaries.

As I have mentioned, however, the finger cannot always be pointed at loyalist extremists – for the role of the British army throughout much of this period was also highly suspect. The death of Aidan McAnespie is one notorious case in point. McAnespie was a well-known Co. Tyrone GAA player who frequently crossed into the Republic via the busy army border checkpoint at Aughnacloy. In February 1988, as he walked along the road, McAnespie was shot in the back by a soldier stationed at the checkpoint. The soldier claimed that his finger had slipped on the trigger: he was immediately whisked away from the site, and later fined for negligent discharge of a weapon. He received a medical discharge from the army in 1990.

The Irish government commissioned a report into the killing – which has never been published; while in 2008, a new Police Service of Northern Ireland investigation into the incident noted the sheer physical effort needed to pull the trigger on a modern firearm, and concluded that the soldier's explanation was 'the least likely explanation' of what had taken place that day. McAnespie's standing within the GAA has contributed to a lasting bitterness concerning this case.[36]

If St Enda's is the most bombed club in Northern Ireland, then Crossmaglen Rangers in South Armagh is the region's most attacked – although in this case, the attacking was done by the British Army. The Rangers club had been founded in October 1887: and for whatever reason – be it location or the hardihood and spirit of the people of the area – it almost immediately became one of the top clubs in the country. It is certainly the case that the club's hinterland was one of the most highly individual districts in Ireland – and it is the case too that the partition settlement in 1921 should never have included this district within the new Northern entity. Traditionally, Crossmaglen was one of the most Gaelic areas in Ireland: its population was dominated by Catholics – and the potential for trouble existed from the moment a stroke of the pen yanked Crossmaglen and its hinterland into a new Protestant state. For decades, however, the area stayed quiet: the people of Crossmaglen got on with their lives, continued to look south, played their Gaelic games – and held the line even after the eruption of trouble in 1969.

Perhaps the preponderance of smuggling in the area had something to do with this wish for a quiet life: the border was unwanted, but it nevertheless provided a trade bonanza in everything from cattle to razor blades to nylon stockings – and the last thing anyone in the area wanted was attention from the security forces. But inevitably the climate changed in the area: the security forces began to pay attention to South Armagh; body and vehicle searches became daily occurrences; resentment simmered – and on the day in 1971 when a nervy young sentry at an army post on the Springfield Road in Belfast responded to a cars backfiring by killing a prominent Crossmaglen resident, Crossmaglen went to war, rapidly acquiring the title 'bandit country' and becoming a no-go area for troops. Smugglers' knowledge of every stream, track and hedge gap in the district turned local IRA volunteers into almost invincible guerrillas.

The British army made matters even worse by building its fortress-like local base immediately adjacent to the Rangers' clubhouse and grounds. Because the base could be serviced only by air – the army dared not use the local roads – GAA activity was continually subject to the racketing noise of helicopters taking off and landing. Take the following broadcast, made by an RTE radio reporter during a match played at the Rangers ground during the Troubles:

> It was in many ways an unforgettable experience. The programme was broadcast from the magnificent GAA club grounds. But this was unlike any surroundings I had ever found myself in before or since. During that live show the crashing sound of helicopters flying overhead and landing outside the complex at times threatened to drown out the programme. The shouts of the British soldiers to each other from the highly fortified watchtowers surrounding the pitch could also be clearly heard.[37]

As the Troubles continued the army progressively took out their wrath at the state of affairs in 'bandit country' by means of various forms of harassment. British soldiers initially used the pitch for their own sports, then as a helicopter landing pad; when GAA games were in progress, players were forced to dive for cover. In 1972, Silverbridge was due to play Crossmaglen: as players waited for the throw-in, a helicopter landed and British solders emerged to clear the pitch; players and spectators were assaulted.

A wall around the ground was demolished, giving easy access to the army. The pitch was repeatedly damaged by the heavy machinery brought in by the troops and by the continuing landing of helicopters. When the club erected special gates on the premises, the army knocked them down with their Saracens and bulldozed them to the ground. The pitch lost its status as a county ground: but the games continued – though how throughout this sort of thing the club managed to achieve the status it did as a leading Irish GAA club beggars belief. Moreover, not alone did the club win county and All-Ireland championships: under Joe McKiernan, who ranks as a great GAA figure, Co. Armagh itself actually won an All-Ireland Senior Championship at Croke Park in 2002.

Part of the reason for the Rangers' continued existence and success derives in part from a fierce determination not to be cowed. In addition, it must be stressed that, while South Armagh was indeed an IRA stronghold, a majority of the club's membership were genuinely GAA supporters only, and not members of the IRA. In a revealing interview for BBC Northern Ireland's documentary *Field of Dreams*, one of the club's stars (and later its manager) Oisin McConville remarked that, 'I was scared shitless, to be honest: it was life or death if you joined [...] there was plenty of shooting and sniper fire [...] there would have been an element of fear at this time. The politics and the soldiers were intimidating. So you could get involved in that – or you could do what I did, and throw yourself into sport.'[38]

Like McConville, the overwhelming majority of the Rangers membership opted for sport – but the attitude of the army towards the club created an atmosphere which was so poisonous it dangerously affected the soldiers also. In the same documentary, McConville describes his emotions on shaking hands with a British soldier – and a spokesperson for the Veterans for Peace group criticizes the authorities, noting that 'Very little regard was given to soldiers as individuals. They could afford to lose a few of us without too much adverse publicity [...] There seemed a wanton risk of soldiers' lives.'

I recall visiting the Rangers' clubhouse in the aftermath of an army raid – and as I inspected the smoke-damaged walls, the tracks of army vehicles churning up the playing pitch, and those of army boots leading back to the barracks, I found myself pondering what my own reaction to such sights would be, were I a twenty-year-old GAA player in Crossmaglen.

It is worth noting that in general, the leadership of the GAA in the Republic remained either unaware of, or at least unmoved by the plight of clubs such as the Rangers. One exception was the Co. Cork player Con Murphy, who won four All-Ireland hurling medals with his county, before becoming GAA president in 1976. Murphy is to be commended on taking up the case of Crossmaglen, and lobbying the British government to ease the pressures being exerted on the club. Years later, Murphy offered an explanation for the club's success which could have applied to the GAA overall:

They were being kept down, their movements were being restricted and the young people of the area were being deprived of playing our national games. I witnessed as a matter of fact young people being chased off that field by soldiers with fixed bayonets. When you are under that kind of pressure and then you get the relief of shaking it off you'll make up for it because the spirit is there and Crossmaglen are winning their All-Ireland championships and to an extent Armagh winning their All-Ireland has proved that is the way we react when we are suppressed. When we get the chance we will fight back with the spirit we have and we'll come good in the end.

*

The GAA, like every other body in Northern Ireland, was forced to come up with measures to cope with the gathering storm. During the first hunger strike of 1980, for example, the organization had issued a statement to the effect that any worthwhile effort based on genuine humanitarian efforts to end the strike should be considered. As the second gathered momentum, it grappled with an even more dangerous situation. The organization issued a statement reiterating the association's adherence to the principles of non-violence but its council declined to debate a motion that condemned violence outright.

This refusal to condemn violence in explicit terms later exposed the association to severe criticism from those who wished the GAA not merely to disassociate from the H block protest, but to throw the full weight of the organization against it. But this was a fraught situation for the GAA. It was no mere bystander, but rather a full participant in this political drama – for five of the hunger strikers were members of the GAA.

The broader political situation also impacted on the organization. The spreading violence across Northern Ireland, and the manner in which the internment laws were implemented, together meant that the lives of hundreds of young GAA members – and consequently their families – became entwined in republican politics. Throughout the conflict, the challenge for the GAA was to show that it loved the sinners while condemning their sins. And there can be no denying the strain placed on the organization, from management to grassroots: Liam Mulvihill, who served as GAA director general from 1979 until 2008, commented on his retirement that the period of the hunger strike had been the most difficult period of his entire service – an observation which is certainly not to be wondered at.

One of the principle reasons why Mulvihill was able to negotiate successfully these turbulent times was the support and guidance he received from Paddy McFlynn, who surely ranks as one of the GAA's greatest presidents. McFlynn strongly empathised with the prisoners' plight and felt that a humanitarian solution to their demands should have been forthcoming – but, just as Luke O'Toole had done before him, he continued the policy of refusing to allow the GAA to become involved in matters political. He came under huge pressure for his attitude, both from the national H block committee which was set up to further the prisoners' demands, and from a wide swathe of opinion from within the GAA itself – particularly in the North, where he was visited in his Co. Down home by deputations seeking to persuade him to change his mind.

Individual clubs staged protests, H Block-related demonstrations erupted during half-time match breaks, and the tensions mounted inexorably. To add to the sense of danger, pro-hunger strike demonstrations inevitably produced a backlash from unionists, and there were some inconclusive moves to bring pressure on the British authorities to withhold funding from the GAA. And in addition to all this, a gesture of sympathy in Cork provoked a backlash from the Irish police which could have had even greater repercussions for the GAA than any unionist objections could achieve.

At the All-Ireland football semi-final in Cork's Páirc Uí Chaoimh on 24 May 1981, Cork secretary Frank Murphy called for a minute's silence for two GAA men who had died in an electrical accident, and for the four hunger strikers who had died to date. Some of the Gardaí who were present during Murphy's gesture claimed afterwards that they had been duped into standing in sympathy with the hunger strikers: in June, their representative Jack Marrinan published an article in the *Irish Independent* complaining on their behalf.

The fact that the GAA had not adopted the motions condemning violence at its March convention was also used against the Association. But the county boards issued statements in response to Marrinan's complaints, stating that Murphy's call for support had clearly made a distinction between the electrocuted men and the hunger strikers, and adding that no one had been deliberately misled. Both sides held their positions but the matter was acutely embarrassing for the GAA: one of the organization's earliest sources of strength, let us not forget, had stemmed from the encouragement given by Eoin O'Duffy, the first Garda commissioner, to rank-and-file members of the new Irish police force to join the GAA. A quarrel with the Garda was the last thing the GAA needed.

Ironically, it was an assault on the Gardaí by H Block campaigners that put an end to this row and swung opinion, including that of the GAA itself, firmly to the side of the police. In July 1981, a ferocious riot broke out outside the British Embassy in Dublin: seasoned demonstrators from Northern Ireland clashed with the police, using weapons that ranged from flag poles to head slashers against the baton-wielding police. In the end the Gardaí dispersed the rioters – but at a cost of 120 police officers injured, compared to 80 demonstrators. The riot raised the spectacle of the Northern Troubles coming south – and nobody in the Republic wanted this.

A general election was held in the Republic in June 1981 – and now the GAA was forced to create a *cordon sanitaire* between itself and the fervid politics of the day. Again, this was a potentially difficult situation – but now, the organization emerged enhanced. Two H Block candidates stood in the election: Paddy Agnew and Kieran Doherty (a hunger striker) were also GAA members: and when their candidacy was announced, Liam Mulvihill moved swiftly to disentangle the GAA from the situation. He issued a statement noting that the

GAA was strictly non-party political: members of the GAA could not, therefore, *officially* support this or that candidate; what they did in their private capacity, of course, was a matter for themselves. Luke O'Toole, ducking and weaving under the assaults of Dublin Castle in the aftermath of 1916 could not have done better. Agnew and Doherty won election to Dáil seats in the constituencies of Louth and Cavan-Monaghan respectively.

Curiously the directive does not appear to have been sent to all county boards – but its existence did enable leading officials to spread the word that the rules of the GAA forbade overt political support. It was as if a large banner hung over Croke Park reading *The heart says one thing, the head another*. And this was the policy that brought the GAA through the H Block crisis, without either forfeiting the support of the police, or suffering the cessation of many key Northern Ireland clubs over lack of support – or, for that matter, experiencing a backlash from those GAA members in the Republic who wished to have nothing to do with the ongoing crisis in Northern Ireland.

*

How pleasant it would be to record the advent of a smooth and happy period of history following the horror of the hunger strikes. But this was not to be: after all, Northern Ireland did not and does not lend itself to smooth history. Take the issues surrounding the rebuilding of West Belfast's Casement Park. In the Republic, the power and influence of the GAA was exemplified in 2004, when the government agreed to grant the organization €109 million – funding which was used to rebuild Dublin's Croke Park, and to refurbish other grounds. But in the North a sourness of attitude toward the rebuilding of Casement Park continued. A report in the *Belfast Telegraph* of 17 March 2016 summarized the position concerning government funding:

> One of the three Northern Ireland sports stadiums is complete and another is almost complete; the third stadium, Casement Park, is still a derelict site.

The GAA and Sinn Féin had hoped to have Casement completed in time for the 1916 commemoration ceremonies – but since that anniversary, the soccer and rugby stadia have been completed with the assistance of official funding; while Casement, for which some £60 million had been promised, still lies idle. Of course, the situation is not a classic Northern Ireland 'them and us' issue: there are valid planning and safety objections which militate against siting a 40,000-seat stadium in a heavily urban part of West Belfast.

In terms of politics, Sinn Féin had made the rebuilding of Casement Park one of its signature issues – much to the annoyance of some residents of the area, who would have been affected by increased crowds; and much to the annoyance too of elements within unionism, which would much rather that Sinn Féin did not get what it wanted. But had any real measure of goodwill been part of the mix, then any real and material objections would have been dealt with, and an agreed version of the stadium built. But the GAA and the authorities could not agree – because the goodwill is not there in sufficient quantities. At the time of writing, Casement remains bogged down in a political and planning quagmire.

This unfortunate episode aside, the GAA has played its part in reforming Northern Ireland in the aftermath of the Good Friday Agreement of 1998. The police force was reborn as the Police Service of Northern Ireland (PSNI) – and the GAA removed the last vestiges of its 'ban' culture, that of preventing members of the security forces from joining the organization. In latter years, of course, the ghosts of the past have thronged in Northern Ireland once more: a sort of overtly performative DUP disdain for all things Irish, including the Irish language and the GAA itself, has collapsed the Northern Ireland executive. It can feel difficult to feel optimistic about the future – and yet the future must be anticipated and planned for, and the GAA must play its part.

And so: what will be the future of the GAA in Northern Ireland? The answer is that the future of the GAA is the future of the nationalist population. The GAA club at Dungiven in Co. Derry has been renamed after Kevin Lynch, one of the dead hunger strikers, and one of the best young hurlers that the province of Ulster has ever produced. His sporting prowess deserves to be remembered and acknowledged – and yet unionists complain that the GAA in Dungiven is glorifying a terrorist. These same unionists who make such criticisms would never dream of attending a GAA match or darkening the door of a GAA club – but there are political silver lodes to be mined by such cries. An old Belfast socialist orator speaking on the steps of City Hall once pointed despairingly at the gulls circling overhead and thundered at his hearers: 'You are like those gulls, but they have more sense than you: if you threw them bread and sashes, they'd go for the bread – but you'd go for the sashes every time.'

The problems of the North will not be solved as I once hoped: by imaginative leadership in the Republic slowly altering the Catholic-laced laws of the state to make the prospect of unification more acceptable to Protestants – for, even though their fears were always ill-grounded and susceptible to manipulation by demagogues like Paisley, they were nevertheless real.

Those policies are over – but there was and there remains a continuing deficit in unionist leadership. Unionism should itself feel confident and capable of extending the hand of friendship to Northern nationalism and to the Republic, a state which has raced ahead economically and socially, while Northern Ireland itself has stagnated in both areas. The North is dominated by public-sector jobs and by the agricultural sector – and yet, astoundingly, the DUP calls on Northern Ireland farmers to leave the European Union and forego its generous subsidies. Brexit will spell ruin for the economy of Northern Ireland, should it go ahead, but the DUP has nailed its colours to the Brexit mast, and it will not take these colours down.

The past of Northern Ireland has always been a numbers game – and its future is too. The future lies in demographics: since the time of the 1991 census, it has been clear that sooner or later, there would be more nationalists than unionists living in Northern Ireland. The stratagems by which census figures were once manipulated are no longer possible, and today it is evident that this day of reckoning is rapidly approaching. The next census is due in 2021 – the centenary of the foundation of Northern Ireland – and it will tell a tale.

Catholics now outnumber Protestants by significant margins at every school level – primary, secondary and tertiary. How will demographics shift the future of Northern Ireland? – and how will Brexit impact on the imaginations of Northern Protestants, if the economy of the United Kingdom sags and unravels in the years to come? A united Ireland looks more likely today than it has done for years – and yet the DUP leadership cannot, or will not, look this future in the eye.

As nationalist confidence waxes and grows in Northern Ireland so will the confidence and the resources of the GAA. The modern association is no threat to Protestant identity: indeed, it would welcome increased Protestant membership, regardless of what Brexit may bring – and in this, it can only be assisted by the decline in influence of the Catholic Church in Ireland.

It can be said with confidence that the GAA has been a great benefit to the island of Ireland and to the Irish tradition. I anticipate the day when it can help to spread those benefits to the inheritors of Ireland's Protestant tradition, and to play its part in cementing together the long-sundered traditions of Irishness.

CHAPTER TEN

Etched in Concrete

Tꜰ ᴇ ʟᴏɴɢ sᴛᴏʀʏ ᴏꜰ ᴛʜᴇ Gᴀᴇʟɪᴄ Aᴛʜʟᴇᴛɪᴄ Assᴏᴄɪᴀᴛɪᴏɴ, the social and political changes it has observed and in which it has participated – these human histories are remembered in many ways. History is commemorated, for example, in the names of the GAA's major sporting trophies – most prominently, of course, that of the Sam Maguire Cup. Its clubs up and down the country remember the past too: think of John Mitchel and Kickham, Fontenoy, Clann na nGael, Wolfe Tone, Robert Emmet and Michael Hogan, and a multitude more iterations of famous battles and figures, all of which evoke those individuals and engagements that deserve to be commemorated.

The past is etched in concrete too: into the walls of stadiums up and down the country, and further afield. Croke Park will always be the principal commemorative site of the GAA, and Thomas Croke's name is one that will not fade: and this exercise in naming and remembering is repeated in, for example, Co. Kerry's Fitzgerald Stadium – named for Dick Fitzgerald, whom we have already met and whose stadium stands in the most beautiful setting of any GAA ground, overlooking the lakes of Killarney. And as we will see, many other counties in Ireland have echoed Kerry's move. History can be selective – and such naming policies has the virtue of keeping the past well and truly alive. In this chapter, I want to focus on a series of vignettes which will, I hope, remind us of the essential humanity of the history told in this book.

*

Not all aspects of the past, of course, are adequately illuminated – and one aspect in particular tends, consciously or unconsciously, to be consistently neglected, by the GAA as by other bodies and individuals. I refer, of course, to women's history: to the part played by women in the life of the GAA, as well as in the independence movement in Ireland. Only one major stadium – Markievicz Stadium in Sligo – is named for a woman. Constance Markievicz was born Constance Gore-Booth, and she grew up at her aristocratic family's Lissadell estate, near Sligo. She became a member of James Connolly's Irish Citizen Army, and was sentenced to death for her part in the events of Easter Week 1916. Her sentence was reduced to life imprisonment: ostensibly this was on the grounds of her gender, though it is clear enough that her class had much to do with the decision to spare her life.

Markievicz was the first woman to be elected to the Westminster parliament; and, as the minister for labour in the first Dáil, was the first female minister in a European cabinet. Her record as an activist and politician speaks for itself: in addition, she is remembered courtesy of the poetry of W. B. Yeats, whose poem 'In memory of Eva Gore-Booth and Con Markievicz' captures her and her sister for all time:

> *The light of evening, Lissadell,*
> *Great windows open to the south,*
> *Two girls in silk kimonos, both*
> *Beautiful, one a gazelle [...]*
> *The innocent and the beautiful*
> *Have no enemy but time.*

In fact, Markievicz's life was largely one of clamour, certainly in her later life: she knew little of the tranquillity which Yeats describes as attending her youth at Lissadell. Perhaps it is appropriate, then, that today she continues to be remembered amid the clamour, high energy, and contestation of a Gaelic football ground. Certainly it is to the credit of the GAA in Sligo that it chooses to honour a famous daughter of the county – a rare female note in a world of male nomenclature.

*

Kenny Stadium at Athenry in Co. Galway sports an unusual name too – though for rather different reasons. While it incorporates the familiar Gaelic and republican traditions, the stadium name also honours a man who at a crucial stage raised a dissident voice against these narratives. On the face of it, of course, Galway's GAA tradition is similar to that of other counties, with the Venn diagram-like overlap between the GAA, the IRB, the Gaelic League and the Volunteers much the same in this as in other counties. As Kevin Jordan writes:

> It was mainly the same people that were involved. So when the Irish Volunteers began in Athenry it was Jordan, Lardiner, Dick Murphy and John Broderick who were involved, the IRB and GAA men. Again this was replicated throughout the county. Amazingly these men were also representative to regional groups, Jordan and Lardiner as County GAA delegates to Dublin, and Murphy to the IRB Connacht Council. The crossover between the three organizations was often blurred and this gave the members a sense of purpose that they were serving Ireland in a political, cultural and military sense.[39]

This 'sense of purpose' accurately describes the GAA position throughout the country in the revolutionary period: but where Galway in particular was concerned, the normal order of things was reversed as 1916 approached – for here, the local GAA membership was enrolled *against* the cause of the Volunteers.

This tension was encapsulated in an historic row between Liam Mellows, sent from Dublin in 1915 to organize the county, and a blacksmith named Tom Kenny – who was not only deeply embedded in both the GAA and the IRB, but was also the founder of a local agrarian society around Craughwell in the east of the county. In the late nineteenth century, the Craughwell district had been the epicentre of agrarian violence and agitation. The local landowner, Lord Clanricarde, was still remembered as being one of the very worst and most negligent of the Famine-era absentee landlords – and Kenny, through his organization of both the GAA and of anti-landlord activities, had become the local hero. His activities made him so notorious in some quarters, indeed, that a querulous civil servant asked in a report: 'Is Ireland to be ruled by a blacksmith and a water bailiff?' (The water bailiff was John MacBride, who was later executed for his part in the 1916 Rising.)

It is certainly the case that Kenny's forge was something of a hotbed of revolutionary activity: and two episodes in particular render Kenny himself a hero or a villain, depending on one's point of view. The first, in 1910, concerned Kenny, a widow named Mary Ryan and the shooting of a man called Martin McGoldrick. The situation was this: Ryan's husband had died in the United States, and she returned to her native Galway to take up the tenancy of a fifteen-acre farm owned by the Clanricarde estate – a farm which Kenny wanted broken up and distributed to landless, impoverished locals. As a result of these local tensions, Ryan found herself at the centre of a bitter and ultimately fatal dispute. Rural agitations, involving either land or nationalism, can be merciless: in this case, Ryan was boycotted; even the local postman would not speak to her; her hay was burned; and shots were fired near her house.

The campaign against Ryan culminated in an attempt to level the walls around her holding, so that it could be classed as unfenced common land. McGoldrick, an RIC policeman guarding the rebuilding of the wall, was shot and killed and three men were subsequently charged. They were acquitted, however, after Kenny visited the jurors. The trio returned to a hero's welcome – but the upheaval deepened the hostility towards Kenny already felt by larger farmers, shopkeepers and the clergy. Later, Kenny took his campaign for land division further, in a particularly cruel and dramatic form: he poisoned the hounds of the famous Galway Blazers Hunt – and now the bourgeoisie turned on him too.

But his supporters did not: indeed, far from being appalled at what Kenny had done, his popular base rallied to his call. The famous contemporary IRA leader Seán Moylan recalled why this was the case:

> Kilmallock, where I was born, is situated amidst the finest lands in the country. It was, therefore the happy hunting ground of the Ascendancy. A walled town, its strategic value ensured the existence there of an English garrison. The annals of the mere Irish existing in the locality were short and simple – poverty, oppression and that contempt which only the Mississippi negro knows. But in a manhood denied its natural rights, resentment of that denial always smoulders.[40]

The Blazers certainly brought profitable business to the county. However, the landless population who followed Kenny and played hurling and Gaelic football, felt not only poverty but also a sense of utter exclusion from their own sense of identity – and moreover, they certainly did not benefit from the Blazers' largesse and resented the 'horse Protestants of the Hunt'. They were therefore easily identified as the enemy: Kenny and the members of his society were attacked and threatened, and Kenny could only come to his door when armed with a revolver. His blacksmith business was ruined.

Nevertheless, Kenny maintained his popularity, particularly in GAA circles – and he was in a position, therefore, to try to harness this popularity against Liam Mellows in 1915. He bitterly resented Mellows' appearance on what he regarded as *his* patch: and he attempted to use the GAA to thwart the plans of his fresh-faced and youthful rival. But in this, he was unsuccessful: Mellows himself described what happened during the summer of 1915 when he attempted to hold manoeuvres involving Volunteer personnel from a number of local villages and companies:

> An attempt was made by Mr. Thomas Kenny, Chairman of the Co. Galway Board of the GAA to upset our plans, by arranging a list of fixtures to be played at Oranmore on the same day.

Despite Kenny's local standing, the manoeuvres were held and the hurling matches fell through. Undaunted, Kenny continued to duel with Mellows throughout 1916 – but again, Mellows got the better of him, forcing him to return cattle he had seized for butchering and distribution to the poor. As for the Rising itself: Kenny was opposed to the whole plan, correctly forecasting failure and slaughter. But the irony is that the rising achieved some limited success in those very areas of Galway where Kenny himself had planted revolutionary seeds – chiefly around Moyode Castle, which Mellows managed to hold for a few days.

Subsequently, both Kenny and Mellows fled to America – where hostilities between the two continued. At length both men returned to Ireland: Mellows would not survive the Civil War, but Kenny came through the revolutionary period unscathed – and went on to train the Galway hurling team that won the All-Ireland in 1923. Hence his name affixed to the walls of the GAA stadium at Athenry.

The Father Griffins GAA club recalls another Galway figure, and another eddy in the history of the GAA. Father Michael Griffin held strong nationalist views: he was happy, indeed, to pose for a photograph in a friend's borrowed Volunteer uniform. One of Griffin's last public appearances, in November 1920, was to join a group of boys playing football on common land outside St Joseph's church in Galway. Then he left them to enter the church, saying he had to 'visit Jesus'.

At the time there was a reign of terror in Galway, with the Black and Tans kidnapping and killing as they wished. IRA retaliation was weaker in the area than in other parts of the country: and at this particular moment, the Tans, the Auxiliaries, and their local adherents were carrying on an uninterrupted campaign of shootings and beatings in an attempt to discover the fate of one Patrick Joyce, believed to have been an informer, who had been kidnapped and shot by the IRA.

Priests were not excused: they too were being beaten and attacked – and at his usual Sunday card game at his home on Galway's Montpellier Terrace, Griffin, who was on duty for sick calls, was warned by his friends that he should 'do a Cogar', should a knock come to his door later in the night. (Cogar McDonagh had successfully resisted a kidnapping attempt by masked members of the security forces by holding on to the jamb of the door and shouting loudly until help arrived.)

Later that same night, 12 November 1920, a knock did come – and Griffin was seen by neighbours to admit a man, whom he evidently recognized, to his home. They spent a short time in the house, before leaving together, talking amiably. A few days later, Griffin's body was found in a bog hole – and the man who enticed him to his death left Galway. He later emerged, to international notoriety, as William Joyce – better known as the 'Lord Haw Haw' who broadcast propaganda from Berlin on behalf of the Nazis in the course of the Second World War. His former British paymasters hanged him in 1946 on a charge of treason.

*

Further south, in Co. Cork, GAA teams who play in either hurling or football All-Irelands are commonly referred to by commentators as the 'Rebels', with Cork the 'Rebel County'. Such terms are not lightly bestowed: and it is certainly the case that Cork earned them. This county saw some of the most ferocious, and most significant, fighting of the War of

Independence, suffered some of the worst reprisals of the period – and witnessed at least one historic episode Ireland could have done very well without: the assassination in August 1922 of Michael Collins himself.

Both the significance of the Cork GAA, and its close relationship with the physical-force tradition in Irish republicanism, are illuminated in the names of the Sam Maguire Cup and the Liam MacCarthy Cup – the perpetual trophies bestowed annually on the winners of the football and hurling All-Irelands. Sam Maguire (1877–1927) was a Protestant who emigrated to London from the Dunmanway district of the county. Maguire became a noted footballer and captain of the London Hibernians, a leading club of the time; subsequently he became chairman of the GAA's London County Board.

Both he and his county board deputy, Liam MacCarthy (1853–1928) were ardent Fenians. It was Maguire, for example, who swore the young Michael Collins into the IRB, along with many another young Irish emigrants in the pre-war period: and the relationship continued: throughout the War of Independence, Maguire was a principal supplier of guns and intelligence to Collins. After his death, a group of admirers came together to donate a handsome silver trophy named in his honour to the GAA. At the time of writing it is arguably the most prized amateur sporting trophy in Europe.

However, hurling comes a very close second in popularity to football – and the trophy for this was donated by the man whose name it bears. MacCarthy too became chairman of the London County Board; and like Maguire, he joined the

Irish Volunteers in London, along with his sons. His Volunteer membership, however, sat rather awkwardly with his position as a councillor in Peckham in south London, and MacCarthy as a rule practised discretion in his public utterances. But at a Volunteer meeting in Dulwich, called to discuss the looming threat of conscription in Ireland as the First World War dragged on, he found that discretion had its limits. Collins asked him how Irish citizens should react to the question of conscription: should they join up or not? – and McCarthy was invited to give a simple 'yes' or 'no'. He replied with neither – but offered instead a Corkonian version of a Delphic utterance: 'If you come from Clonakilty, then to Clonakilty you must go.' Collins and some of his hearers correctly interpreted this as a direction to go home and fight, which they duly did.

The MacCarthy Cup in particular was born out of the national struggle – and it was not created merely to commemorate MacCarthy's memory. During his lifetime he had purchased £500 worth of shares in the crucial National Loan, which was floated to further the resistance effort, and which was organized by Collins. When the loan was repaid, MacCarthy and his two sons spent the money on commissioning the trophy itself, which was then presented to the GAA in 1924.

Today, one can readily trace Cork's association with the War of Independence through the jerseys of two of its most famous hurling teams: the county side which has so often electrified Croke Park; and Glen Rovers, one of the most famous GAA clubs in the country. It was the fame he won at both levels which led the former Glen star and county player,

Jack Lynch (1917–99) to be invited to become a Fianna Fáil candidate; he would subsequently go on to become taoiseach of Ireland.

Today the Glen Rovers jerseys carry a black loop, which was adopted by the club in 1916 as a tribute to the executed Irish leaders; the county team, meanwhile, wears red. Back in 1919, the county colours were blue and saffron: these were the colours of Lord Clare's regiment, drawn from the 'Wild Geese', those European regiments of exiled Irish which fought for Catholic monarchs in Europe, and which swept the field at the battle of Fontenoy in 1745. They were first presented to the Cork team in 1913 by the legendary GAA player and administrator, J. J. Walsh: he had earlier organized a successful trip to Fontenoy, as a means of reminding a contemporary generation that past military glory could be won again.

Within five years, Walsh's thesis was bloodily contested on the streets of Cork, in conflict between crown forces and the IRA. Shortly before a Munster semi-final in 1919, troops entered a GAA premises and stole the Cork team jerseys – this by way of laying a marker on the GAA that the authorities were aware of the frequent cross-over in membership between the IRA and team players. Seán McCarthy, a famous GAA player – and one who in fact exemplified this cross-over – allied with Tom Irwin, a fellow GAA player and republican, to persuade another club to donate its jerseys so as to save the day. This GAA club was the forbiddingly-named Cork Total Abstinence Society, which had recently merged with St Finbarr's. The two GAA men were successful in their quest, and emerged triumphantly with the trophies of the visit – a set of red jerseys with a Total Abstinence badge on the front. Cork won in subsequent matches and the lucky jerseys were adopted as the new team colours – needless to say, without the badge!

But the subsequent history of Tom Irwin, who was also one of the finest field athletes ever produced by the county of Cork, illustrates the brutalities and misunderstandings of war that have been the cause of so much loss of innocent life. Out of the blue, Irwin received a death threat telling him he had twenty-four hours to leave Cork. He panicked and made his way to Belfast – but it was later discovered that the threat had come not from the IRA but from a group of criminals whom he had witnessed conducting a robbery. However, Irwin emigrated to South Africa from Belfast despite being officially cleared by the IRA: his friend Seán McCarthy had his case investigated, and publicly set the record straight – but Irwin refused to set foot in Ireland again. He died at Cape Town in 1956.[41]

J. J. Walsh was another Corkonian with GAA clubs named in his honour. He emerged from his post within the shattered GPO building in 1916 to be sentenced to death: he was reprieved and later came out of Frongoch a senior figure in the IRB. As a result, he was close to the centre of the planning that led both to the subsequent armed struggles and to the first Dáil – and he helped to secure the key support that passed the Treaty on which today's Irish Republic is built.

Walsh was born in 1880 of farming stock, a few miles from Bandon. The town was once a Protestant bastion – though by the time Walsh came to maturity, Richard Boyle, Earl of Cork and Catholic-hating landowner who built the town, had long vanished in the dust of history; and a deep and growing rift had opened between local Catholics seeking Home Rule and Protestants seeking the maintenance of the union with Britain.

Walsh was a talented Gaelic footballer: and he was one of a small and discreet group that organized a highly significant public meeting in Cork in December 1913. The intention of the meeting was to further the Home Rule argument by establishing a chapter of the Irish Volunteers in the city. As was IRB policy elsewhere, Walsh's affiliation to the Brotherhood was not referenced; instead, he appeared ostensibly – or perhaps ostentatiously – in his capacity as chairman of the GAA's Cork County Board, and in the hope of providing a certain gravitas to the gathering. It proved to be an uproarious meeting: and his presence at it did him no good at all, for an enraged member of the Ancient Order of Hibernians hit him with a chair, and he was forced to seek hospital attention. As we know, the AOH was closely allied to Redmond: and this incident, relatively minor in itself, foretold the later and rather more dangerous conflict between republicans and the AOH in Co. Monaghan explored earlier in this book.

This Cork meeting also highlighted divisions within the GAA itself over the familiar issue of whether the organization should be a political or a purely sporting organization. Some members of the GAA in Cork disagreed strongly with Walsh's presence at the meeting, but Walsh easily rode out the criticism. Forceful and efficient, he was unambiguously a proponent of the physical-force tradition – for example, declaring in 1918 that 'the only way to deal with John Bull is through the barrel of a rifle'.

Walsh's influence on the GAA in fact extended well beyond Cork, in that professionalising reforms he had introduced in his native county were subsequently copied throughout Ireland. He pioneered the use of auditors to supply regular accounts to county boards; he also introduced turnstiles to collect fees before games – and the result of the latter was, as one respected commentator noted delightedly, that: 'Gate receipts increased to levels that were not thought possible earlier.' [42]

At the conclusion of the revolutionary period, Walsh went on to become a government minister, and one of the country's most successful businessmen. He saw to it that some of the increased revenues now flowing into newly stable GAA coffers were used to buy railway shares: this provided the GAA with the valuable facility of being able to arrange trains for important matches, thereby greatly increasing attendances.

Walsh's financial success led to his reliving a sequel to one of his GAA exploits – in the unexpected environs of the skies above the Brazilian rainforest, long after the War of Independence had concluded. In 1910, he had organized a demonstration against a visit to Cork made by Winston Churchill, then first lord of the admiralty. Greatly to Walsh's annoyance, Churchill had been given the red-carpet treatment, complete with official welcome and lavish dinners. The following September, Walsh saw to it that the officers and cadets on a visit to Cork aboard the German training ship *Hansa* were invited to the semi-final of the Cork county hurling semi-final (which was contested that year by Redmond's and Sarsfield's).

The German visit – which was made, let us not forget, against a rising sense of geopolitical tension in Europe in advance of the First World War – was a huge success. Huge crowds witnessed a flotilla of German long boats rowing up the River Lee; German melodies were played at the sports ground – and the mariners were cheered to the echo as they took to the boats to row back down the fast-flowing river to the *Hansa* which was moored in the harbour at Queenstown.

The visit also, however, saw a tragedy barely averted. In the crush of spectators that accompanied the embarkation, a boy fell into the river and was swept downstream. Without hesitation, the ship's captain, Hans von Schiller, together with a cadet, dived in fully clothed and managed to hold the boy's head out of water until help arrived from the Lee Rowing Club, where the Germans had moored their boats. Schiller was subsequently decorated by Kaiser Wilhelm II for his courage: he went on to become a German naval hero during the Great War – and subsequently a famous airship pilot.

Indeed, Schiller captained the Zeppelin *Hindenberg* as it cut the journey from South America to Europe to less than half the fourteen days taken by the great ocean liners of the day – with Walsh, on holiday with his wife, a passenger on the European leg of the journey. Schiller met them aboard, telling them they were the first Irish people to travel on the airship – and remarking too how much he liked the Irish because they were, in effect, the reason for his earning a decoration from the

Kaiser. Schiller was astounded to discover, in the course of this conversation, that Walsh was not merely Irish – but was the very man who had honoured the *Hansa*, and in effect won him his decoration. Walsh and his wife became the airship's most prized passengers.

Schiller's luck would hold subsequently – for he was delayed and failed to join the *Hindenburg* on its last flight. The airship's cataclysmic mid-air explosion, as it docked in New Jersey in May 1937, ended the airship era – but Schiller resumed his naval career, surviving the Second World War, and eventually becoming a successful author. Walsh's luck held also. He continued to enjoy business success and paid for the Cork senior hurling team's training expenses out of his own pocket – although he was canny enough to demand regular receipts! In effect, however, no verification was required, for the team's improved performances spoke for themselves.

Jim Hurley was another Cork icon of the GAA – and a figure who participated in the War of Independence, before going on to carve out a significant place in Irish society. Hurley commanded one of Collins's guerrilla 'flying columns' at the tender age of eighteen: and was evaluated by Tom Barry as being 'probably the youngest and certainly one of the best battalion Commanders in Ireland'. Hurley took part in some highly charged IRA episodes, including the ferocious gunfight at Burgatia House near Rosscarbery in February 1921.

He is also remembered as one of the finest hurlers ever produced by the county: this ranking bestowed by certain Cork aficionados of the game, who enjoy attempting the nearly impossible task of contrasting one generation's heroes with those of another. Certainly Hurley is placed on a pedestal with Christy Ring, whose career falls outside our time frame, but who at the very least would be adjudged to be to hurling what Muhammad Ali was to boxing.

After the War of Independence had subsided, Hurley returned to his studies, and wound up as registrar of University College Cork. The story is told that one day he was struck by the appearance of a passing student and enquired who he was. The student's identity was revealed, and – 'I thought so,' nodded Hurley, 'I shot his father.' He shot someone else, too: he had a hand in the ambush that killed Michael Collins himself. Many years later, Collins's nephew – also Michael – was sitting in the family home at Booterstown, south Dublin, when he noticed a man passing by the house once, twice, three times. The young Michael alerted his father Johnny to the fact that the house seemed to be under surveillance. Johnny hailed the stranger – who turned out to be Hurley. He explained that he was trying to summon the courage to knock: Johnny then hugged him and welcomed him into the house. 'We were so young,' Hurley said again and again. 'We were so young.'

For his part, the younger Michael Collins subsequently had the experience of going to Munster and Croke Park finals – seated between his father and Jim Hurley. Johnny Collins himself never allowed the many memorials erected to his brother's name to record any details save the year of his birth and of his death; no reference was permitted to the manner in which Michael Collins died.

The name of Tom Barry himself, the legendary commander of a famous 'flying column', is of course etched indelibly into Cork's GAA and revolutionary history – but other Barrys have left their mark too. Three in particular come to mind – all, so far as I know, unrelated. They are Tadhg Barry, Denis Barry, and Jimmy 'Tough' Barry: and let us look now at the first of these men.

The culture of political funerals is extremely important in Irish society: such occasions express both respect for the person who has died, and respect for (though not necessarily agreement with) their cause or viewpoint. The O'Donovan Rossa funeral, and its accompanying oration by Patrick Pearse – which I referenced earlier – is generally reckoned to be the apotheosis of Irish political funerals; and a springboard for the 1916 Rising. That funeral was reckoned to be one of the largest seen in Ireland during the revolutionary period – but in fact, it was rivalled in size by the funeral of the Cork GAA figure and trade unionist Tadhg Barry.

Barry promoted the causes of the GAA, the independence movement and the trade union movement with equal fervour. One of his most lasting contributions to the GAA was a handbook on hurling and how it should be played. He was born in Cork's Blarney Street of working-class parents in 1880, and went to school in the famous North Monastery run by the Christian Brothers. He was a founding member of Sinn Féin, was a leading member of the Sunday's Well GAA club, wrote a widely read GAA column for the Cork *Free Press* under the pseudonym 'An Ciotog', and was a member both of the county and national GAA boards. He trained Cork's first camogie team and became a respected referee – a difficult enough accomplishment in GAA circles at the time.

'An Ciotog' literally translates as a left-hander, and the term carried a political significance for Barry. Quite apart from being an active Volunteer officer, he was a prominent member of the Irish Transport and General Workers' Union: in short, he could be taken as the epitome of those who worked for independence not merely in order to secure freedom, but to achieve explicitly *socialist* goals. As with Tom Kenny in Galway, Tadhg Barry's GAA activities were bound up in the concept of a national struggle – and through the worst of the upheaval of this period, he worked to secure better living conditions for farm workers, organizing strikes in their ranks; and in those of railway workers, the better to hamper the British war effort. So it was that the Auxiliaries made a particular point of setting fire to the offices of the union during the burning of central Cork in December 1920.

Following a series of arrests, and periods on hunger strike, Barry and several other Cork city councillors were finally arrested as they met to elect a successor to the office of Lord Mayor of Cork – Terence MacSwiney having died while on hunger strike in October 1920. Barry and his comrades were Interned in Ballykinlar in Co. Down; here, one of his fellow internees was future taoiseach Sean Lemass. At Ballykinlar, Barry became something of a celebrity amongst his fellow prisoners, due to his custom of flying the red flag of socialism over his hut. Such an emblem, however, was obviously a red rag to the sentries: on 15 November 1921, as Barry farewelled some comrades who were leaving the camp, a sentry shot him through the heart.

Michael Collins did not share Barry's socialist philosophy: in fact, he ordered the removal of two paragraphs from the Democratic Programme, which was written by Barry's trade union colleague Cathal O'Shannon for the first Dáil in 1919, explicitly because they were 'too socialistic'. Notwithstanding these political differences, however, Collins's regard for Barry was such that he left the Treaty talks in London (by then reaching a critical stage), and returned to Cork to join Barry's vast funeral cortège. The Treaty was signed less than three weeks later.

The second Barry was Denis, or 'Dinny', a noted hurler. He was interned in 1916, and on his release became active in the Volunteers. We have already looked at the attempt by Sinn Féin to subvert the system of British administration in Ireland through the establishment of a parallel system of justice and policing: a republican police force was established – and Barry ran the Cork city operation, and worked closely with Lord Mayor Tómas Mac Curtain and his successor MacSwiney. He became friendly also with Michael Collins – whose Dáil election he helped ensure by checking that the votes were counted accurately.

Ironically, Denis Barry had also worked – even more actively – to ensure that W. T. Cosgrave would figure among the wave of successful Sinn Féin election candidates who broke over the Irish political landscape after 1916; Cosgrave was first elected in a Kilkenny by-election in 1917. Fate decreed that Cosgrave would become head of the Cumann na nGaedheal Free State government in 1922, and the principal figure charged with upholding the Treaty after Collins's death. But Barry himself opposed the Treaty: with the result that he was interned at Newbridge in Co. Kildare – a camp with the unenviable distinction of having executed the greatest number of IRA prisoners during the Civil War.

Barry might have been better off facing the firing squad: instead, he elected to join a mass hunger strike by republican prisoners in October 1922; he died a month later. At this time, the mercurial Daniel Cohalan was the Catholic Bishop of Cork: previously, he had welcomed onto hallowed ground the body of Terence MacSwiney, who had also died on hunger strike. Later, however, he had changed his tune, excommunicating those individuals (on both sides of the Treaty debate) who had taken part in reprisal ambushes and killings – and now he refused Barry's coffin from entering any church in his diocese. But, as was the case with many an Irish patriot who suffered 'a belt of the crozier' in life or death, Denis Barry's memory survived the strictures of the bishop; and his reputation remains high with both GAA followers and republican sympathizers.

If ever a man earned his nickname it was the third – or 'Tough' – Barry in our story. Jimmy Barry was an extraordinary athlete and all-round sportsman: for he was a top hurler, a Gaelic football player and – unusually for an athlete engaged in those sports – an excellent swimmer and All-Ireland champion diver too. He had earned his distinctive nickname by dint of being a noted boxer who, finding himself interned on Cork's Spike Island for having played an enthusiastic part in a prison riot which wrecked the building, organized and participated in bouts as a means of raising funds for the IRA.

Later, Jimmy Barry was a courageous and active volunteer during the Tan war. He fought in the anti-Treaty side in the Civil War – but it was in the aftermath of that fratricidal conflict that he demonstrated the part the GAA could play in healing the wounds of civil strife. Barry became the trainer of the Cork county hurling team which won an extraordinary fifteen All-Irelands. As Kerry was to Gaelic football, so Cork was to hurling in those years: in the period 1926–31, Barry's team won four All-Irelands in a row. No GAA follower would think of disputing Jimmy Barry's claim that Cork hurlers were like mushrooms: they sprouted overnight – but unlike mushrooms they had staying power.

In fact, the mushroom motif, and Barry's assessment of the resilience of the Corkonian, would be amply borne out a few days after the terrible events of Bloody Sunday in November 1920. The IRA in Co. Cork had responded, exacting a terrible vengeance in the form of an ambush at Kilmichael which claimed the lives of eighteen Auxiliaries; the militia's response to this was of course the burning of Cork city centre in December of that year.

All of these tales focus on the part played by fighting men – but Co. Cork also provides stories of the parts played by women in the War of Independence. The help given to these men by women was, after all, indispensable – though certainly not always acknowledged – and the cause of feminism within the GAA was considerably advanced by one incident in particular. This involved Tómas Mac Curtain, who was a senior IRA officer as well as Lord Mayor of Cork – and he turned up at a meeting of the Cork County Board one evening and announced that arms were available if the money for them could be found. The treasurer consulted his records and found that there was £187 in the accounts: he handed it over to Mac Curtain, who, in the event, did not seem to have used the money.[43] But the Lord Mayor's visit prompted the meeting to set up an arms fund by arranging a series of camogie matches – the feeling being that the police would be less likely to break up women's matches. A game was accordingly arranged between the local Knockavilla and Ballinhassig camogie teams; Tim Herlihy, at this time a champion sprinter, was appointed to referee the game.[44]

Herlihy's athletic prowess was put to the test when the RIC invaded the pitch and attempted to capture him. With loud shouts of 'play on' ringing in their ears, the RIC withdrew – and the courageous women *did* play on. Now, however, the military was summoned, and soldiers with fixed bayonets drove terrified women and children across the surrounding fields and ditches. Other camogie matches that day were played with more success and the arms fund benefitted.

This game took place in the townland of Belrose, which lies east of Cork city – and not far from the site of one of the most famous engagements of the War of Independence. This was the battle at Crossbarry in March 1921 where an IRA section, outnumbered by at least eight to one, successfully engaged in a day-long battle with a British force that is said to have been one thousand strong. British casualties were heavy – thirty-nine dead and forty-one wounded – while the IRA division, commanded by Tom Barry, saw only three of its members killed and three wounded.

Amongst those who took part in this engagement were the famous Cork university hurler Eugene 'Nudge' Callanan and Con Lucey, IRA medical officer and winner of an All-Ireland hurling medal the previous year. The most significant IRA casualty that day, however, was Charlie Hurley, commandant of the IRA's Third Brigade: he had been scheduled to take part; but an injury sustained in a previous engagement caused him to be stood down. He died, in fact, of what might be termed an excess of honesty: he had been forced to get about, on account of his injury, by means of a pony and trap. Seán McCarthy warned Hurley that the British had mounted a particular hunt for him, acting on information obtained by torture from a prisoner in Cork Gaol – but Hurley nevertheless insisted on returning the pony and trap to their owner, Denis Ford. He was killed the following day, as he sought to flee a British ambush at Ford's house.

In 1971 – the year the GAA ban on foreign games was finally lifted – Hurley received a tribute at the official opening of the Bandon GAA club named in his honour. Liam Deasy, who had succeeded Hurley as commander of the Third Brigade, noted in his oration that 'The country owed more to the GAA in peace and war than any other influence': and quoted the words of General Douglas MacArthur, which are to be seen today inscribed on the walls of the sporting complex at the West Point military academy in New York.

> *Upon the fields of friendly strife*
> *Are sown the seeds that upon*
> *Other fields, on other days*
> *Will bear the fruits of victory*[45]

The applause which followed Deasy's words demonstrated that the lines quoted above found an echo in yet another generation of GAA supporters.

The wells of Cork seem never to run dry. Pádraig Ó'Caoimh, for example, succeeded Luke O'Toole at the helm of the GAA in 1929 – and he remained in this position for thirty-five years. Today, Cork's fine GAA stadium at Páirc Uí Chaoimh is named in his honour. Interestingly, Ó'Caoimh – as was the case with many an IRA and GAA man – was the son of an RIC father. He was a hurling star in his day, playing for the Cork county team; and he fought against the Free State in the Civil War, and was interned for his pains. Under his leadership, the GAA developed rapidly, and invested heavily in football and hurling facilities. Croke Park was extended and expanded so that new covered stands accommodated ever-increasing All-Ireland multitudes (crowds of close to 85,000 were commonplace).

In his speech and demeanour, Ó'Caoimh was careful to sound and appear as an individual devoted solely to the GAA's sporting past, present and future: but it is the case that he also maintained a discreet loyalty to the organization's political heritage. Indeed, I accidentally witnessed this trait for myself. The year was 1957 and Éamon de Valera had just reopened the Curragh internment camp and was busily snuffing out, as we have seen previously, a renewed IRA campaign on the Irish border. I was interviewing Ó'Caoimh in his office at Croke Park, and he kept me waiting while he transacted some business on the phone. At length he finished, turned to me, smiled apologetically, and explained that 'We were arranging to send a few dozen footballs to the lads in the Curragh.' Today's Páirc Uí Chaoimh is one of the finest stadiums in Ireland, and a fitting commemoration of an excellent individual.

*

Co. Tipperary's place in GAA history shines in its own light. The town of Thurles in itself enshrines the memory of the GAA's founders and that of Thomas Croke; while the county's own Michael Hogan will forever be associated with the events of November 1920 at Croke Park. And at least one other Tipperary player deserves special mention: Tom Semple (1879–1943), of the famous Blues GAA club of Thurles, may be justly compared to Dick Fitzgerald of Kerry in terms of what he contributed to Tipperary hurling.

Semple is credited with being the first man to introduce systematic training to the county. His personal prowess as a hurler helped to bring many victories to the county, including the 1908 All-Ireland Hurling trophy; and wins in the Munster hurling championships of 1906, 1907 and 1909. Amongst this string of Tipperary victories, the last in particular stands out. The enemy in this case was Cork: and following a hard-fought first half in which quarter was neither asked or given, Tipperary trailed its rivals by four points. Then, off the field, Cork made a fatal error that stung Semple's pride into action.

Supporters of the Rebel County had a habit of bringing carrier pigeons to matches, so that results could be sent home with despatch. In this case, however, the Cork supporters jumped the gun: scenting victory, they released the pigeons to bring the gloating news to the banks of the Lee. When Semple saw the pigeons released at half-time, he called the 'matchless men of Tipperary' together, pointed in affront to the departing birds – and then, bandaged and bloodied though he was, managed in the second half of the game to score a goal himself. Tipperary swept to a sweet victory, by 2-10 to 2-6. Seldom in the annals of sport has the gentle pigeon had such an inflammatory effect!

The association of Semple with Croke is not accidental. The strong-minded Semple was the driving force behind a collection raised in 1905 to erect a memorial to Croke's memory: and Semple did not hesitate in the process to take action against the GAA's central council – which wanted the archbishop commemorated at Croke Park itself. Eventually, the row was settled by a particularly GAA compromise: £1,000 of the £2,400 fund was set aside towards the rebuilding of Thurles's Confraternity Hall, which was to be named Croke Memorial Hall. It was not, however, until 1920 that the foundation stone for the building was laid on Liberty Square in the town: the occasion – appropriately enough for a project dear to Semple's outlook – was marked by a fiery speech delivered by the then Archbishop of Cashel John Harty, in the presence of a body of distinctly unappreciative Black and Tans.[46]

By that time war was raging throughout the province of Munster: Tipperary had become a cauldron of ambush and reprisal; and Tom Semple had become Michael Collins's principal courier ferrying news between Tipperary and Collins himself. Collins, of course, embodied Kipling's dictum: he was able to walk with kings while not losing the common touch – and this he translated into an effective tactic in guerrilla warfare. When, for example, a colleague suggested to him that the manager of a certain hotel would be a valuable source of information (for a projected assassination attempt), Collins replied that 'No, we need the boots.' Semple was not a 'boots' per se – but he was the all-important guard on the train to Dublin, with eyes and ears trained to see and hear everything. Collins knew who would work and who would not.

Semple had a special pocket sewn into his uniform greatcoat: and throughout the Black and Tan war, he maintained a reliable information flow to Collins. How he survived to do so, though, is surely a miracle. For this was a tall and commanding figure, and one that exuded presence: quite simply, Semple was immediately recognizable throughout the county and further afield; and his exploits as a hurler and later work as a referee and iron-handed steward merely added to this element of recognizability.

The Black and Tans certainly suspected him of being an IRA man – and till the end of his life Semple carried on his face a noticeable black spot, which was an emblem of these suspicions. He sustained this beauty mark after being taken into Black and Tan custody for questioning. Empty revolvers were placed against his face and the triggers pulled – but Semple didn't break and emerged from his ordeal to continue his courier activities. He sided with Collins in the Civil War; subsequently, his training of teams and his other GAA activities played a significant role in the necessary building of bridges that took place, in Tipperary as elsewhere, in the aftermath of that bitter conflict.

*

In the story of GAA involvement in the independence movement, the silent testimony of the naming of a club or of a stadium is often the most eloquent statement of the named person's contribution to the history of both sport and politics. So it is with Fraher Field at Dungarvan in Co. Waterford. Dan Fraher was a Fenian, a Gaelic leader and a founder member of the GAA. At the time of writing, Waterford hurling is enjoying a resurgence: and the county team is currently one of the most exciting sides in the All-Ireland Championship. In many ways, this success can be chased back to Fraher's lasting legacy.

Fraher ran his own moderately successful business at Dungarvan – a drapery store known as the 'Gaelic Outfitting Store'. He was a friend of Patrick Pearse: to such an extent, indeed, that his son Maurice was the first boarder to enter St Enda's, Pearse's school in Dublin. Fraher's son-in-law Pat Whelan – better known as Pax Ó'Faoláin – became commanding officer of First Battalion, West Waterford Brigade of the Volunteers. Like many a lad in the area, Whelan had learnt his hurling and football on a field made available to the GAA by Fraher.

Fraher leased the field from a local landowner, and at first he used it for a variety of public entertainments, including the holding of circuses and the staging of the local agricultural show. Over time, however, Fraher developed the land into a functioning GAA field, so that by the early part of the last century three All-Irelands were staged at the venue. Fraher and his family also used the field to show their appreciation of Pearse's influence in a very practical manner. Following the execution of Pearse and his brother Willie in 1916, their widowed mother Margaret and their sisters Margaret and Mary Brigid fell on financial hard times. Fraher began to stage benefit matches, the proceeds of which went to the Pearse family.

After Fraher's death, the field passed to Whelan's sons. They in their turn gave it to the GAA, which over the years developed it to its present position as one of Munster's finest stadiums.

*

As with Waterford, Kilkenny's name resonates rather more clearly in the annals of the GAA, than in those of the Volunteers. This is despite that fact that in the aftermath of 1916, the county of Kilkenny was one of the first counties to elect a Sinn Féin TD – W. T. Cosgrave, who as I mentioned would later become independent Ireland's first leader. Kilkenny is of course the country's premier hurling county: the Cats have won so many All-Irelands that, at one stage in the years before this book was written, there were suggestions that some way should be found to bar the county from competition, so impossible did it appear to defeat the county on the field! Irish hurling has since heaved a sigh of relief, as natural selection has ensured that other counties grew stronger and won on their merits.

Today, Kilkenny's Nowlan Park stands as a reminder of the man who helped to make this record possible. James Nowlan was one of the architects of the GAA: he is the very man who advised GAA men to join the Volunteers so that they could learn to shoot straight. Nowlan was the longest serving president in the history of the GAA: he was appointed in 1901 and remained in his post until 1921. He was a cooper by trade, and became an alderman on Kilkenny Corporation in 1898. Nowlan was also a keen disciple of the Celtic Revival: aside from the GAA, his other major interests in life were the Gaelic League, Sinn Féin – and the IRB above all.

His known sympathies consigned him to deportation in the aftermath of the Rising; and then to gaol in Cork in September 1919 for being found in possession of a revolver. He was widely respected within the GAA, and he unashamedly used his influence to promote the interests of the IRB within the association. A Celtic cross is set over his grave at Glasnevin; and the GAA in modern times has continued its tribute by naming a new trophy in his honour – under-21 All-Ireland hurlers today play for the James Nowlan Cup.

But in this county of exemplary hurlers, there are other names to be remembered. Jackie Brett was a youthful hero of both the GAA and the Volunteers: he played football for Mullinahone, Co. Tipperary, and at the age of eighteen ran out for that county on Bloody Sunday. Brett survived the bloodshed of that day: and in later days, he would earn a considerable reputation amongst other Volunteers for his service in the cause of independence – first as a dispatch rider, and then a member of the Kilkenny 'flying column'.

Eventually, however, tragedy came to Brett. In April 1921, he was cleaning his rifle, when it accidentally discharged and killed him.[47] Aware of his reputation, the Black and Tans were keen to prevent a public funeral being held: and so they entered the district in force. Brett's remains were thus buried temporarily at Castlejohn in Co. Tipperary: but in order to prevent the Black and Tans dishonouring his corpse, his comrades dug up the coffin and secretly buried it in a turnip field. In August 1921, with the Treaty and a degree of peace approaching, his colleagues reburied Brett in consecrated ground in his native Mullinahone, in southern Tipperary, close to the border with Kilkenny, in what the historian Jim Maher has described as 'the biggest funeral ever known in the county'.[48]

Kilkenny may not have had many ambushes and actions on the scale of Crossbarry or the burning of Cork – but as Brett's funeral indicates, the sympathies of a majority of the people of this area were with the GAA and the Volunteers.

Epilogue

WHITHER THE GAA, AS IT AND THE ISLAND OF IRELAND witnesses this ongoing decade of centenaries? As we have seen, the organization both influenced and was influenced by the struggle for Home Rule, the Rising, the War of Independence and the Civil War – to name but a few. It is woven into the stuff of Ireland, and it is not possible to write a history of these years – or a history of the twentieth century in Ireland – without being mindful of its presence. But what of the future?

The challenges which the organization faces today are, needless to say, entirely different from those of its early years: in a few words, it is not the *survival* of the organization which is at stake but its *ethos*. Specifically, the GAA must address the question of how to preserve and nurture the ideal of voluntarism in the face of commercial and financial success. The players who attract the supporters filling the huge stadiums throughout the country because of the skills they have honed in countless hours of training: these individuals are increasingly well educated, and are pursuing demanding careers. Inevitably, the issue of paying these players for their time and their energy is becoming a pressing issue, and one that that the GAA will be forced to address. After all, it is generally understood, though not officially acknowledged, that certain managers already receive recompense, and players do receive expenses – although none of the sums involved remotely resemble the sort of money available in, for example, the game of soccer. More transparency is obviously required on this longstanding issue.

In June 2018, another controversy arose which penetrated to the heart of the GAA's ethos – and which also usefully illuminated the nature of its structures, which allows so much autonomy to county boards. After much light and heat, one could say that this controversy was resolved in favour of *localism* – in favour, that is, of the parish and county tradition which places honour ahead of monetary return.

This issue first developed when Kildare were drawn against Mayo in the All-Ireland Championships series. The GAA central committee directed that this popular (and highly lucrative) fixture be played at Croke Park: but the Kildare team manager Cian O'Neill – mindful of the advantages of a local draw for his team – issued a ringing declaration that the game would be played locally (in Kildare) or nowhere. There was a wave of support throughout the country for this position: GAA fans everywhere saw the issue as being between the Goliath of Croke Park and the David of the Kildare ground at Newbridge, which holds only eight and a half thousand spectators (Croke Park, though it would not have been filled for this fixture, holds approximately ten times that number.) After three days of heated debate, on and off the national airwaves, Goliath yielded to David. Localism triumphed and Kildare won. Charles

Kickham would have been pleased – for the moment. Certainly the president of the GAA, John Moran, got the message after a Leinster final replay, scheduled around the same time, had to be transferred from Croke Park to Sempel Stadium because a Michael Bublé concert was taking place in Croke Park on the eve of the game. He announced that henceforth no further concerts would be held in the championship months of July and August. Bublé fans bring in revenue, but it is the fans' support of their local teams that keeps the GAA alive.

Kickham would not have been so pleased at the fact that the GAA had to back down again in a major controversy that broke out only a few weeks later, at the end of July 2018. The GAA's rules initially prompted an official refusal to allow a Manchester United v. Celtic all-star soccer match to be played at Cork's Pairc Ui Chaoimh to help the widow and children of Liam Miller, the former GAA player and later Celtic and Manchester United star, who had died at the age of thirty-six. But both the public and the wider GAA family reacted vigorously against this manifestation of the 'old' GAA man mentality and, with the aid of pressure from social media, forced the GAA to reconsider its position. Officialdom had been correct in citing the rule book, but wrong in overlooking the fact that times have changed and the issue is no longer resisting foreign games, but one of assisting the widow and the orphans of a much-loved Cork sportsman.

For an association founded – literally – on parochialism, the internationalisation of the GAA is incredible. As I write this, my great-granddaughter Molly plays for the women's

Gaelic football team of Copenhagen – and Molly is but one of many, because there are thousands of such youthful players throughout the world. There are flourishing GAA clubs everywhere one looks, from Asia to the Middle East, Australia to North America – though sadly in this last theatre, isolationism and the curtailment of the Green Card system is stemming the flow of immigrants who once filled the ranks of GAA clubs across America.

Those airport buses I mentioned at the outset of this book – the ones taking young Irish immigrants from the bus stop outside Cuala on journeys to the four corners of the world – are still operational. If anything, they are becoming ever more frequent, as they whisk Ireland's university graduates off to the airport and away, to the sort of blue-chip jobs across the globe that their parents could only have dreamed of. In fact, it's quite likely that many of them are going to jobs in international companies founded and owned by Irish nationals! And as they go the GAA goes with them, energising the lives and amplifying the voices of the vast and potentially enormously powerful Irish diaspora. There are upwards of seventy million Irish or Irish descendants around the globe – and their cultural, political and sporting clout has barely been tapped.

For decades, however, successive Irish governments have held an ambivalent attitude to the diaspora. Once out of sight, Irish emigrants were also firmly out of mind; and if anything, they were held to be a potentially menacing or destabilizing force in Irish politics. Their views and opinions – changed and broadened dangerously, perhaps, by the influence of the wider world – were best kept at bay; and their right to vote circumscribed or removed, lest they interrupt the delicate calculations of Irish national elections. Even today, Irish governments hesitate to grant voting rights to Irish emigrants abroad for this very reason. Witness the extraordinary scenes in the marriage equality and abortion referendums of 2015 and 2018: temporary Irish migrants were forced to return home *in person* to vote (and they came in their thousands, from as far away as Australia); unlike other countries, the Irish government did not provide facilities for their emigrants to save on the expense and trouble of travelling by voting in consulates and embassies abroad.

The attitude of the GAA to our migrants, by contrast, is wholly different, and this manifests itself in a myriad ways. The organization plays an important role in filling the gaps which exist in the social and welfare structures available abroad to Irish emigrants. Where once the young emigrant was virtually compelled to go to the pub to make contacts and find out about job opportunities, now the GAA performs this function to an ever-increasing and impressive degree. This sense of community and cohesion works in other ways too: long-term observers of the Irish scene in New York, for example, will tell you how attendance at Gaelic Park matches and social functions resulted in innumerable marriages, and an accretion of strength to the Irish community in the city. And as with New York, so it is with the world: similar stories can be told of GAA clubs across the United States and further afield. The pub is of course still a vital component of many an Irish emigrant's life – but the

GAA provides a valuable alternative to the potentially harmful effects of this source of consolation.

And this quiet, necessary work takes time and sacrifice. One cannot do better than point to the case of my friend Niall O'Dowd, who fifty-odd years ago founded the *Irish Voice*, New York's influential Irish-American newspaper and – later – website. Back in the late 1960s, Niall was a teacher in Dublin, and a skilful player with the Louth county GAA team. He was brought out to Chicago, his passage paid by means of a 'whiparound' among local GAA members.

To accommodate Niall his GAA sponsor had to share his bed with Niall and move his wife to the sofa. A loyal GAA wife, she accepted this banishment uncomplainingly, accept on those occasions when, usually after midnight, her husband delivered a full throated rendition of his favourite song "The green green grass of home". Even GAA loyalty could not prevent the wife from angrily bringing such impromptu concerts to an end! Niall moved on from Chicago to San Francisco where he found an audience amongst the emigrants for his first newspaper *The Irishman*, which campaigned on issues such as an improved allocation of green cards to Irish migrants.

Niall subsequently moved again – this time to New York, where he became a significant figure in the Irish community, making the acquaintance of many senior American mainstream politicians and other important figures. Eventually he decided to turn his attention to the problem of Northern Ireland, and set about founding a network of industrialists, politicians, trade unionists, professionals and helpers from every walk of life. He became the link between the White House and the IRA, he criss-crossed the Atlantic on innumerable flights during his peace efforts, and his work helped to feed a gathering momentum. The Kennedy family came on board: Jean Kennedy Smith became the US ambassador to Dublin, and Ted Kennedy became President Clinton's most important political American advisor on the Irish situation – and the Good Friday Agreement of 1998 was the eventual result. A form of peace, then, has come to Ireland – and it is to be hoped that Brexit will not cause that peace to unravel.

The GAA was bound up, as we have seen, with the Troubles in Northern Ireland, and played its part in bringing the violence to an end – and perhaps we can derive a measure of comfort from a possible change in unionist attitudes to the organization and its games. In June 2018, DUP leader Arlene Foster attended the Ulster Gaelic football final between Donegal and her home county of Fermanagh: by no means a small step, and noted as such. Again, we cannot know what a Brexit-shadowed future will bring to Northern Ireland – but the GAA will play its part, through work and through gesture, in helping to assure the future of the peace process. And in the meantime, the GAA continues its work of building for the future elsewhere too, both at home and abroad. Abroad, the activity is ongoing, with hundreds of GAA volunteers assisting newcomers in getting a start in life. For each of them, the GAA is part of what they are. And at home, on the playing fields of Cuala and in a multitude of such fields across Ireland, this knowledge and identity are equally potent, equally cheering, equally and uniquely grounding.

Appendices

The Rules of the Games

Hurling

1. The ground shall, when convenient, be at least 200 yards long by 150 yards broad, or as near to that size as can be got.
2. There shall be boundary lines all around the ground, at a distance of at least five yards from the fence.
3. The goal should be two upright posts, twenty feet apart, with a cross-bar ten feet from the ground. A goal is won when the ball is driven between the posts and under the crossbar.
4. The ball is not to be lifted off the ground with the hand, when in play.
5. There shall not be less than fourteen or more than twenty-one players at the side in regular matches.
6. There shall be an umpire for each side and a referee who will decide in cases where the umpires disagree. The referee keeps the time and throws up the ball at the commencement of each goal.
7. The time of play shall be one hour and twenty minutes. Sides to be changed at half-time.
8. Before commencing play hurlers shall draw up in two lines

in the centre of the field opposite to each other and catch hands or hurleys across, then separate. The referee then throws the ball along the ground between the players or up high over their heads.

9. No player to catch, trip or push from behind. Penalty, disqualification to the offender and free puck to the opposite side.

10. No player to bring his hurley intentionally in contact with the person of another player. Penalty, same as in Rule 9.

11. If the ball is driven over the sideline it shall be thrown in towards the middle of the ground by the referee or one of the umpires; but if it rebounds into the ground it shall be considered in play.

12. If the ball is driven over the end-lines and not through the goal, the player who is defending the goal shall have a free puck from the goal. No player of the opposite side to approach nearer than twenty yards until the ball is struck. The other players to stand on the goal-line. But if the ball is driven over the goal-line by a player whose goal it is, the opposite side shall have a free puck on the ground twenty yards out from the goalposts. Players whose goal it is to stand on the goal-line until the ball is struck. N.B: hitting both right and left is allowable.

Camogie

The rules for camogie are essentially the same as those for hurling. The scoring systems are identical: three points for a goal and one for over the bar. There are, however, certain differences: camogie matches are ten minutes shorter than hurling games; the base of the hurl is somewhat smaller than in the men's game; the sliotar (ball) is also slightly smaller; and use of the hand pass is allowed. As in men's hurling, protective helmets must be worn.

Football

1. There shall not be less than 15 or more than 21 players a side.
2. There shall be two umpires and a referee. Where the umpires disagree, the referee's decision shall be final.
3. The ground shall be at least 120 yards long by 80 in breadth and properly marked by boundary lines. Boundary lines to be at least five yards from the fences.
4. Goalposts shall stand at each end in the centre of the goal-line. They shall be 15 feet apart, with cross-bar eight feet from the ground.
5. The captains of each team shall toss for choice of sides before commencing play and the players shall stand in two ranks opposite each other, until the ball is thrown up, each man holding the hand of one of the other side.
6. Pushing or tripping from behind, holding from behind, or butting with the head shall be deemed foul and players so offending shall be asked to stand aside and may not afterwards take any part in the match, nor can his side substitute another man.

7. The time of actual play shall be one hour. Sides to be changed at half-time.

8. The match shall be decided by the greater number of goals. If no goal be kicked, the match shall be deemed a draw. A goal is scored when the ball is kicked through the goalposts under the crossbar.

9. When the ball is kicked over the sideline it shall be thrown back in any direction by a player of the other side. If kicked over the goalline by a player of the other side, the goal-keeper whose line it crosses shall have a free kick. No player on the other side to approach nearer than 25 yards of him till the ball is kicked.

10. The umpires and referee shall have, during the match, full power to disqualify any player or order him to stand aside and discontinue play for any act which they may consider unfair as set out in Rule 6.[49]

Handball

As I mentioned earlier, handball is said to have been Thomas Croke's favourite sport. The GAA eventually threw its weight behind the development of the sport; it also received a boost in the early days of the state from the Gardaí under the sports-minded Eoin O'Duffy, when handball alleys were constructed at police stations throughout the country. At the time of writing, the handball alley at Croke Park is one of the best handball alleys in Europe. Prior to the foundation of the GAA, handball was the most widely played sport in Ireland.

Games are played in an alley which can either be open or enclosed with a high wall on one end and walls on either side. The game resembles squash, although played, of course, with the hand rather than rackets; and it can be played with either two or four contestants. It is played with a small hard rubber ball, and demands great hand-eye coordination, agility and physical strength.

Athletics

As the GAA was initially mainly concerned with athletics, Cusack also drew up rules governing these forms of activity.

The rules for weight-throwing were given in *United Ireland* of 14 February. The remainder of the athletic rules were published in that paper's issue of 21 February, when General Rules were also given.

1. Every competitor must wear complete clothing from the shoulders to the knees, e.g. sleeved jersey and loose drawers.
2. Any competitor may be excluded from taking part in the sports except properly attired.
3. Competitors must be limited to amateurs, except in cases where committees put on events for money prizes. No person competing for a money prize can afterwards compete as an amateur.
4. All betting must be put down if possible.

It was further decreed that the Central Committee could

suspend anyone guilty of any malpractice connected with athletics.

5. All entries must be made in the real name of the competitor.

Writings

The writings that sparked the movement, beginning with a letter from Michael Cusack that proposed the formation of an 'Irish Association'.

Michael Cusack to Maurice Davin: 26 August 1884

Dear Mr. Davin,

The Irish Association with its members must be formed before the end of this year. The Association could organize the whole country within the year 1885. We could then safely hold the projected national gathering in 1886. The business must be worked from Munster. Suppose we held a meeting of delegates in some central place in Tipperary on the 1st of November next. Don't bother your head about Dublin. The place couldn't well be worse than it is. We'll have to look to the provinces for men. Dublin will have to fall in or keep up the connection with England. I have written to Cork this day telling them that you have responded most heartily. I am sure Mr. Stack of Listowel will look after North Kerry. Although I am not a member of the National League, I think I am not without influence with several of its leading members.

The national press will give me room for signs when I am ready. The shamrock is also at my disposal. I hope to see it enlarged in about a month and then the education of the people could start in earnest. The paragraphs on athletics in 'United Ireland' are exploding like shells in the enemy's ranks. Of course they know it is my doing and therefore the paper is not likely to hang fire soon. I have found it to be utterly hopeless to revive our national pastimes without the assistance of the leaders of the people and I have not hesitated to urge my claim with a persistence that brooks no refusal. After a protracted struggle I won all round. Our business now is to work together caring for none but the Irish people and quietly shoving aside all who would denationalise these people. I'll write to you again when business is a little further advanced. With many thanks.

I am yours faithfully.
Michael Cusack

'A Word about Irish Athletics'

Written by Michael Cusack and published in *United Ireland* and the *Irishman*, October 1884.

No movement, having for its object the social and political advancement of a nation from the tyranny of imported and enforced customs and manners can be regarded as perfect if it has not made adequate provision for the preservation and cultivation of the National pastimes of the people. Voluntary neglect of such pastimes is a sure sign of national decay. [...] The strength and energy of a race are largely dependent on the National pastimes for the development of a spirit of courage and endurance. A war-like race is ever fond of games requiring skill, strength and staying power. [...] But when a race is declining in martial spirit, no matter from what cause, the national games are neglected at first and then forgotten. [...] A so–called revival of athletics was inaugurated in Ireland. The new movement did not originate with those who had ever had any sympathy with Ireland or the Irish people. Accordingly, labourers, tradesmen, artists and even policemen and soldiers were excluded from the few competitions which constituted the lame and halting programme of the promoters. Two years ago every man who did not make his living either wholly or partly by athletics was allowed to take part. But with this concession came a law which is as intolerable as its existence in Ireland is degrading. The law is this, that all Athletic meetings shall be held under the rules of the Amateur Athletic Association of England and that any person competing at any meeting not held under those rules should be ineligible to compete anywhere. The management of nearly all the meetings held in Ireland since has been entrusted to persons hostile to all the dearest aspirations of the Irish people. Every effort has been made to make the meetings look as English as possible – foot races, betting and flagrant cheating being their most prominent features. Swarms of pot–hunting mashers sprang into existence. They formed 'Harrier' clubs for the purpose of training all through the winter after the fashion of English professional athletes, that they might be able to win and pawn the prizes offered for competition in the summer. We tell the Irish people to take the management of their games into their own hands, encouraging and promoting in every way, every form of athletics which is purely Irish and to remove with one sweep everything foreign and iniquitous in the present system. The vast majority of athletes in Ireland are Nationalists. These gentlemen should take the matter in hand at once and draft laws for the guidance of the promoters of meetings in Ireland next year. The people pay for the expense of meetings and the representatives of the people should have the controlling power. It is only by such an arrangement that Irish athletics can be revived and that the incomparable strength and physique of our race will be preserved.[50]

Letter from Archbishop Croke to Michael Cusack

Archbishop Thomas William Croke's letter to Michael Cusack indicates Croke's acceptance of the role of Patron of the Gaelic Athletic Association (*United Ireland*, 27 December 1884). The letter was subsequently published in a number of nationalist newspapers including *United Ireland*.

What follows is a GAA-edited transcript of the document.

To Mr. Michael Cusack, Hon. Secretary of the Gaelic Athletic Association.

My Dear Sir – I beg to acknowledge the receipt of your communication inviting me to become a patron of the 'Gaelic Athletic Association', of which you are, it appears, hon. secretary I accede to your request with the utmost pleasure. One of the most painful, let me assure you, and, at the same time, one of the most frequently recurring reflections that, as an Irishman, I am compelled to make in connection with the present aspect of things in this country, is derived from the ugly and irritating fact that we are daily importing from England not only her manufactured goods, which has practically strangled our own manufacturing appliances, but, together with her fashions, her accent, her vicious literature, her music, her dances, and her manifold mannerisms, her games also her pastimes, to the utter discredit of our own grand national sports, and the sore humiliation, as I believe, of every genuine son and daughter of the old land. Ball playing, hurling, football, kicking according to Irish rules [...] and all such favourite exercises and amusements amongst men and boys, may now be said to be not only dead and buried, but in several localities to be entirely forgotten and unknown. And what have we got in their stead? We have got such foreign and fantastical field sports as lawn-tennis, polo, croquet, cricket, and the like – very excellent, I believe, and health-giving exercises in their way, still not racy of the soil, but rather alien to it, as are, indeed, for the most part the men and women who first imported and still continue to patronise them. [...] And unfortunately, it is not our national sports alone that are held in dishonour, and dying out, but even our suggestive national celebrations are being gradually effaced and extinguished, one after another, as well. Who hears now of snap-apple, or bonfire night? They are all things of the past, too vulgar to be spoken of, except in ridicule, by the degenerate dandies of the day. No doubt, there is something pleasing to the eye in the 'get up' of a modern young man who, arrayed in light attire, with parti-coloured cap on and racket in hand, is making his way, with or without companion, to the tennis ground. But, for my part, I should vastly prefer to behold, or think of, the youthful athletes whom I used to see in my early days at fair and pattern, bereft of shoes and coat, and thus prepared to play hand-ball, to fly over any number of horses, to throw the 'sledge' or 'winding stone', and to test each others' mettle and activity by the trying ordeal of 'three leaps', or a 'hop, step, and a jump.' Indeed if we continue travelling for the next score of years in the same direction that we have been going in for some time, contemning [despising] the sports practised by our forefathers, effacing our national features as though we were ashamed of them, and putting on, with England's stuff and broadcloths, her 'masher' habits and such other effeminate follies as she may recommend, we had better at once, and publicly, adjure our nationality, clap hands for joy at the sight of the Union Jack, and place 'England's bloody red' exultingly above 'the green'. Depreciating, as I do, any such dire and disgraceful consummation, and seeing in your society of athletes something altogether opposed to it, I shall be happy to do for it all that I can, and authorise you now formally to place my name on the roll (sic) of your patrons. In conclusion, I earnestly hope that our national journals will not disdain, in future, to give suitable notices of those Irish sports and pastimes which your society means to patronise and promote, and that the masters and pupils of our Irish colleges will not henceforth exclude from their athletic programmes such manly exercises as I have just referred to and commemorated.

T. W. Croke Archbishop of Cashel[51]

It is worth noting, however, that Thomas Croke was *not* Michael Cusack's first choice as Patron of the GAA. A delegation of the association's founders had first approached a neighbouring bishop, Bishop Patrick Duggan of the Clonfert diocese in east Co. Galway. Duggan was known as a nationalist sympathiser: and he seemed like the perfect candidate and advocate. According to myth, Duggan had enthusiastically accepted the GAA's proposal, at a dinner held in his Loughrea residence, when his manservant ('Mike') entered with a document. The bishop perused the paper gravely and in silence, and then he turned to the manservant and said: 'Mike, we will have to kill another pig.'

The document was said to have been a copy of the Papal rescript, condemning the Land League's boycotting campaign which was then in full spate across Ireland. A similar letter was at that very moment being delivered to Catholic prelates all over Ireland.

As I say, so the myth goes.

Unfortunately – as so often happens to good stories in Ireland – the bare facts cast a dispiriting light on a good anecdote. This particular papal rescript in fact lay some years in the future: instead, while Duggan certainly welcomed the offer to become Patron of the GAA, the bald truth is that he was then in his seventies – and so he suggested that the younger Croke would make a better candidate for the job.

As proved to be the case: Croke, as we have seen, did become an indispensable figure in the GAA's early years and the organization recognizes this by adopting his letter of acceptance as the GAA's Magna Carta.

A Note on Police Surveillance

The calibre of RIC membership in a given district inevitably influenced the extent and worth of the knowledge of IRB and GAA activity which the organization was able to garner.

It is clear from even a cursory perusal of contemporary RIC reports that the authorities could, in general terms, rely on fairly accurate intelligence: and could track both Fenians and athletes across Ireland by means of a combination of observation and paid informants.

Take the following report the southwestern division of the RIC. The district is Cork, the year is 1891, and the memorandum contained the following:

The IRB organization has played a considerable part in political affairs. With very few exceptions all the prominent members have taken the Parnellite side in the split and have worked steadily to further the interests of that section of the Nationalist party...

We have already seen how clashes between IRB and clerical interests were a ubiquitous feature of the GAA's infancy. The following police assessment of the effect of such a clash, meanwhile, indicates how near such tension came to stifling the organization in its infancy. It also – once again – illustrates the importance of the leadership of Croke in overcoming the quarrels which resulted:

The GAA which promised in 1887 and 1888 to be a considerable factor in the political history of Ireland, is at the present moment tottering to its fall. It is torn by dissensions, and in finance has been the victim of fraud. The clerical wing particularly seems to have gone out of hand, and to be completely disorganised. [...] However in Cork, there is much talk amongst the IRB section of reorganising the association, and running it purely as a Fenian branch. This may work for a time in larger cities, but in rural districts will end in failure.

To bolster this argument the police gave a statistical breakdown of the effect of the Fenian clerical division as follows:

We now have 44 branches in the division as compared with 72 last year under clerical influence – and 50 as compared with 63 under Fenian control, showing in all a decrease of 41 branches.

The RIC reports issuing from the northern division, meanwhile, illustrate the importance of informers in keeping track of the GAA's activities. A report of July 1888 opens with the big news of the year: 'A new informant who has been secured during the month in the City of Derry'. The informant has provided the police with intelligence that 'although the IRB is strong there, there was never such disorganization existing amongst them than at present.' The informant added for good measure that the GAA membership is 'just now dissatisfied about their subscriptions being unaccounted.'

The informant's assessment was that there was no one in Derry who could keep the Fenians in control – and the police report underlines the continuing close relationship between the Fenians and the GAA in Ulster in general, recording that:

On the night of the 20th of May there was a large IRB meeting in Newry which was held in the GAA club rooms there. A match had been played during the day near the town between the members of a GAA branch from Dundalk and a Newry club and after the members had been entertained in the evening in the club rooms some were asked to retire and the remainder of about 80 in number formed an IRB meeting.

It was resolved that as the football season was nearly out and as few opportunities offered during the summer of their meeting together under the guise of the GAA, they should hold IRB meetings regularly, at least once a month and keep the organisation in proper working order.

Indeed, this difficulty – gathering IRB members together when the GAA season was not in full swing – was very real. The RIC kept a meticulous watch on the growth of the organization, noting that:

'Two new branches of the GAA have been lately formed. [...] The association is steadily increasing, but it still continues in this division without any exception to be under the nominal control of the clerical party...

Dissent or no dissent, the police persistently regarded the GAA as a threat, and Dublin Castle was informed that:

Meetings are everywhere attended by the local police and open supervision is being kept on all members suspected of being connected to the Fenian organisation.

Later, as the period of the War of Independence loomed, and the GAA and the Gaelic League grew in strength, this policy of observation grew into outright obstruction and other forms of overt challenge: the police would sometimes break up GAA matches or cut down goalposts. The RIC demanded the right to attend GAA matches free of charge in order to keep proceedings under observation: friction arose at various grounds as ticket-sellers attempted to counter this tactic by demanding payment for admission to the stadiums – payments which the RIC inevitably disputed.

All this surveillance-shading-into-harassment was not of course dictated by mere police busy-bodyism. Rather, it was a manifestation of the authorities' ever-developing concern at the state of politics in Ireland, and their sense that the GAA was the ultimate barometer of the growth of cultural, political and potentially active revolutionary activities which might challenge London's hegemony.

Notes

In the following, BMH stands for Irish Bureau of Military History.

1 O'Keeffe to Roberts, 4 March 1984, copy in author's possession.
2 William Nolan (ed.), *The Gaelic Athletic Association, 1884–2000*, quoting a memoir of Larry Wren. Geography Publications, Dublin, 2005.
3 Mark Tierney, *Croke of Cashel*. Gill and Macmillan, Dublin, 1976.
4 Ibid.
5 P.D. Mehigan, quoted in Sean Kilfeather (ed.), *Vintage Carbery: P.D. Mehigan*. Beaver Row Press, Dublin, 1984.
6 O'Ceallaigh, Seamus *The Story of the GAA*, Gaelic Athletic Publications, Limerick, 1977.
7 P.D. Mehigan, quoted in Sean Kilfeather (ed.), *Vintage Carbery*. Beaver Row Press, Dublin, 1984.
8 Nolan, quoting from a memoir of Tommy Moore.
9 http://www.theirishstory.com/2014/05/23/an-abundance-of-first-class-recruits-the-gaa-and-the-irish-volunteers-1913-15/#.Wt3bDi7wbX4.
10 John Redmond, Woodenbridge speech, 20 September 1914.
11 Anthony Gaughan, *Austin Stack: Portrait of a Separatist*. Kingdom Books, Tralee, 1977.
12 http://traleetoday.ie/52242-2/.
13 Tadhg Kennedy, BMH statement.
14 Edward McGrath, BMH statement.
15 *Freeman's Journal*, 5 August 1918.
16 Tim Pat Coogan, *The Twelve Apostles*. Head of Zeus, London, 2017.

17 http://www.tara.tcd.ie/bitstream/handle/2262/57090/
   Killing%20and%20Bloody%20Sunday,%20November%20
   1920.pdf;sequence=1.
18 Oscar Traynor, BMH statement.
19 Tom Ryan, BMH statement.
20 Jack Shouldice, BMH statement.
21 Harry Colley, BMH statement.
22 Tom Ryan, BMH statement.
23 Marcus de Burca, David Gorry, Jim Wren (eds), *The Gaelic Athletic Association in Dublin 1884–2000*. Geography Publications, Dublin, 2005.
24 Foley, Michael, *The Bloodied Field*, O'Brien Press, Dublin, 2014.
25 Catherine Byrne, BMH statement.
26 Coogan, *The Twelve Apostles*, Head of Zeus, London, 2017, and *Michael Collins*, Hutchinson, London, 1990.
27 James McGuill, BMH statement.
28 This episode is described in Coogan, *Michael Collins*.
29 Quoted in Coogan, *On the Blanket*. Palgrave Macmillan, New York. 1980.
30 Ibid.
31 Rugby in Ireland, north and south of the border, is governed by one body – the Irish Rugby Football Union (IRFU). This has led to the unusual situation whereby the Ireland rugby team includes players from two separate national-political entities. Rugby in Ulster is strongly unionist and middle class. In 1995, the IRFU commissioned the songwriter Phil Coulter to write a politically neutral anthem for the Ireland rugby team, to represent both Northern Ireland and the Republic of Ireland. The resulting song, 'Ireland's Call', is played alongside the Irish national anthem, *'Amhrán na bhFiann'* ('The Soldier's Song') at international matches.
32 See Sathesh Alagappan, 'North and South: Football and Irish Partition'. theirishstory.com.
33 Northern Ireland qualified for their first ever European Championships, UEFA Euro 2016, played in France, after

beating Greece 3–1 at Windsor Park on 8 October 2015. It was the first time in 30 years that Northern Ireland had qualified for a major tournament. At the tournament itself, O'Neill led the side to the second round, in which they lost narrowly to Wales, but recorded a surprise victory over Ukraine in the group stages.

34 Quoted in Andra Jackson, *Independent* (London), 10 March 1994

35 Ibid.

36 On 19 June 2018, the soldier in question was charged with the manslaughter of Aidan McAnespie by reason of gross negligence.

37 Weeshie Fogarty Con Murphy, Tribute article http://www.terracetalk.com/articles/Tributes/107/Con-Murphy.

38 Stephen Gordon, 'Old enemies at field of dreams', *Sunday Life*, 20 March 2016.

39 Kevin Jordan, *Rebellion in Galway*. Galway, Kevin Jordan, 2016.

40 Seán Moylan, BMH statement.

41 Described in Jim Cronin, *Making Connections: A Cork GAA Miscellany*. Cork County Board GAA, Cork, 2005.

42 Ibid.

43 Ibid.

44 Ibid.

45 *Southern Star*, 22 May 1971.

46 The Dr John Harty Cup for Munster schools hurling is named in his honour – as is the playing field of Murroe GAA club (Harty's local club) in County Limerick.

47 Jim Maher, *The Flying Column: West Kilkenny, 1916–21*. Geography Publications, Dublin, 2015.

48 Ibid.

49 The rules for hurling and football were published in *United Ireland* on 7 February 1885.

50 *United Ireland*, 11 October 1884.

51 The Gaelic Athletic Association', *Freeman's Journal*, 24 December 1884.

Bibliography

Beecher, Sean, *The Blues: A History of St Finbarr's Hurling and Football Club.* Goldy Angel Press, Cork, 1984.

Clayton, Xander, *Aud.* G.A.C, Plymouth, 2007.

Corry, Eoghan, *An Illustrated History of the GAA.* Gill & Macmillan, Dublin, 2005.

Cronin, Jim, *Making Connections: A Cork GAA Miscellany.* Cork County Board GAA, Cork, 2005.

Cronin, Mike and John M. Regan (eds), *Ireland: The Politics of Independence.* Macmillan, London, and St Martin's Press, New York, 2000.

Cronin, Mike, Murphy, William and Rouse, Paul, (eds), *The Gaelic Athletic Association, 1864–2009.* Irish Academic Press, Dublin, and Portland, Oregon, 2009.

Cronin, Mike, Rouse, Paul and Duncan, Mark, *The GAA County by County.* Collins Press, Cork, 2011.

Cronin, Mike, Durcan, Mark and Rouse, Paul, *The GAA, A People's History.* Collins Press, Cork, 2014.

Cummins, Gerry and de Burca, Éanna, *The Frank Burke Story.* Print Irish, 2016.

De Burca, Marcus, *The GAA: A History.* GAA, Dublin, 1980.

Dwyer, T. Ryle, *Tans, Terror, and Troubles: Kerry's Real Fighting Story, 1913–23.* Mercier Press, Cork, 2001.

Fogarty, Philip, *Tipperary's GAA Story.* Tipperary Star, Thurles, 1960.

Foley, Michael, *The Bloodied Field.* O'Brien Press, Dublin 2014.

Gaughan, J. Anthony, *Austin Stack: Portrait of a Separatist.* Kingdom Books, Dublin, 1977.

Graham, John Patrick, *Killeevan Sarsfields GFC: A Centenary History 1915–2015 and a Parish Record*. Published by the Author, Newbliss, Co. Monaghan, 2016.

Hall, Donal and Maguire, Martin, *County Louth and the Irish Revolution*. Irish Academic Press, Kildare, 2017.

Henry, William, *Pathway to Rebellion: Galway, 1916*. Mercier Press, Cork, 2016.

Hogan, Sean, *The Black and Tans in North Tipperary: Policing Revolution and War, 1919–1922*. Untold Stories Publications, 2013.

Humphries, Tom, *Green Fields: Gaelic Sport in Ireland*. Weidenfeld and Nicolson, London, 1996.

Jordan, Kevin, *Rebellion in County Galway*. Privately published, Galway 2016.

Looney, Tom, *Dick Fitzgerald: King in a Kingdom of Kings*. Currach Press, Dublin, 2008.

Maher, Jim, *The Flying Column: West Kilkenny, 1916–21*. Geography Publications, Dublin, 2015.

Mannion, Marie (ed.), *Centenary Reflections, 1916*. Galway County Libraries, Galway, 1916.

Martin, Joseph, *The GAA in Tyrone: The Road to Greatness*. Tyrone GAA Board, Dungannon, 2003.

McAnallen, Donal, Hassan, David and Hegarty, Roddy, *The Evolution of the GAA*. Stair Uladh (Ulster Historical Foundation), Belfast, 2009.

The Nemo Rangers Story. Litho Press, Middleton; and *The Nicks of Time*, Litho Press, Middleton.

Nolan, William (ed.), *Tipperary History and Society*. Geography Publications, Dublin, 1985.

Nolan, William (ed.), *The Gaelic Athletic Association in Dublin*. Geography Publications, Dublin, 2005.

Ó'Broin, Leon, *Revolutionary Underground*. Gill & Macmillan, Dublin, 1976.

Ó'Ceallaigh, Seamus, *The Story of the GAA*. Gaelic Athletic Publications, Limerick, 1977.

Ó'Donnchú, Liam, *Tom Semple and the Thurles Blues*. Walsh Colour Printing, Kerry, 2015.

Ó'Laoi, Padraic, *Annals of the GAA in Galway*. Galway County Libraries, Galway, 1994.

Ó'Tuathaigh, Gearóid (ed.), *The GAA and Revolution in Ireland, 1913–1923*. Collins Press, Cork, 2015.

Puirséal, Pádraig, *The GAA in its Time*. Ward River Press, Dublin, 1984.

Tierney, Mark, *Croke of Cashel*. Gill & Macmillan, Dublin, 1976.

Twohig, Patrick J., *Autobiography of a Freedom Fighter*. Tower Books, Cork, 1996.

Journals and pamphlets

Eire-Ireland, Spring–Summer, 2013: Irish-American Cultural Institute, Morristown, NJ. This edition is devoted to a valuable discussion of topics such as the Irish language and the GAA and to the development of sport within Irish society, with particular reference to the evolution of the GAA.

Kenny, Tom, 'Galway Politics and Society, 1910–23'. Four Courts Press 2011, Maynooth Studies in Local History, no. 25.

O'Mahony, Sean, 'The First Hunger Striker, Thomas Ashe, 1917'. Elo Publications, Dublin, 2001.

Moore, Martin, 'The Call to Arms'. Walsh Colour Print, Castleisland, 2016.

'The Gaelic Athletic Association through History and Documents', 1870–1920, GAA Museum, Dublin, 2008.

Index

The GAA and the War of Independence (Tim Pat Coogan)